Brian Carter was born in Paignton, South Devon, where he still lives. He has been walking and climbing the British hills since boyhood. The author of eight previous books including *A Black Fox Running, Jack, Dartmoor – The Threatened Wilderness* and *Nightworld,* he writes a daily country and conservation column for the South Devon newspaper, *The Herald Express.* Currently he is writing a new animal novel to be published by Century.

WALKING IN THE WILD

*Over 50 Celtic Walks in Devon, Wales and the
Hebridean Isles*

Brian Carter

CENTURY

LONDON MELBOURNE AUCKLAND JOHANNESBURG

First published in 1988 by Century Hutchinson Ltd,
Brookmount House, 62–65 Chandos Place, Covent Garden,
London WC2N 4NW

Century Hutchinson Australia Pty Ltd, PO Box 496,
16–22 Church Street, Hawthorn, Victoria 3122,
Australia

Century Hutchinson New Zealand Limited, PO Box 40-086,
Glenfield, Auckland 10, New Zealand

Century Hutchinson South Africa (Pty) Ltd, PO Box 337,
Bergvlei, 2012 South Africa

Set by Vision Typesetting, Manchester
Printed and bound in Great Britain by
Mackays of Chatham Ltd, Chatham, Kent

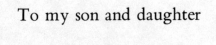

To my son and daughter

Contents

Introduction

The poet Edward Thomas knew all about the joys of lone walking, preferably across country. He could march through the night to emerge spiritually refreshed at dawn.

There is immense satisfaction in tramping over turf or rock in pursuit of contentment and well-being. For me it's the journey that counts and not the destination, which is often vague. I love the actual business of walking. I like to stride through my thoughts receiving whatever Nature has to offer – a sunrise, a line of peaks, cottage roofs, distance lying smoky and unreal in the gathering dusk. Sometimes a lane or a country road is enough, although a glimpse of hills will set the excitement churning in my guts.

On high ground the physical thing is dominant and I'm aware of my body and the damp heat rising under my clothes as yesterday's beer leaks from the pores. Occasionally I walk all night. More than once the hills or the sea cliffs by moonlight have provided consolation if not inspiration, and I've returned from them a happier man.

Hiking across Celtic Britain you run the risk of bumping into a whole posse of literary ghosts and if you are keeping your own company there's no need to apologise for striking up brief platonic relationships with people who aren't there. Hazlitt, Belloc, Borrow and Edward Thomas are among the more obvious fellow travellers, although the Welsh mediaeval poet, Dafydd ap Gwilym, has made his presence felt. Hazlitt springs to the defence of loners: 'I cannot see the wit of walking and talking at the same time,' he wrote. '. . .I like solitude . . . Give me the clear blue sky over my head and the green turf beneath my feet, a winding road before me, and a three hours march to dinner.' I know the feeling!

This is a Loner's Guide, and a book for couples, a few kindred spirits or small family groups. I'm not a herd animal but to come out of hill solitude into human company can be most pleasant. Once, not so long ago, entering Hay-on-Wye with frost heightening the brilliance of the stars above the dusk haze, I could smell dinners cooking. The evening was rich with the aroma of food, and pub warmth was beckoning. So I went in search of both.

The wild ways can still lead into happy surprises if you are prepared to abandon the car and the town and strike out into the lanes or over the hills. Then quietude, which at first may be disconcerting, soon registers to defeat stress and sluice the spirit. On the other hand, a country walk needn't be a heavy experience. It can simply do the heart and bowels the world of good and sharpen appetites blunted by urban life.

I have a long list of favourite walks from Devon to the Hebridean Isle of Mull. Some are thrilling wilderness routes over mountains and moors; others are coastal paths through the seasons; the rest are strolls along country lanes and roads, from village to village.

During my walks I've never been encumbered by a heavy back pack; nor have I entered a Youth Hostel. Hostels are admirable places but they aren't my sort of refuge at day's end. I still rough it in a bivouac on the hills if I have to, preferring a sleeping bag among the rocks to a night under canvas. This was central to my boyhood and youth but now I love to set off from a cottage base in the wilderness or from an inn. Almost as attractive as walking away from the pub breakfast into the mountains for the day is the prospect of the hot bath, good food and drink waiting behind evening and weariness when I return.

I also like to mix my walking. Homeric journeys over ridges and across valleys continue to appeal and I can't contemplate them on the map without emotion. Traversing a bleak Scottish deer forest or the Glyders followed by the Snowdon Horseshoe is good for the soul – providing you are fit. And I glory in a brisk up-and-down morning on the South Devon Coastal Footpath or an afternoon ramble through the lanes of mid-Wales. Every once in a while I push myself hard, burning off the physical and mental flab on high rock. Then, blissfully shattered, I've always felt I've earnt the comforts of the bar and the fireside.

Walking is one of the enduring pleasures of my life, and West Britain continues to provide all I require as a wilderness romantic. At times the Celtic connection isn't obvious, especially in South Devon with its wealth of Anglo-Saxon place names. But it is there and sooner or later you discover it.

The older I get the more I fear for the places where I walk, and the wilderness places are obviously vulnerable to human selfishness. I hope these walks will win enough converts and attract enough kindred spirits to protect the corners of Western Britain that I love. But go to them alone or with a loved one or a couple of friends. Respect solitude.

It is important to understand that the walks are described as I experienced them, through the seasons and at different periods of my life. Teetotallers may be disenchanted by my obvious admiration for the British pub. I plead with them to stiffen the upper lip and walk with me – as far as the inn where we'll part company on friendly terms.

The distances given are approximate but fairly accurate and they are given in good English miles. I hate the modern trend towards the metric, so the mountains are so many *feet* high, the pub a few hundred *yards* down the road where a *pint* of cider will do me any day. Allow extra time for bad weather and steep mountain slopes or scrambles.

Moorsense, Mountainsense

Wild places offer adventure but walking them alone can be hazardous unless you treat them with respect. Plenty of books examine the survival business in detail but I feel compelled to list a few points. Beginners should always have experienced companions, although I didn't.

Footwear: A wide range of strong, lightweight boots is available these days. I value mine above all my other equipment.

Waterproofs: A windproof, waterproof cagoule or anorak is essential. I always carry my 'Ultimate' Goretex in my rucksack with waterproof over-trousers which I hate.

In the rucksack: This is a matter of personal choice, but as I get out on the moors and mountains all year round I tend to be cautious. Bad weather can put the careless in peril and even summer wind and rain claim their victims. Spare sweater and T-shirt, spare woollen stockings, waterproof mittens, plastic bivouac bag (survival bag), food, compass, whistle, torch, camera, map.

The contents of your light day pack will depend on how far and where you intend to go. The bivvy bag, for instance, may be scoffed at but walkers be-nighted through injury will welcome the sleeping-bag-type protection it provides.

Whistle: Lost in mist or darkness. Six long regular blasts every minute (within reason!).

Torch: Injured in darkness. Six regular flashes every minute should attract search parties.

Map: I carry an Ordnance Survey map, preferably one of the Outdoor Leisure $2\frac{1}{2}$ inches to 1 mile series.

Compass: Ambitious walkers must be able to walk to a compass bearing. Learn how to do it or get someone to teach you.

Towel: Very useful if you decide to take a dip.

Weather: Plan an escape route. When bad weather closes get to the road no matter if it's miles from where you intend going. In fog a stream will eventually bring you to a dwelling or a road. Following streams off mountains in this way isn't to be recommended because they take the most direct line, i.e. over crags as waterfalls!

Bogs: Reeds, marsh grass and cotton grass warn you to steer clear of the mires. If you get onto a real bog that quakes underfoot as if you are walking on a duvet across porridge you'll soon get off! So plan your route.

Rivers: A flash flood can turn a stream into a torrent and tired walkers aren't advised to ford rivers after a heavy downpour.

Fitness: Break yourself in easily. Make sure you pace yourself and don't take on too much too soon. Break in your boots. Make sure your rucksack fits snugly. Soon you'll be gliding along with the ease of a deer. Summer walking can be pure joy but it would be unwise to try it alone until you are sure of yourself and know your limitations.

The route: Leave word of your intended route, time of departure and when you hope to get back. Tell someone or leave a card stuck on the inside of the windscreen of your car. Finally, don't leave valuables in your car. The vehicle vultures who break into motors don't miss much. I always try to park mine in full view of the road.

Dartmoor danger area: Details of range firing programmes are obtainable by answering service on the following numbers: Torquay 24592, Exeter 70164, Plymouth 701924, Okehampton 2939.

Remember: Moorsense and Mountainsense make sense.

Grading of the walks

Ⓐ: Easy and gentle.
Ⓑ: More demanding.
Ⓒ: Strenuous.
Ⓓ: Difficult (involving scrambling).

DEVON

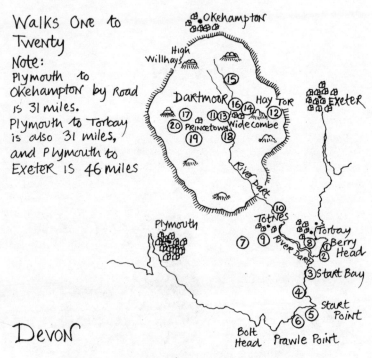

Walks One to Twenty

Note:
Plymouth to Okehampton by Road is 31 miles.
Plymouth to Torbay is also 31 miles, and Plymouth to Exeter is 46 miles

Okehampton

High Willhays

Dartmoor

Hay Tor

Exeter

⑮

⑯ ⑭

⑰ ⑪⑬ ⑫

⑳ Princetown   Widecombe

⑲ ⑱

River Dart

⑩

Totnes

Plymouth

⑦ ⑨

River Dart

⑧ Torbay

② Berry Head

③ Start Bay

④

⑤ Start Point

⑥

Bolt Head   Prawle Point

Devon

- Dartmoor and the South of the county including the coast.
(Not to scale)

1

The South Devon Coast

The beauty of walking is that you can take your time or swing along like one of those Victorian walkaholics who thought nothing of clocking fifty miles in a day. But I doubt if even the hardest Victorian could have done fifty miles in one go along the South West way. The switchback of steep up and down sections makes you aware of leg muscles – painfully so if those muscles are unaccustomed to hard exercise. Anyone thinking of attempting the twelve miles of coastal path from Berry Head to Kingswear should bank some stamina beforehand. All the hills rise dramatically from sea level to four hundred feet or more.

WALK ONE
Berry Head to Mansands and back.

Length: 6 miles
Grade Ⓑ

A pleasant spring adventure for all ages but especially for parents with youngsters and a love of nature.

Berry Head is a celebrated limestone promontory jutting out into the English Channel east of Brixham. It is arguably one of the most beautiful Country Parks in Britain and is worth

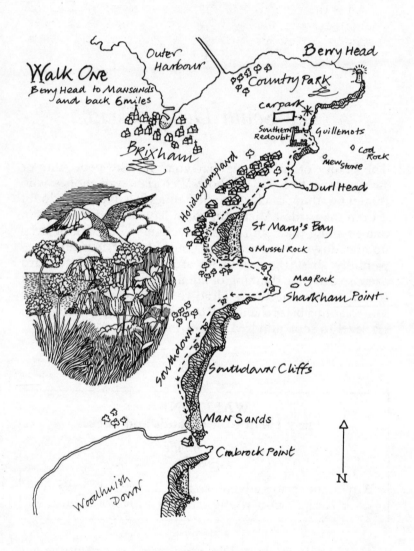

Walk One
Berry Head to Mansands
and back 6 miles

Outer Harbour

Berry Head

Country Park

carpark

Southern Redoubt

Guillemots

Cod Rock

Mew Stone

Durl Head

Brixham

Holiday camp land

Nursery

St Mary's Bay

Mussel Rock

Mag Rock

Sharkham Point

Southdown

Southdown Cliffs

Man Sands

Crabrock Point

Woodhuish Down

N

exploring with its wealth of wild flowers, migrant songbirds and seabird colonies.

Towards the end of the headland, beyond the coastguard station, is the Light and magnificent views of the Channel where the parade of shipping provides an endless spectacle. Through the telescope you may spot gannets diving into the sea or porpoises and dolphins swimming past Cod Rock.

Berry Head has two forts dating from the Napoleonic Wars, and under the ramparts of the Southern Redoubt is one of the most important guillemot loomeries on the Channel Coast. During the spring, rafts of these birds will be on the water doing their ceremonial dances or preening themselves. Above the colony are the fulmar and kittiwake ledges. The yodelling cries of herring gulls rise above the boom and bark of great black-backed gulls and the piping of oystercatchers.

I'm a Devonian with a Welsh mother, and this part of the Celtic coast is my home territory. I used to come here as a kid from Paignton just after Hitler's War for the gulls' egg harvest. Some of the climbs we attempted then have been given heroic names in the guide books but for me these seacliffs will always play host to the little phantoms of the 1940s in their black daps (gym shoes), patched shorts and hand-me-down woollies.

That day at the end of March I had put nearly four decades between myself and the primary school past. I walked over the turf through the Southern Redoubt to climb the wall and pick up the path again where it ran beside the fields. The last snow of winter had come in the night like a cruel trick, yet along the clifftops the dog violets were blooming among the dead bracken and slush. Gulls, ravens and daws beat into the north-west wind that was responsible for the arctic spell. So I had the path to myself and the raw weather lent an edge of excitement to a walk I had taken hundreds of times. The wind was raking the Channel, lifting waves to peaks that dissolved in foam. Near Durl Head I put up a rabbit and watched it vanish into the blackthorn scrub.

The morning blazed and glittered, but the snow on the hills faded to green where pasture met cliff. Durl Head was also free of snow. The stack at the foot of the dark slabs was cut off from the mainland by the tide. I stood a moment and let the wind thump my back. A cock pheasant lifted from the bracken in a firework explosion of wings while I was looking across St Mary's Bay. The cormorants were unimpressed. They sat upright on Mussel Rock and watched the gulls scrummaging on the sea at the Sharkham Point sewage feast. But the pheasant's departure had fused the nerves in my fingertips.

The path rolled on before me, and beyond two clifftop meadows it traced the seaside boundaries of a holiday camp. Nipping through a gap in the hedge I dropped a pound of tiny meat-flavoured biscuits for the tribe of feral cats that lived among the chalets. I'd met a few of the scruffy toms and shes as they slunk through the thorn and bramble thickets in pursuit of food. I liked their style.

Walking on, I let a rough flight of steps guide me out of the blackthorns and down onto the grey sands and shillet litter of St Mary's Bay. (There is an alternative route that brings you above the beach when the tide is high.) The beach was deserted and a joy to trudge over with its ranks of oystercatchers and gulls in hasty retreat. Waiting at the far end were more steps cut from the cliff to take me back to the path. About thirty yards further on I turned left through a gate and crunched along the track beneath the trees to Sharkham Point. Here the walk abandoned its associations with holidaycampland and I was suddenly on the promontory faced by the soul-piercing beauty of white downs sweeping to the distant bulk of Scabbacombe Head. Despite the wintry tingle in the air blackbirds and thrushes sang from the gorse and thorns as I turned inland, vaulted the stile and dropped into a pasture. The cold failed to mask the smell of the muck spreading which was stronger than the smell of the sea.

I crossed the field leaving behind me the last of Torbay's urban sprawl. The grass was soft underfoot. Above Southdown big thunderheads sailed into the blue left behind by other clouds which the wind had blown out to sea. The sun flashed through gulls' wings and I took another stile in my stride and jogged along the mud path, over the stream and more restrictive woodwork to make the steep ascent through the snow onto the downs. The enormous landslips falling to the crags and the sea were highrise accommodation for rabbits. They were quartered ceaselessly by buzzards and foxes. Here Man didn't have all the say. Beside the clifftop fence the tracks of wild animals were printed on the snow.

The shoulder of Southdown was streaked with white and the primroses were shrivelled on the banks. My boots crunched and squeaked through deep snow and lifting my eyes from the footprints of voles, badgers, rabbits and small birds I saw the Channel racing before the wind to Scab-bacombe Head and the horizon. Now that wind had the bite I had first encountered on Berry Head. The solitude captured me and made me happy. Trees and shrubs above the steeps were alive and singing and the pastures on the other side of the path were dotted with sheep.

Knee-deep drifts blocked the top of the hillside which dropped abruptly to Mansands and the nameless coombe. Clouds were massing above Woodhuish Down whose flanks swept the eye to Woodhuish Farm and the sweet silhouette of upland that flowed seaward to Downend Point. The white countryside was braided with dark hedges and blotched with even darker copses.

Melt-water was pouring off the slope. It washed the slush and mud from my boots as I worked my way down to Mansands and the waves which were standing up uncertainly in the offshore wind before collapsing and sliding back to come again. The pebble beach had changed little since my childhood despite the efforts to tidy it up; but behind it the marsh which had once attracted thousands of wildfowl had gone. The lane climbed from the lime kiln up to Woodhuish to remind me of the way things were in the black dap days, and Coastguard Cottages above their low crag to the south of the beach had survived. But I await with dread those 'improvements' which sound the death knell for wild corners – the picnic areas, car parks and lavatories.

The two humps of Woodhuish Down looked particularly inviting under snow I decided as I found a sheltered hollow on the beach and fished the thermos and lunchpack out of my rucksack. Mansands remained empty while I ate the brown bread and peanut butter and swigged the coffee. Behind me the sky was clouding over and I got my things together and ran for the cottages and took refuge in a little lean-to shed. Snow fell white across Sharkham and the sky darkened rapidly until blackness prevailed. Flakes whirled around the garden. Then the full force of the squall hit Mansands, and the roundabout flicker of snow became horizontal scribbles. Distances were erased and the wind was a high-pitched whine in the telephone wires.

Peering out I saw snow billowing along the coombe but beneath the noise was the faint piping of oystercatchers. The world had shrunk but some brightness showed above Hillhead and moments later the storm passed. Behind it came the sun. The last flakes fluttered down and Sharkham Point was there again, hardening to brown and green. The sea took on its familiar brilliance.

The walk back wasn't boring for it offered different views of the ground I had covered. Berry Head from the south was magnificent. Even on dull days limestone seems to generate its own light. On that occasion the rock was radiant.

Note: The name Woodhuish Down doesn't occur on the Ordnance Survey map – but it should! It is the down between Mansands and Scabbacombe.

WALK TWO
Higher Brownstone Carpark, Mansands, Outer Froward Point and Higher Brownstone again.

Length: 7 miles
Grade Ⓑ

Lanes, seacliffs and wildlife. In mid-May it is ravishing.

I parked the car at Higher Brownstone carpark with the morning still young and no one about. It was good to walk in a T-shirt and old denim trousers tucked into the red climbing stockings. My pack wasn't heavy and I felt fit enough to cross the Alps.

Leaving the carpark I came east along the narrow country

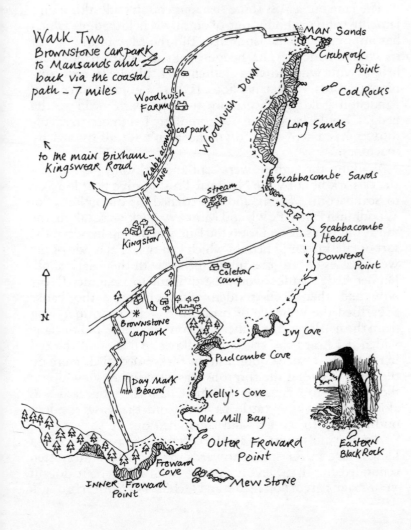

Walk Two

Brownstone car park
to Mansands and
back via the coastal
path – 7 miles

Man Sands

Crabrock Point

Cod Rocks

Woodhuish Farm

Woodhuish Down

Long Sands

car park

Scabbacombe Lane

to the main Brixham–Kingswear Road

Scabbacombe Sands

stream

Scabbacombe Head

Downend Point

Kingston

Coleton Camp

Brownstone car park

Ivy Cove

Puddcombe Cove

Kelly's Cove

Day Mark Beacon

Old Mill Bay

Outer Froward Point

Eastern Black Rock

Froward Cove

Inner Froward Point

Mew Stone

N

road past the farm bailiff's white and blue house. Under the eaves which face the sunrise were the domed nests of house martins, but despite the recent heatwave the birds had yet to return from Africa. At the entrance to the Coleton Fishacre drive which leads to the house and gardens owned by the National Trust I swung sharp left and lengthened my stride to put the handful of houses behind me and take the right hand fork a little later for Mansands by way of Scabbacombe Lane.

The lane ran across some spacious countryside although I lamented the grubbing-out of so many field hedges which has impoverished the landscape. But the May morning had its compensations. The hedge banks at either hand were bright with wild flowers – stitchwort, bluebells, red campion, primroses and dandelions. Is there a gold warmer than dandelion gold? A few more trees growing wild in the hedges would have been welcome but I suppose the flail-mower has a will of its own and aren't we all owned by machines?

Walking through flower-scent and larksong I came past the carpark built by the National Trust to give people access to Scabbacombe Sands, and approached the outbuildings of Woodhuish Farm. Fowls and Muscovy duck were taking the sun at the wayside and soon the lane was diving between the sort of tall, unkempt hedges which I admire. Each side of me were masses of ramsons filling the air with their dark stink. Higher hedge banks would be difficult to imagine. Every now and then well-trodden paths climbing the banks advertised the presence of badgers. A yellowhammer sang from the nettles and as I emerged from the shade and the lane widened I heard the cries of swallows. All around the old byres and barns of Woodhuish the fork-tailed birds were on the wing. Beyond the rooftops was a sweeping view down the coombe to Mansands and the Channel. A buzzard was aloft and mewling, cattle bawled from the vast, modern outbuildings to the left, and I marched on.

Among life's most pleasant experiences is a walk down a Devon lane in the spring towards the sea. My father often reminded me that Devon rhymed with Heaven. It does if your dialect gives you Deb'n and Heb'n! The notion brought a smile to my face as the lane narrowed into the roughest of stone tracks to make the long descent to Mansands. An old border collie overtook me without a sideways glance and loped away.

The track skirted the water meadows in the bottom of the coombe and ran into the pebbles of the beach close to the lime kiln. But I went over the stile near Coastguard Cottages into the field where sheep and lambs were grazing. Moments later I was climbing onto Woodhuish Down.

The path was the frontier between the pasture and the wild steeps. Off Crabrock Point lay a reef called Cod Rocks (why always Cod? All along the coast of England and Wales, scores of Cod Rocks). The steeps of bracken, gorse, thorn and bramble were a self-managed Nature reserve and the home of many creatures. They were visited by hawks and falcons and favoured by stoats, foxes and badgers. During a walk a few years ago I saw a stoat leap onto a rabbit and ride it like a jockey while the poor doomed victim screamed in terror. But now the larks were singing their celebration of life and I had found the sort of rhythm that mocks distance and gradient.

To climb out of seabird cries into larksong is to hit a spiritual high. Landward was the last hump of the downs. Beyond the inevitable stile was a wheatfield and flat walking towards the dark cliffs of Scabbacombe Head and the flanks of the coombe that rose like a green wall between Coleton Camp and Downend.

Over the next stile a short distance further on there was a long, grassy loss of height and just a child of a hill between me and Scabbacombe. Dafydd ap Gwilym would have loved it there on the sands. Off the beach of pebbles and shingle the sea was green and inviting. Scattered along the shore were half a dozen nudists wearing nothing but sunglasses. A lot of private parts were cooking in public and walking amongst the exposed flesh I felt embarrassingly over-dressed.

Flickering back and forth across the cliffs under the headland were many fulmars. Those tube-nosed seabirds colonised Scabbacombe Head in 1946. Successive generations have returned each year to keep their bargain with birth.

I climbed a very steep section of the path and a little beyond the bench chose to follow it directly up to the top of the head rather than take the alternative which ran along the clifftops. The seaward slopes had been swaled in early April and were covered with primroses and bluebells. I walked over Downend Point above the cave where house martins nest and the small coves and inlets which I explored in the 1940s in search of gulls' eggs. (We ate the eggs in omelettes or Mam used them in her cake mix.) The fields on my right reached down to the fence and there was the attractive marriage of farmland and wilderness.

Every gorse thicket had its linnets, and thrift was blooming above the crags. Out to sea a big container ship was creeping up the Channel. Trawlers were running south and the low thrum of their engines carried across the water. Most of the promontories and inlets below were nameless. The steeps of bracken, bramble and thorn protected them from people and whenever I passed a badger's sett or saw a cormorant spreading its wings in the sun I wanted to cheer.

The path zig-zagged into a coombe and ran on around a gorse-clad shoulder to make a similar ascent onto the turf above the steeps of Ivy Cove. I put the stile behind me and trudged on through the deep grass of a lovely clifftop meadow to be confronted by the vision of the Mew Stone. The great rock with its stacks, jagged towers and reefs stood a few hundred yards off Outer Froward Point. But a lot of good walking separated me from Froward and I had decided to saunter over the meadow and drop down to pick up the path again before it vanished into deep gorse. Soon I was in the lower gardens of Coleton Fishacre, the house D'Oyley Carte built.

The way through the conifers was depressingly neat but it brought me into contact with grey squirrels and left me in the sunshine again on the other side of Pudcombe Cove looking down into the small swimming pool on the beach where D'Oyley and his guests used to splash about.

Then the path followed its erratic course down into a goyal choked with scrub willow and thorn, over a wooden bridge across a stream and right along the edge of high vertical cliffs to Kelly's Cove. The steep drop to the rocky point beloved of anglers dumped me on the turf with the Mew Stone dark in the sun-dazzle off the point to my right. Another uphill slog and I was above Old Mill Bay where shags and cormorants nested. For some strange reason the small copse of sycamores had been felled by those in authority but their stumps were difficult to ignore as I approached Outer Froward Point and its zig-zags.

Once on the point I eased off my rucksack and changed my T-shirt before attacking the homemade pasty and pouring the apple juice into my face. Across the tidal rips the Mew Stone was catching the sun. Gulls and cormorants squabbled over breeding space on rock thick with guano. The ebb had exposed the surrounding mussel reefs and skerries. Between the outlying rocks congers lurked and a grey seal could sometimes be seen fishing for pollock.

I settled back among the thrift and sea campion and turned my binoculars on the razorbill that was sunning itself on one of the stacks. Then I packed up and moved on to climb the north side of the point into the clifftop Monterey pines. The giant trees were full of squirrels and the movement of foliage in the wind set the sun-dappled shadows dancing before me. The odd bunker and gun emplacement in the undergrowth were reminders of the war. Some of the buildings have been claimed by the Devon Trust for Nature Conservation. The wood is managed by the Trust.

Coming out of the pines I turned right onto a narrow road which climbed straight up to the Day Mark Beacon. This is an eighty-foot stone tower standing on eight stone legs in the middle of a field. It was erected by the Dart Harbour Commission in 1864 and throughout the Victorian Age was a navigational aid to seamen heading for Dartmouth.

Despite the obvious military influence on the road which pursues a series of right-angled turns all the way to Brownstone carpark I loved the final leg of this walk. A cock partridge crowed from the drystone wall that separated the hayfield from the wheat, and the dark green corn was rustling as it shifted and caught the sun. I began to sing in a voice that has emptied public bars throughout Britain; then the larks took over.

Note: The coastal part of this walk and the first walk combined – Berry Head to Outer Froward Point and back – is delightful, providing about 17 miles of hard exercise in magnificent surroundings.

WALK THREE
Strete Gate to Torcross and back.

Length: 4½ miles
Grade Ⓐ

If you like birdwatching this walk has a lot to offer but even if ornithology is low on your list of interests you'll find it stimulating.

The wind was blowing hard off Start Bay when I left Strete Gate and trudged south along Slapton Sands through the grey autumn morning. The countryside on the right was loud with seasonal colour but I was following the splendid curve of Start Bay on a beach as tawny as an old lion. Ahead, blurred by the drift of spray, was Start Point and the lighthouse. Down on the tideline anglers were casting into the surf and the thunder of the waves was a fine Wagnerian touch.

The walking wasn't easy. Gritty sand which 'gives' underfoot demands effort but there was always the rough turf between the beach and the road if I tired of the graft. I was glad to be in the teeth of the gale with the sting of spray on my face and my mind focused on the moment. Then the wind 'shoulder-charged' me and sent me staggering, and I recalled other walks on the beaches of Mull and other autumns.

Start Bay is vast. Its storm-raked waters have claimed many crab fishermen from the hamlets of Beesands and Hallsands. And in April 1944, over 750 American servicemen perished here when their landing craft were sunk by German E boats during training for the Invasion of Europe. It is a beautiful, treacherous bay with beaches that suddenly shelve

Walk Three
Strete Gate to TORCROSS and back – 4½ miles

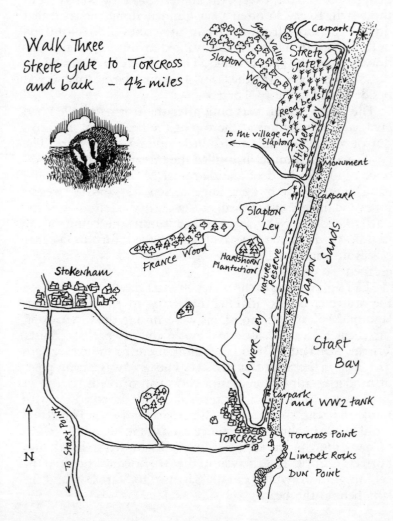

Carpark

Slapton Wood

Saea Valley

Strete Gate

Reed beds

to the village of Slapton

Higher Ley

Monument

Carpark

Slapton Ley

France Wood

Hartshorn Plantation

Slapton Sands

nature Reserve

Stokenham

Lower Ley

Start Bay

Carpark and WW2 tank

TORCROSS

Torcross Point

Limpet Rocks

Dun Point

To Start Point

N

to surprise the bather. There is no shelter for men caught by bad weather in open boats.

The morning of grey sky and grey wind and the sea a steady roar was brewing its own melancholy. I came to the memorial raised by the US Government as a tribute to the civilian population evacuated from the South Hams when the area was used for simulated warfare – with live ammunition! Sand, spray and seabirds were flying and few people were about, except the anglers and they were part of the beach. Every so often a car gunned along the road that divides the shore from the freshwater lakes of Slapton Ley.

I returned to the beach and walked on among small boats drawn up on the pebble banks. The surf was ferocious but its noise could not muffle the cries of wading birds. I wandered beside it and came to Torcross.

The new sea wall was built after the storms of 1984 had savaged the buildings at the top of the beach, but Torcross out of season was still a nice little middle-class resort. The coach-tripper summer had filled the tills and the hamlet was once again the kind of seaside resort M'sieur Hulot would have favoured had he been English. Sensible sandals, tweeds, pipes and hand-knitted cardigans were in evidence. Here the Fifties lived on. Why are seaside autumns the haunt of the middle-aged? When we pass forty do we return to familiar places in search of those bits of our past that seem to have escaped Time?

I had a glass of ale in the thatched Start Bay Inn and walked the seafront before making my way to the fresh-water lagoon. Mallard and moorhens were among the lily pads off the reeds of Slapton Lower Ley. In the car park the rusty World War II tank stood as a monument to the Americans drowned in the Start Bay disaster. The tank was a grim piece of modern sculpture against a backdrop of reeds.

Otters, which are rarely seen, share the Lower Ley with mink and both species hunt pike, roach and eels. The elvers would have negotiated the sluice back in the spring of 1944 as the tank crew practised the killing skills needed to break into Fortress Europe. But the war in the Atlantic never halted the eels' migration swim from the Sargasso to Start Bay and the lake behind the beach.

The wind gusted strong but the wildfowl flighting in splashed down without incident. Three men in beards, Barbours and Hunter wellies lifted their binoculars and scanned the far shore for rarities. One of them yawned and glanced at me but my blue Goretex cagoule wasn't 'Twitcher' garb and like the ducks out on the water I was of no great interest.

A mud path runs alongside the leys and the shoreline reedbeds almost uninterrupted from Torcross carpark to Strete Gate, but the rough ground between the road and the beach sometimes provided a better vantage point. The waters and their margins are a Nature Reserve that attract birdwatchers and twitchers from all over Britain. The twitcher collects names. He will travel hundreds of miles to tick off a new bird. When word gets around that a rarity has been spotted at Slapton the twitchers flock to the Higher and Lower Leys. Many are knowledgeable conservationists in love with wildlife; others are just curious.

Autumn brings avian celebrities to the lakes and as I walked I kept a lookout for great crested grebes, sandpipers and greenshank as well as the usual sort of wildfowl the Ley can flush from its reeds and tiny bays to delight the RSPB enthusiast. The scene was gentle on the eye. Landward was the swell of farmland and the dark mass of France Wood on the hillside. Seaward the shingle ridge was taking some of the sting out of the wind. The coot in the water under the reeds sailed across calm reaches.

I came over the Slapton village road to the Higher Ley which was dense with reeds and scrub willow. I've seen a marsh harrier here, hunting low for water voles and water birds, its head swinging from side to side as it sailed over the undergrowth, oblivious to the traffic speeding along the road. The Gara Valley reedbeds were thrashing about in the gale and few birds were on the wing although in the early autumn this is a popular gathering point for migrants.

At Strete Gate the wind rose and cuffed me off balance. Then I was in the car aware of what I had left behind me and the warm unpleasant smell of the upholstery. I switched on the ignition and Radio 3. Dvořák's Symphony Number 8 might have been written for the occasion.

17

WALK FOUR
Torcross to Hallsands and back through the lanes via Stokenham.

Length: 7½ miles
Grade Ⓑ

By the sea and home through the lanes. Spring and autumn offer their own delights.

Mike Taylor and I were a couple of middle-aged ruffians in shorts and boots, shouldering rucksacks and wearing the sort of broad smiles which make passers-by uneasy. Mike is large and bulky with a full, grey-streaked ginger moustache and thinning fair hair. The summer morning at Torcross was cloudless and the deckchairs on the prom were already taken by sunbathers when we climbed the steps beside the Tor Cross Hotel with the intention of walking south along the beach and the coastal path.

The very first headland above the hotel had its botanical surprise. The cliff face was hidden by a great mass of Hottentot Fig, an alien and exotic wild flower whose real home is South Africa. The flowers were large, yellow discs; the leaves were fleshy – like little waxed fingers. 'One of your prostrate perennials,' I said.

Mike lidded his eyes, stroked his moustache, nodded and walked on down the steps. The beach was deserted and the tide still ebbing. At high water walking this stretch is difficult unless you're wearing a diving suit, but the coastal path is always waiting above the shore and you can follow it all the way to Hallsands and beyond if you choose.

Our boots sank in the wet, gritty shingle while out on Start Bay the pleasure boats were making easier and swifter progress. Waves broke with hypnotic regularity and the breeze coming off the sea made breathing pleasant. The beach carried the sun's lustre on pebbles and broken shells. On the horizon was the silhouette of Start Point and the lighthouse. Through the heat dance it could have been a mirage. Then we passed a family in bathing costumes and were pursued for

18

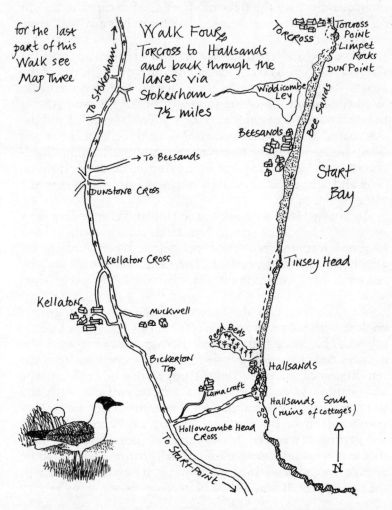

for the last
part of this
Walk see
Map Three

Walk Four
Torcross to Hallsands
and back through the
lanes via
Stokenham
7½ miles

To Stokenham

Torcross

Torcross
Point
Limpet
Rocks
DUN Point

Widdicombe
Ley

Bee Sands

→ To Beesands

Beesands

Dunstone Cross

Start
Bay

Kellaton Cross

Tinsey Head

Kellaton

Muckwell

Reed Beds

Bickerton
Top

Hallsands

Lamacraft

Hallsands South
(ruins of cottages)

Hollowcombe Head
Cross

To Start Point

N

a few yards by a wet golden retriever. Beyond Limpet Rocks and Dun Point it was necessary to take to the top of the shore to have a look at the fresh-water lake of Widdicombe Ley. There it was, holding the sunlight south of the village football pitch and the ugly caravan site which will soon be gone.

The soccer field brought back memories of games laid to rest in my youth and early twenties. I played here in mighty gales and sea winds full of flying shells and starfish. Legend maintains that half the Beesands team used to turn up straight off the crab boats with their football boots hung around their necks.

Dawdling and chatting we arrived at Beesands and the Cricket Inn, a pub facing the bay on the road at the top of the beach. Anglers were trying their luck along the wavebreak. We brought our pints and pasties out onto the wall among the crab pots and gazed across the sea. Gulls wheeled and the sky soared and arched over us. Out in the Channel gannets were diving or maybe it was a troupe of performing angels cooling off. Start Point was occupying more of the horizon now and we set off towards it, screwing up our eyes in the glare of the beach.

At Tinsey Head we took to the path and climbed up for a view of Hallsands across farmland which hadn't been hastened into the economic cul-de-sac where hedges are grubbed-out and trees felled. The fields were small and the copses untidy. 'God protect it all from the developers,' Mike said.

We walked on to the bottom of the coombe that was choked with tall reeds and osiers for about a quarter of a mile inland. The place had created its own character over the decades and the wildlife it sheltered had benefited from the remoteness of the place and the popularity of Widdicombe and Slapton Leys. Apart from the beauty of the reeds and scrub willow it was another of those important migratory points for birds. But these self-managing Nature Reserves are getting fewer and fewer, and we hoped the reedbed would receive some sort of official designation as one of those Sites of Special Scientific Interest to put it beyond the reach of the developers. It was one of Nature's great successes and all we had to do to preserve it was leave it alone. Alas, there is this awful compulsion in modern man to 'tidy-up' Nature and reduce it to the level of a municipal park or to bury it under his leisure schemes.

Hallsands North had a pleasant run-down air about it, but the pond beyond the rough little carpark which had gradually filled with silt since the war to become wetland would soon be dug out by Heritage Coast work teams as a conservation area. The planting of summer-leafing trees among the wetland vegetation at the back of the pond would enrich the habitat. The water would bring in the wildfowl.

The Hallsands Hotel standing on the bluff to the south was off-white and seemed to have been dazed by the wind-battering it took throughout the autumn and winter. But it offered a cool bar and cool Devon cider. Beyond the hotel were dangerous cliffs, nesting gulls, sea campion and four cottages perched in a row along the top of the crags and the path.

We came on to Hallsands South and the ruins of the village which was destroyed in the great storms of 1917. Here the compacted mud path gave way to pebbles. Ahead was the bulk of Start Point and we were part of the sadness of a lost way of life. All that remained of the small fishing community was a chimney breast, the wall of a cottage, the shell of a building, a heap or two of stones and thrift shaking in the breeze.

We went down to one of the sandy inlets, peeled off and swam. Then we sunbathed and talked about the storm which had ended everything. It must have been monumental. Despite the sun and the season I felt lonely, and I rarely get that feeling in unspoilt wilderness. A similar sensation ambushes me when I stand among the shells of the crofts on the Isle of Mull which were emptied by the clearances. There is that soft alarm of silence and the past coming alive to prickle the skin.

Other visitors came and went but never in large numbers. We retraced our steps and sat in the grass on the clifftop in front of the holiday flats and tea room. Snatches of conversation lapped at the edges of our own occasional remarks and the Punch and Judy chatter of the gulls. Behind us was a cosy, commercial oasis with its holiday cottages and heated swimming pool; before us the vastness of Start Bay. Nostalgia prevailed and we idled away the afternoon and early evening until the sun had vanished from Hallsands and we felt it was time to walk the lanes and country roads back to Torcross.

The sudden change from coast to farmland really appealed to me. There were gone-wild hedges dividing small fields on hillsides that glided up into the sky. We passed a mare and her foal sprawled in the deep grass below one of those old spinneys borrowed from a less destructive age. Whenever there was a field gate there was the gleam of grass and swallows hawking winged insects.

Near the top of the lane the countryside opened up and we ignored the sign pointing to Lamacraft and strode on to Hollowcombe Head Cross. The sun was going down on the South Hams as we followed the Kingsbridge Road above astonishing views of the fields and hills. The hamlet of Kellaton was scattered in the coombe to the west and the breeze carried the smell of sheep from the pastures to the east. It was a landscape that offered little resistance to the wind. Autumn would edit it even more severely to winter's bleakness.

The summer dusk closed around us. We passed the Muckwell Farm turning and tall stands of cow parsley on the verge and left Kellaton Cross behind. Just before Dunstone Cross was a gateway glimpse of high farmland spilling to the Dart Estuary. Now we were walking downhill between rounded hedges which were begging for trees. But at least we could look over our right shoulders to the sea. Our progress into dusk was wordless now. We swung up past the big pink house of Lower Widdicombe Farm and before dropping again were treated to the spectacle of Chillington's clustered lights. Distances were fading to darkness, the half-dark of summer. Other lights revealed other communities tucked away in coombes or on hillsides. Cars cruised by. Start Point lighthouse flashed. It needed an owl cry to complete the night but only gulls winging overhead were in voice. The South Hams were vanishing and the stars burnt with hazy brilliance.

After Mattiscombe Cross a long downhill stretch brought us to the A379 and we followed it right before crossing the road to enter Stokenham. Lights were on in the downstairs windows of cottages beside the road. We came past the post office and The Tradesman's Arms to The Church House Inn and the prospect of a good, hot curry. It wasn't far from Stokenham to Torcross where our lift would collect us at the appointed hour to take us home. The cider was smooth and we were sun-flushed and relaxed and ready to eat.

WALK FIVE
Start Point to Lannacombe and back through the lanes.

Length: 4½ miles
Grade Ⓐ

Any time of the year this stroll has a lot to offer.

From the carpark on Start Point I could look down on Start Bay and the ruins of the deserted hamlet, Hallsands South. Winter rain was hammering out of the strong south-westerly wind and distance was gone. I tied the drawstring of the cagoule hood under my chin and went through the gate to follow the road to the end of the Point and the lighthouse. In the spring the northern flanks which fall to the crags above Shoelodge Cove and Freshwater Bay are yellow with primroses. Despite the weather daws and gulls were on the wing. The wind would sweep them over the jagged spine of rock where the Point became wilder, and they would come wobbling on the turmoil of air down the steeps.

The entrance to the courtyard front of the lighthouse and lightkeeper's house is barred by another gate carrying a 'PRIVATE' notice. The lighthouse is one of those Victorian gems I've been drawn to since childhood. The white buildings are a startling contrast to the grey sea, the grey rocks and the grey weather. But the Union Jack snapping

Hallsands

Sturt

Bay

Hollowcombe Head
Cross

Hollowcombe
Farm

N

WT Station

Car park

Shoelodge Cove

Start Farm

Freshwater Bay

Lannacombe
Cottage

Kings Head Rock

Lannacombe
Beach

Great
Mattiscombe
Sand

Foxhole
Cove

Start
Point

Lannacombe Bay

Blackstone
Lake

Peartree
Point

Great Sleaden
Rock

Black
Stone

Walk Five
Start Point to Lannacombe
and back through the lanes
4½ miles

and cracking like a whip on the flag pole brought a splash of colour to the scene.

I retreated a few yards and climbed onto the rock spine. The wind had me fighting to keep my balance for a moment. Off the end of the Point big dark swells were sliding over the two rocks called Black Stone. The tide ran between them and the mainland through the rips of Blackstone Lake. I turned and walked the Point's backbone of rock, pausing on an eminence that was covered in grey lichen to squint into the rain towards Peartree Point which is high and has an Alpine profile.

The path descended the steeps and ran towards Peartree through the dead bracken and thrift, at times along the cliff edge above places like Foxhole Cove until it reached the broad terrace of turf overlooking Great Sleaden Rock and the skerries which are covered at high tide.

Throughout my life I've bivouacked here from time to time under the Point to be woken in the night by the tidal waters roaring between the rocks. The cliffs of Peartree offer spectacular yet easy climbs and I did many of them with my daughter Rebecca when she was at primary school.

Peartree Point is the beginning of the fantastic rock formations which run parallel to the shore for miles. Anyone with time to spare would do well to scramble up some of them rather than dutifully trudging the well-worn track. Even these outcrops offer the chance to stand in the sky, and here you will encounter the sort of beauty which may inspire you to confide inner thoughts.

Looking across Lannacombe Bay I was surprised to see a dark line moving landwards over the water. Approaching the reefs which guard the approach to Great Mattiscombe Sand the 'line' became a wave which stood up as high as a double-decker bus in the offshore wind and swept to the shore. We had had a week of gales and storms until the sudden shift in wind. Perhaps this had produced the curious phenomenon.

I walked around the Point, taking care above Peartree Cove with its vertical cliffs waiting to claim the unwary. I could hear the surf thunder and raced on to stare down onto the beach of Great Mattiscombe. The foam of wavebreak was sliding down the sands in a torrent and another roller was climbing like a dark wall out of the bay and gliding to the shore. Where the sloping sand met rock it broke and churned white over the beach to splash the base of the cliffs. A minute or so separated each wave.

The rain had stopped and I pulled back my hood and let the wind shake the sweat out of my hair as I followed the path along the 'raised beach' under Start Farm, striding past gorse-clad slopes and relict cliffs with more strange outcrops on the skyline. The shore was a long rock platform broken by coves and inlets, but I was fascinated by those curious formations poking out of the escarpment to my right. King's Head Rock possessed all the characteristics of a Dartmoor Tor. It was as if the moors had pushed right down to the coast. I looked back at the fine profile of Peartree through the Celtic gloom, then up again at King's Head Rock. Sheep were fattening themselves in the field between the escarp and the shore. The track was stony. On my left were the mussel beds, reefs and tide pools. Waves continued to smash over them and retreat. The rain returned, veiling King's Head Rock, but it could not dim the yellow bloom of gorse which lit the way to Lannacombe Beach.

Rain haze descended on the great headlands to the south west, and the thunder of the waves engulfing the beach startled me. I came down to find the stream pouring through a sluice into the undertow. No one was about.

Here I turned off the coastal path and walked the cart-track inland between hillsides of gorse and thorn. The noise of the sea chased me, growing fainter as the track became a narrow lane. To the left was the marshy lap of the coombe with its thorn and salix and wild looking copses on the hillside; to my right were bare fields. The hedgerow ash and hazel, thrashing about in the wind, were delightful after the seascape and shore.

Soon I passed a house buried among the trees, and some caravans at the top of the coombe, and came to a crossroads where I took the right-hand lane which was signposted Hollowcombe. The rain crumbled away once more and I pulled off my cagoule and stuffed it in the rucksack. A long steep hill brought me past two white cottages with black slate roofs and a little red gate next to a white one. Then I paused to take in the beauty of Hollowcombe Farm and its bullock yard, ruined outbuildings and faded white house.

A brisk pace brought me on to Hollowcombe Head Cross and another right-hand turn which led to the WT station and Start Farm before I reached the carpark.

WALK SIX
Start Point to Prawle Point and back.

Length: 8 miles
Grade Ⓑ

In the spring the beauty of this coastal classic can knock you out. But try it on a wild winter's day. The first section of this walk from Start Point to Lannacombe is also a shorter walk and is covered in Walk Five.

Noon was an oven and we were in it, cooking. The heatwave of early May showed no signs of breaking but we came down to Lannacombe Beach with the memory of Start Point's primrose scent fresh in our minds. I smiled at my wife. Patsy's face had caught the sun and she looked like the young girl I had met at the local 'hop' back in another age.

Children shouldering shrimp nets picked their way over the rocks and pebbles on the beach. We went past the half dozen parked cars up the track beyond Lannacombe Cottage. The thorns on the left had been angled by the wind and here we met hordes of St Mark's flies. They got in the hair and nose and mouth, but fortunately there were only pockets of them.

The day was heavy with the musk of gorse and loud with birdsong. A jet roared overhead leaving a fading vapour trail among the odd wisp of high cloud. We sauntered past a house that stood under red brick chimneys. There were crab pots on the salt-sprayed lawns and in the crabpot sheds beside the track. Yet another blackthorn thicket waited round the

Walk Six

Start Point to Prawle Point and back — 8 miles (The beginning of this walk is on Map Five)

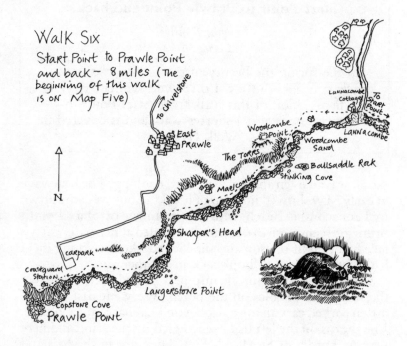

To Chivelstone

Lannacombe Cottage

To Start Point

East Prawle

Woodcombe Point

Lannacombe

The Torrs

Woodcombe Sand

Ballsaddle Rock

Stinking Cove

Malcombe

N

Sharper's Head

carpark

Coastguard Station

Langerstone Point

Copstone Cove

Prawle Point

bend and Patsy was swiping at the St Mark's flies again. Spitting the big black insects off my lips I wondered if I would manage to stick to my philosophy of weighing each creature for its worth! The flies get their name from St Mark's Day, April 25th, when they are said to emerge from the larvae.

Among the trees overlooking Woodcombe Sand were the rooftops of a very attractive house although it had no right to be there. We walked towards the sound of running water, into a coombe where the greenery of fern, dock and cow parsley and a great jungle of aquatic plants practically hid the stream. Here scrub willow flourished and the blackthorn was in late blossom. Then the path looped seaward again and we had a view of the house through the trees.

The hills on our right displayed those jagged outcrops which look so artificial they reminded me of rocks in Botticelli landscapes. An imbecile had carved his initials on the bole of a solitary ash tree just beyond the gap in the wall which the path used to escape from the bracken onto the extremity of Woodcombe Point. At either hand were masses of bluebells and stitchwort, but our eyes were drawn to the sea. The water stretching to the horizon was all sun-sparkle and the boatmen hauling crab pots offshore registered like a mirage. The loveliness of the coast curved into the blue vagueness of fine weather and the walking along what appeared to be raised beaches was easy.

We decided this was one of the finest stretches of the British coast. The beaches were small, sandy and deserted, and the farmland dividing the shore from the escarpment of relict cliffs was drenched in birdsong. The Point, with its pinnacles and rock towers, fell in steeps of gorse, thorn and ivy to the fields. Everything wore the sunlight that had brought out the St Mark's flies to plague us as we walked through the gorse and climbed a stile in the drystone wall to drop into a green meadow. Offshore was Ballsaddle Rock and we were standing on the edge of a low seacliff above Stinking Cove. The narrow beach was deserted but there were footprints on the sands, something I rarely find on Hebridean beaches out of season. Behind us Jersey heifers lay chewing the cud and the meadow sloped gently up to Maelcombe House.

'I'd like to live there,' Patsy said, crouching to tighten a bootlace. 'It doesn't look out of place like some of the properties we've seen on the coast.'

It was one of those mock-Tudor, half-timber dwellings built I'd say in the twenties or thirties. Set back in pines and summer-leafing trees, with beehives against the garden wall and an old stone byre and a midden down by the shore, the house would have sent Daphne du Maurier scuttling off to the typewriter. Anyway, I was going to buy it as soon as it came on the market.

'Along with your cottage on Mull and your Herefordshire farmhouse and your Welsh pub,' Patsy said. 'Apart from the writing you'll have to get a newspaper round in the evenings if you want half your dreams to come true.'

Below the next field was a beach which we had to visit and flop down on to sunbathe. I consulted the map. The rocks on the hill dominating Maelcombe House were called Torrs, and torr is the Gaelic equivalent of the Devonian tor. It confirmed another of those Celtic connections and meant 'rock on a hill'.

When the skin on my nose began to tighten and sting I suggested we moved on towards the buttresses of Langerstone Point. Crossing the pasture we discovered three calves – one black, one brown and one dun and white – dozing in the sun. All the fields were small, bounded by exquisite drystone walls or hedges like Wordsworth's 'little lines of sportive wood run wild'. They awakened memories of my childhood when much of the English countryside looked that way. A cuckoo called across the meadow as we walked from field to field into the past. An old sheep regarded us suspiciously while her lamb lifted a hindfoot to scratch an ear. The path hugged the top of the shore wherever it could and the sandstone cliffs separating beach and farmland were rarely over ten feet high.

In the next field the young wheat was limp in the heat behind a magnificent, fat drystone wall composed of layers of small stones. Patsy found a baby's dummy at the entrance to the adjoining field – lying there like an element of surrealist painting.

Langerstone Point beckoned and as we approached the

'buttresses' became rock towers jutting from a hillside that wasn't very impressive the closer we walked. And by the time we stood under it in the heat ripple the illusion of a solid mass had fallen apart. It was a collection of torrs on the escarpment.

We sat in the grass above the rock sprawl and mussel reefs on the tip of the point and stared over the sea to the horizon. The brilliance of the water hurt our eyes but fainter now the cuckoo called and being what we were and where we were was enough. It was difficult to imagine a spring without blackthorn blossom, swallows and cuckoos. The place and the sunlight filled me with optimism and I thought of Richard Jefferies and what he had written in *The Story of My Heart*. 'From Nature, from the universe . . . we take energy, grandeur and beauty.'

A raven left the torr and flew silently towards Maelcombe and we walked on beside clumps of flowering thrift through the fields into the slow dance of the flies. And the profile of Prawle Point was printed on haze at journey's end. A big arch of rock jutted from the foot of its cliffs into the sea.

One by one the drystone walls were left behind and the Point was proving to be a dramatic marriage of crag and turf as it filled the bottom of the sky. We lengthened our stride until the final meadow was reached beyond the World War II bunkers which were covered with grass and sheep. On the hillside to the right was a row of red cottages. The signpost where the path ended and the meadow began told us Lannacombe was two miles away. 'It seemed further,' Patsy said.

Unlike the other points Prawle was impressive even at close range. We had passed Willow Cove, Landing Cove and Western Cove, and apart from the fishermen back at Woodcombe had seen no other human beings.

Patsy took the path to the top of Prawle Point while I came over Copstone Cove to climb the friendly buttresses and grass terraces which were all atilt. Before long I was hauling onto the summit west of the Coastguard Station. Patsy joined me in the grass and we unpacked the lunch and ate and drank and stretched out to sunbathe. A pair of woodbrown butterflies tangled in courtship dance against the misty blue sky. Yachts crept across the mouth of the Kingsbridge Estuary and white sails were bellying between us and Bolt Head. The yellow gorse of Prawle Point made the sea seem very blue.

The return by the same route was delightful.

Note: Walkers who really like to stretch their legs won't flinch from a combination of walks 3, 4, 5 and 6, cutting out the lanes sections. Begin at Strete Gate and follow the coast all the way to Prawle Point – about 14 miles. How you get back depends on you. Either contemplate returning by the same route or have transport waiting at Prawle Point.

2

The South Devon Countryside

Beyond holidaycampland and the well-known tourist trails of South Devon is a less-visited area of quiet beauty. It is a countryside of low, rolling hills, small farms and villages, deep coombes, thatch and slate roofs and church towers poking out of trees. The soil is red, the Devon accent a pleasant burr and the pink wash of the buildings waiting down a lane splashed with liquid cowdung is a welcome sight at the end of your walk.

South Devon is green and gentle. In the spring it is full of the fragrance of apple blossom once you leave the main roads behind you. From the South Hams to the outskirts of Torbay there are corners which haven't changed much in the last sixty years. Many of them retain that bee-haunted, sun-washed tranquility I encountered so often when I was a boy back in the Forties.

WALK SEVEN
Harbertonford and Harberton. The lanes of the South Hams.

Length: 6 miles
Grade Ⓐ

Perfect for a Sunday morning in early summer.

Almost opposite The Maltsters Arms at Harbertonford was the Diptford Road. The Victorian church and its grey steeple

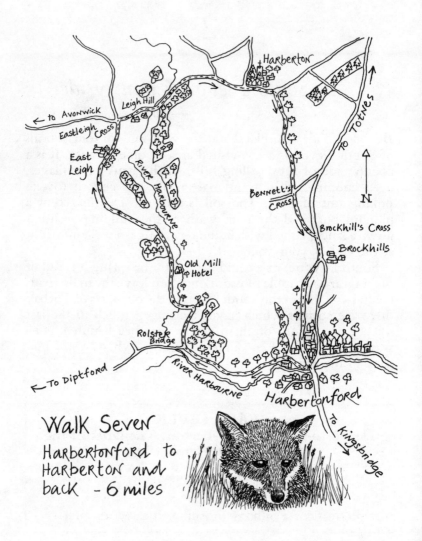

To Avonwick
Leigh Hill
Eastleigh Cross
East Leigh
River Harbourne
Harberton
To Totnes
N
Bennett's Cross
Brockhill's Cross
Brockhills
Old Mill Hotel
Rolster Bridge
To Diptford
River Harbourne
Harbertonford
To Kingsbridge

Walk Seven
Harbertonford to Harberton and back - 6 miles

were very South Hams although I could feel echoes of Dyfed in my surroundings – an old part of the village, the small cottages in a row, the country road, peacefulness. Swallows and house martins were flying high like votes of confidence for the meteorologists who had promised continuing good weather.

Harbertonford is one of those villages which haven't been entirely taken over by commuters or holiday-homers. I play for the local soccer club in the South Devon League. The pitch is a sheep pasture beside the River Harbourne. During the season there is a boom with a salmon net attached across the narrow river to catch the ball whenever it goes in the water. Steve Jane, the Club Secretary, fishes it out with a landing net on a pole.

The rooks cawing from their nests in the trees on the rise above the Harbourne brought those matches poignantly alive as I walked past the old woollen mill. All the blackthorn blossom and luminous greenery of May couldn't entirely swamp the vision of big Jeff Palfrey ploughing through the mud to head in a goal or little Les Steer doing a ferret job on some ball-playing opponent. We usually lost but the game remains one of those wholesome Devon happenings that make my week.

Down in the coombe the river twisted through fields, its banks lined with trees. Beyond the old farm was a hanging copse and I was walking under birdsong through a tunnel of golden green oak leaves.

At Rolster Bridge there was the opportunity to turn left for Diptford, Avonwick and South Brent but I chose to follow the road around the bend beside stands of dog mercury and other wild flowers into more open countryside. On the 'S' bend was a white cottage and another little bridge where I paused and looked in the water for trout. Mink had colonized the Harbourne years ago and I've been lucky enough to see otters between Sandwell Old Manor further upstream and Bow Creek. The river became the Aishbourne in my novel about otters called *The Moon in the Weir*.

Beyond the bridge the road which was no more than a lane with a good surface ran alongside the river which was almost hidden behind the trees on the near bank. At the roadside was a house called Greenwinds and in the top of the coombe was the Old Mill Restaurant and Country Hotel. Here the Harbourne was as narrow as a stream and could have been cleared in a leap by an active pensioner. The coombe was enclosed by hills. Friesian cattle had been aesthetically arranged on a sloping green pasture nearby.

Then the lane swung away from the river and I was climbing a hill between hedges bright with the blue, white, pink and gold flowers of the season. There were lots of harts tongue and campion, stitchwort, bluebells and dandelions. The lane carried me into spring with glimpses of young wheat through a gateway.

At the top of the hill I looked back over humpy farmland and copses. Larks were shrilling close to hysteria and among the songs of the other small birds I recognised the sweet refrain of the blackcap. The smell of the countryside washed over me and I was shedding the last of the tension I had brought with me from Torbay and my work.

A few yards further on Eastleigh Farm masked the beginning of the descent past an orchard and more buildings to Eastleigh Cross and the road to Harberton. The lovely white house on the hillside was barred with shadows of the oaks which were breaking into leaf. Down in the coombe there were cottages and a smallholding then the bridge which featured so often in *The Moon in the Weir*. A few pig houses stood on the mud beside the Harbourne which had widened to river size again. The sun-dappled water was on my left as I came up the hill under a wood of mature trees to the right.

The bed of the valley beyond the river was beautiful with its reedy little fields and lady's smocks, hedges and clumps of willow and alder. The shadows of the wood housed the music of birds and I was walking between the sound of the Harbourne and the rustle of leaves. Down on the water meadows cattle were grazing. A car passed, grating through the gears. I came over the brow of the hill and saw the tower of Harberton Church above the rooftops of the village.

The road down into the outskirts of Harberton was braided with cattle dung. The hedgebanks were high and the hedges plump and leafy. At the crossroads I turned left to walk through the village, up St Clements' Terrace with its typical South Hams architecture of little windows and doorways under porches, to the square in front of The Church House Inn. The pub is 13th century, a low white building. Behind the church was another of those classic South Hams houses, its weather-tiled walls gleaming.

I like village churches, especially those with literary connections – Kilvert's churches at Clyro and Bredwardine, Grasmere Church where Wordsworth is buried, others elsewhere for similar reasons. A grey stone building like Harberton's church appears to grow out of the landscape. Remove such an edifice and the immediate countryside is diminished.

I went into a churchyard that was full of the scent of new mown grass. A blackbird was singing in the yew tree and from somewhere beyond the far headstones came the bugling of domestic geese. The church and the village were in one of those quiet coombes surrounded by native trees. I didn't enter the church. The swallow-haunted sunlight and the blackbird's melody were too seductive to abandon.

The swifts which had only returned a day or so ago from Africa were screaming as they hunted the sky high above me for insects. Only larksong can challenge that joyful summer sound. A cuckoo calling across the chestnut candles after rain is the voice of the English spring.

Closing the iron gates behind me I turned left and took the path down past cottage gardens and a delightful black and white house to the road that led me left again out of Harberton. The wayside bank was enormous and there were enough deciduous trees to bring a smile to my face. I ate a salad roll as I followed the road right at the fork for Harbertonford. And here it climbed uphill beneath the shade of big, beautiful oaks and beeches. One giant had fallen and I stopped to marvel at the mass of roots in the hedge bank. Then I was ambling along under a row of mature beeches, their 'rind' all sun-dappled. A little further on was a byre standing under a mossy roof where a wren was singing such a loud song for such a small bird.

There were trees in their prime each side of the lane leading to Bennett's Cross. The verges were masses of cow parsley and sycamore seedlings, and as the lane levelled out and the trees ended I could look across acres of Devon farmland. Many of the hills had their own spinneys. They rose above a sea of small fields.

I sauntered on to Brockhill's Cross and the busy A381 to walk cautiously down towards Harbertonford and a pint of good ale at The Maltsters.

WALK EIGHT
Waddeton, Stoke Gabriel, Higher Yalberton and back.

Length: 8 miles
Grade Ⓐ

An escape from the summer tourist crush. Bring a plastic container in your rucksack for the cider.

Rooks were at their nests in the tops of the tall fir trees of Waddeton Court. The birds constantly came and went above the thatched roofs of the three pink cottages in the centre of Waddeton hamlet, a community of probably less than fifty souls. It was an idyllic spring setting. Where the roads and lanes met a fine summer-leafing tree was gathering the wind and sun to its foliage.

I took the Stoke Gabriel road and the cawing of the rooks pursued me as I came past Home Farm and on up the slight hill by East Farm and its unpretentious house. Orchards gave way to fields of wheat and I walked beneath oak leaves alongside a hedge where wild angelica swayed in the draught of passing cars. It was heartwarming to find so many mature trees in the hedges.

Everywhere were oaks and glimpses of red soil. Then I found another pink cottage at the wayside. Behind the overgrown garden was a field of buttercups and a gentle vision of countryside running to the sky which was patched with the high cloud of settled weather. Cock crow and the quacking of ducks drifted down from Waddeton. The wind murmured in the branches above me.

From the entrance to Sandridge Barton on the left it was possible to gaze across the Dart Valley to high farmland. Over the leaf-glitter was the river and the boats at their moorings and the houses of Dittisham. The sun burned into the back of my neck. Swallows shrilled.

I passed the stony track which led to Sandridge and swung right with the bend between meadows and wheatfields. From somewhere far off a farmdog barked. The pasture on the right was bounded by a hedge of gnarled trees in which time and neglect had left a few gaps. Through one of those I could see Lower Well Farm in its wooded coombe. The frantic bleating of the sheep contrasted with their placid grazing. A large group of them lay in the shade of an oak in the middle of the field. Behind Lower Well Farm was an orchard and horses taking their ease. I was on the brow of the hill looking over my right shoulder to the roofs and chimneys of the farm which I had visited as a boy. The surface of the road was leaf-shadowed where it widened and the right-hand verge was hidden by stands of cow parsley and angelica which were a triumph for the conservation lobby. Striding downhill I could look into a tree-filled goyal (a little coombe) to the apple blossom and tiled roofs of Middle Well House. And soon I was standing on Port Bridge – another childhood haunt. Leaning over the parapet to look downstream I had an orchard behind me and cream coloured houses each side of the brook in front of me. Pigeons were strutting and cooing in the loft of Port Bridge Cottage and the brook ran shallow over stones. A cattle lorry rumbled by.

Walking on I turned left at the Old Forge into a narrow, leafy lane away from the noise of the traffic. The cottage garden was full of soft fruit bushes and beyond it was a buttercup meadow. Immense hedges rose on the opposite side of the lane and I was in another of those tunnels of foliage. But on the left behind a screen of alders was a pond with lily pads and flags. The big house beside it is called Byter Mill and peering through the stone arch into its courtyard I saw the stream tumbling over a waterfall.

The right hand side of the lane was a bank of ferns and nettles under trees. Here and there were badger paths but my path ran on to climb over the head of Mill Pool. The stream cut through a wetland of grass and rushes to meet the brackish water of the creek. Mink live there now.

Before long I was passing the first of Stoke Gabriel's outlying housing development. 'Development' in this context can be a sinister word. Often all it means is the destruction of the countryside, and there, high on the bank, were the villas and bungalows which were central to somebody's rural dream. They had nice views but were not nice to look at.

I turned back to the creek and the shelduck cruising on the brown water. The far side of Mill Pool was wooded and I preferred it to the development on my right with those box buildings and their expensive views.

Eventually the lane turned away from the creek and ran on between fences and walls under the plaint of starling chicks and eaves clotted with nests. And there beyond the apple blossom was Stoke Gabriel Church. I met villagers and walked through the drone of a hover mower, up Coombe Shute with its pink and white cottages, and down again past The Victoria and Albert Inn before the hill brought me face to face with The Church House Inn. This is one of my favourite pubs. It is centuries old, an eccentric black and white building with a deep porch and an enormous fireplace. I come here for the Devon accent, the farmhouse cider and the euchre – that most Celtic of card games. The place was one of my dad's weekend watering holes and I served part of my apprenticeship as a scrumpy drinker in the bar.

The lounge has an unusual permanent resident. On display in a cabinet on the wall is a mummified cat which was found in the roof of a nearby cottage during repairs to the structure. Cleo is centuries old and her body was probably placed in the building as a kind of phantom mousetrap to frighten away vermin. Or she could be linked with witchcraft superstitions. Evil witches were said to enter cats whenever the ladies fancied a little shape-shifting but if one got into a dead cat she could do the household no harm.

The cobbled drive in front of the pub leads to the Church of St Mary and St Gabriel where generations of villagers are buried. There is a saying: 'Every year the River Dart claims a heart.' Sitting outside the pub at a wooden table sipping half

41

of rough I thought of some of the men the river had taken. The Church House Inn is used by the local salmon fishermen who seine net the tidal waters of the Dart throughout the season. In the evenings they gather to discuss the fishing and deliberate on world affairs. Geoff and Margaret Bradford run a good pub and the shepherd's pie I quarried into was most satisfactory. The sparrows nesting under the penthouse porch also thought so and gathered at my feet with bright-eyed expectancy.

My walk took me on post some shops and a little carpark to ignore the road dipping to the left for the quay and the river and turn right to climb away from the lovely village school and the village hall. At the top of the hill was a walled orchard among the houses which lent a Samuel Palmer aspect to the scene. But where the road swung left beyond the apple trees the builders were at work. New Wimpey Homes were going up on an estate called Old Orchard after its original name. The irony was chilling.

I came out of Stoke Gabriel to stride past Rydon Acres which is a posh housing estate immured in serene privacy. Soon I was in the countryside again. Traffic swished by and I left Four Cross Lanes to come down Whitehill by the farm. The green parkland would soon be covered in caravans and mobiles. In front of the reception centre stood a crop of chalets.

I hurried on and found myself above the orchards of the coombe that links Lower and Higher Yalberton. Then I turned into Yalberton Road and was besieged by more memories. On the right was Hunts Farm and ciderworks; and further down was the thatched farmhouse of Churchwards. The sign boldly displayed at the roadside read: 'Scrumpy Cider Sales this way'. There was the weighbridge and the loft above the mill where I once worked at every process of cider-making. Vic Churchward was a good tolerant boss. He had to be with me and my hands like horse's hooves and my mind always elsewhere.

By the farmhouse door was a smaller sign: 'M. and V.I. Churchward, Cidermakers'. The hill brought me to the sales shed and the vats and a big notice carrying the legend – 'Prize Farm Cider'. And I can vouch for it. Churchward's superb agricultural wine, constipation's great enemy – sweet, medium sweet and dry! My dad drank gallons of the dry when it was called rough, and he lived to a ripe old age. I was weaned on it and still drink the odd quart with half a pound of Stilton or a pair of kippers. Of course, scrumpy can destroy the daft or the unwary or tourists that don't pay it the respect it deserves. Large quantities can loosen the teeth and the bowels, numb the mind and unscrew the kneecaps to leave the victim legless, witless and useless. Yet my father pursued it as if it were the Holy Grail and he only had a day to live. He came here on many a Sunday to sniff around the sherry casks where the golden juice was stored. Maybe his ghost still wanders through the shed, for heaven is where the heart is.

Leaving Churchwards I climbed a short distance up the hill and took the sharp right hand fork into Lower Yalberton Road to walk the coombeside above the apple trees into Lower Yalberton. The farmhouse at the crossroads was startling white but the notice in the yard told me to 'Beware of the Dog', so I swung left and came up the hill between tall hedges. On one side was gentle farmland; on the other, caravan parks. The occasional rustle in the hedge was a small creature panicking at my approach. I passed a copse which had probably been planted as pheasant cover, and some meadows, all on the right, which made it possible to ignore the caravandalism across the road. The sudden urban shock of the STC (Standard Telephone and Cables) factory can be survived in the knowledge that you can walk away from it into larksong and farmland.

Waddeton Road provided an escape from the industrial intrusion. Beyond the last yard and shed were cornfields and meadows. Rooks spread their wings and lifted off the yellow surface where silage had been cut. At the roadside was a pigeon killed by a car, but the larks went on singing and the laughter of children carried across the fields from the outskirts of Torbay. Ahead on the distant skyline was a small copse. I walked towards it and came to Great Tree where the road divided, but Great Tree was really Great Tree Stump – hollow and massive. I kept to the left of it and sauntered through the north of Waddeton and the smell of cows. Thatch and mossy stone stood between me and Waddeton

Barton – a beautiful farm. The yard was running with cattle urine and the outbuildings had seen a lot of history. A cock crowed and was answered by another but as I approached Waddeton Court the rooks filled the day and my thoughts with their cawing.

WALK NINE
Totnes, Ashprington, Bow Bridge and back.

Length: 8 miles
Grade Ⓑ

Out above the River Dart and back through the lanes.
An autumn journey for all age groups.

Totnes is one of the oldest boroughs in England with a Norman castle, market place and Guild Hall, some good pubs and bookshops, an old Sandstone church and pleasant houses on both banks of the River Dart.

I left the Plains by the riverside delicatessen early one autumn morning and walked down the river through Reeves timber yard. From the worksheds came the whine of saws. Timber was stacked all along the quay.

It was a day of high wind and showers and I had an appetite for walking. At the Steam Packet Inn with its riverside beer garden I turned right and climbed the hill for about fifty yards until the lane, signposted 'Footpath to Ashprington', took me sharp left up Sharpham Drive.

To begin with the surface was 'civilised'. The gale roared in shrubberies which only partly concealed the suburban villas. All the golds and browns of the season were thrashing about in a chaos of light and shade. Leaves and birds whizzed by. Then the sky darkened briefly and rain hammered down. Tantalising glimpses of the river valley presented themselves through gaps in the hedge on my left as the sun came out again and the shower swept by.

The Dart, the Celtic river of oaks, was holding the light. From its birthplace on the moors to its estuary it has so much

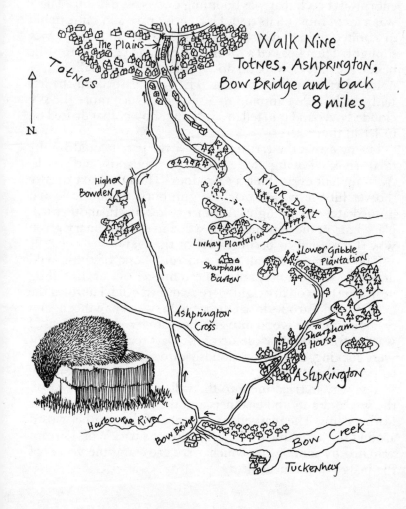

RAT TERY 3

Totnes

The Plains

Walk Nine
Totnes, Ashprington,
Bow Bridge and back
8 miles

N

Higher Bowden

River Dart

Reeds

Linhay Plantation

Lower Gribble Plantation

Sharpham Barton

Ashprington Cross

To Sharpham House

Ashprington

Harbourne River

Bow Bridge

Bow Creek

Tuckenhay

to offer. And I liked the way urban Totnes ended abruptly in countryside where the far banks lay under small rounded hills. Here, the rich hues of the season were patched with the sere of stubble and the red of plough.

Beyond the house called Foxgloves the path became a stony track, running with water. It was a real country lane, high hedged and alive with wind. Leaves and branches were in disarray, and I was walking up a noisy passage broken on the left with views down the fieldside to the river. Before long I passed through a copse of roaring young trees and one enormous beech that was booming out its own music. There was a lot of moss on its rind. I hit a brisk pace and came uphill in conifer gloom which was pierced here and there with sunlight. Then I passed a lovely old oak and climbed the stile beside the gate to walk on down a ride between walls of tree noise, alert for falling boughs. The Dart flashed on the left with the hillside climbing to a spinney. Once more the sky clouded over and rain fell in a stinging shower that drifted on to let in the sun.

I came down the cart track. Over the gate I could see the tidal river flowing wide through wetlands and reeds. Autumn lent everything a splendour. Then the next squally shower hit me with a machine gun burst of rain followed immediately by sunlight. Another stile beneath another oak placed me in the dancing shadows of an extraordinary green way. I emerged to become part of the view.

The morning was all rain and sun – one of those wild dramas a Westcountry autumn can muster out of the fading year. The trees on my right were tarnished gold. I jumped the next stile and strode down the track between hawthorns and on alongside the wood into another shower. And suddenly I was confronted by a close-up of the Dart reedbeds. The reeds were rocking, and racing cloudshadows brought movement to everything.

The way hurried me into the valley with duck rising off the wetland guts and channers and the reeds curling at their feathery tips. The marvellous urgency of the weather closed around me as I came to the bridge over a trickle of a stream watched by some goats which were browsing the verges of the hedge in the next field.

The reedbeds were between me and the river and on the coombeside above the goatfield were the houses of Lower Sharpham Barton. Shelduck splashed down among the reeds – not without difficulty in the wind. The showers had left a glitter behind them and I walked over it across parkland dotted with trees. Then a signpost on the right-hand side of the track proclaimed the public footpath to Ashprington. It was necessary because the path wasn't visible. Undeterred I ambled up through a pasture where Jersey cattle grazed and entered Lower Gribble Plantation and its violence of conifers. Light burst through the branches but after a while the path climbed out of the trees with the copse on its left and a hedgebank opposite. It carried me down to the gates of the Sharpham Estate. Here it joined the lane and I walked on beneath the boughs of an oak. All my life I've been in love with the native British trees. They are a joy to the eye.

I was whistling as I swung down the hill in the teeth of the gale. Hills covered in small fields undulated away to the sky and its stampede of clouds. Birds took to the air only if they were heavily insured. But there below me was the crenellated tower of Ashprington Church and moments later I was in the village.

The small Parish Church of St David and its blunt red tower and superb lych gate proved to be another of those subtle Celtic connections. There aren't many churches in England dedicated to the patron saint of Wales, a man who was the inspiration of Celtic Christianity in the sixth century. But it wasn't just the name that fascinated me. Ashprington's Holy Well is also dedicated to St David and a Celtic chapel once stood on the site of the present church. Perhaps the saint himself prayed here on his way from Wales to France, but it's more likely the oratory was founded by some of his followers. Bow Creek, one of the sheltered inlets of the Dart, was less than half a mile away down in the coombe. It was typical of the sort of tidal creeks favoured by Celtic Christians hugging the coast in their boats during the missionary years of the religion. A chapel among the trees up on the hillside wouldn't attract attention.

I went through the lychgates and poked around in the churchyard while the gale continued to fill the sky with noise

47

and flying leaves. Behind the tower was a goyal and a duckpond with a handful of cider apple trees. The gardens of the village reached into the meadows.

It was a relief to get into the porch and out of the wind. St David's Chapel became the Parish Church in the 13th century and the interior was mediaeval although its austerity, smallness and lack of gloom were reminders of its origins. I had a look at the plastered walls, the Norman font and the modern carving on the pulpit. It was all very pleasing. So I dropped some coins in the wallbox and departed.

A shower had fallen while I was in the churchyard. Ashprington is a neat village of stone cottages and tiled roofs. I found the granite cross in the centre of the community and read the names of the local war dead. The chestnut on the corner was rocking and roaring and a small boy was darting about collecting conkers.

In front of the war memorial was The Durrant Arms standing next to a handsome white house. I walked on, down the hill, with well-cared-for cottages on my left in small gardens. Rain gusted through the village and a scrawny black farm cat ran before it. The sun shone. A rainbow arched over the roofs. The air was cool and smelt of woodsmoke and I was going to Bow Bridge. At Ashprington Post Office Stores I bought a pie and ate it as I walked. From the paddock above Coombe Farm a cock crowed. How I love that sound! It reminds me of the summers I spent in the fields of Ashprington, picking strawberries, and of my young companions with their teeth flashing white in sunburnt faces.

A small bus called the Harbourne Shuttle came up the hill through the stink of cat's pee outside the farm on my left. I walked on and had my first glimpse of the creek. The rooks were absent from rookeries which looked as if they would lose all their nests to the wind.

At Bow Bridge Cross the signs read: Tuckenhay, Cornworthy, Yetson House, Ashprington, Totnes and Harbertonford. I crossed the grey bow bridge over the Harbourne and found half a dozen mallard ducks dozing on the wooden benches and tables beside the river across the road from The Waterman's Arms. The pub provides gourmet bar food, from fresh Dart salmon to roast beef, and good ale; but it was too early and the place was shut. So I sat among the ducks in my cagoule and wondered what Dorothy Wordsworth might have written in her journal if she had visited Bow Creek. The water clattered over shallows of stones and shillets but its cheerful sound could only be heard when the roar of the gale faded every now and then.

To be free to walk with a pack on my back wherever I choose is a great privilege, and as I went back over the bridge to take the Harbertonford Road I recalled how Richard Hannay felt after his escape from London into the Scottish countryside. The hill was long and steep but the gates in the hedge on my left opened into gold and brown views of the Harbourne valley and the play of cloudshadows.

At Ashprington Cross I came straight over the road into the unsignposted lane that led back to Totnes. In *The Thirty Nine Steps* Hannay regretted kicking his heels in Town when he could have been on the hills losing the flab of easy living. The Rut is a fate we can avoid, if not permanently then at weekends or in the long evenings of spring and summer. The lane leading into mystery or even adventure and romance is always there where the houses end and the living world begins.

From the broad ridge I could look down on the reedbeds of the Dart again over hedges that screamed, or gaze across the fields to my left towards the dark hills of Dartmoor. Huge trees soared above the hedges with one colossal beech fit to grace the lawns of Heaven booming and swaying. Very few cars passed.

Beyond Higher Bowden the lane took a right-angled turn and wound down into the valley presenting a superb view of Totnes. The town is a beautifully self-contained community, carefully laid out with none of the urban sprawl and ribbon development which have destroyed less thoughtful communities.

On the far horizon was the silhouette of one of Dartmoor's most celebrated granite outcrops – Hay Tor. Rain fell across the sun and I walked down through the suburbs of Totnes to the quay.

WALK TEN
Huxham's Cross to Rattery and back.

Length: 6 miles
Grade Ⓐ

A lovely route throughout the year but spring can be magical although on Christmas Eve it takes on a special charm.

Late one afternoon, a few days before Christmas, I felt the need to sample the outdoor flavour of the closing year. There had been a light snowfall on frost, but mild weather was forecast for Christmas Day although every kid in Devon was praying for blizzards.

Public transport regularly passes the Cross but I had taken the car that day. The sky was clear as I left Huxham's Cross and dodged through the traffic over the road to Buckfastleigh before darting up the side road to Rattery. For me this is a lane-walker's dream. It takes you away from the 20th century, with six miles of pleasant walking, three there and three back – and a pub fire to break the journey.

The air was windless, the colours a mixture of soft greys, blues, sepia and white. I strode up the avenue of oaks through a hush broken by my footfalls, the far-off cries of rooks and daws, and the diminishing noise of the traffic. Cold masked everything. It left a tingle on my face and made the actual physical side of the business delightful.

The gates in the hedges provided the 'windows' onto what stretched beyond the immediate. Dartington and Totnes lay under chimney smoke, surrounded by the pigeon colours of early winter. Lights were coming on. The sun had gone down and rabbits' scuts vanished into the hedges when I started walking again, ever uphill. The communities below seemed snug set against the cold. Where the way levelled out below a tracery of beech branches I could look to the right and see Hay Tor standing on white moorland hills beyond the South Devon countryside. Nearly all the local hills were crowned with copses. Westward the sunset sky fed off the

Walk Ten

- Huxham's Cross to Rattery and back 6 miles

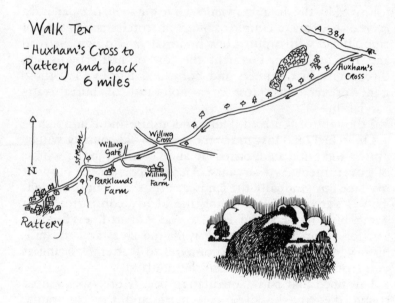

hush. Then the lane was climbing steeply and I felt I was on a causeway that ran over a landscape I had known for a lifetime. The hedgebanks were scarred with rabbit and badger runs. Sheep cried out to each other and the rising, falling ridge brought me gradually higher – several hundred feet above the sea.

On these sorts of walks I always carry an old Ordnance Survey map because I hate the modern trend towards the metric with the height of the hills given not in English but in foreign metres. Give me a signpost with a place name followed by the distance in *miles*. Give me a *pint* of cider and a *quart* of beer and a couple of *inches* of scotch, half a *pound* of ripe Stilton with a pub a few hundred *yards* down the road and I'm at home. I lament the loss of half-crowns and threepenny bits, tanners and bobs, and I grieve for those gone-forever shires lost in a holocaust of bureaucratic vandalism.

I thought of Rutland, Huntingdonshire and Radnorshire as I marched on. How much more of the old country will be gutted and bulldozed, tarted-up and sacrificed to the whims of government civil servants? Anger deepened the glow of my face but gradually the landscape took me out of myself. Then a car passed, reminding me of my compartment in Time, but I had Edward Thomas and Robert Louis Stevenson for company. When we walk the lanes and the hills history walks with us. '4 kilometres to Rattery' glaring at you from a signpost wouldn't be England.

I stopped and had a meditative pee. More oaks waited round the five hundred feet mark and the panorama, bounded by the darkening moors, lifted me to a spiritual high. Sunset's fade-away was restful. In the opposite direction lights twinkled all the way to the sea although the hills of Totnes hid the coast.

On the hill stood three beeches and a Scots pine. In the hedge bottoms snow had drifted and lying amongst it was the body of a grey squirrel. There were no marks on it and it was still warm. Another road accident victim, I thought, miserably, as I placed it in the top of the hedge, face upwards, and came on to the crossroads. Here I followed the Rattery – South Brent lane down into the last of the light.

At first the hedges were tall but they became lower and when I passed the drive which led to Willing Farm I saw the steeple of Rattery church ahead over pale fields. The way crossed a coombe before sweeping up the clear, star-filled twilight and down under arching nut bushes into the village. It wasn't dark enough to conceal the charms of the old house on the right. Stars gleamed on slate roofs and the first white-washed cottages came into view. But the marriage of old and new wasn't everywhere harmonious. Up an incline beyond West Mead was a funny little bungalow it would be hard to love but further on West Mead Cottage and Laurel Cottage displayed clean white walls and slate-roofed porches. The lights and decorations in the lower windows reminded me that it was close to Christmas.

There wasn't much thatch in Rattery but I wasn't looking for it. Beyond some modern houses I came upon a little architectural curiosity of a cottage called Vines. Even in the dimpsey its whitewash and thatch stood out in a village dominated by slate – and so did the gnomes! They were set in the top of the wall that contained a garden so small two sparring tom cats would have felt cramped in it. I came on up the hill past a nook full of cottages which I couldn't resist. At the end of this amazing cul-de-sac was a thatched dwelling too beautiful to be real. But before I could have a closer look a big dog rushed out of a shed and scared me. Muttering threats I retreated and tried to swagger nonchalantly past the village hall while the dog barked and more lights came on.

Rattery Post Office Stores was still open and I bought some buns and wolfed them in the darkfall outside with the cold nipping my ears and nose and the universe immense and starry above me. I could smell food cooking in the kitchen of the nearby Church House Inn so I followed my nose across the car park which had once been the village green. The church was a blank silhouette against the sky but the pub was ablaze with lights. I went inside to find a wood fire burning in the bar. It suited my mood, for the pub had the smallness I associate with things belonging to the distant past. So I heaved my rucksack onto the settle and joined it after purchasing something hot in a large mug. The piping treble of carol singers would have supplied the classic postscript but you

53

3

Dartmoor

The granite plateau can be seen from almost anywhere in South Devon. Here the cultivated land ends and wilderness begins. Among the often spectacular outcrops, the tors, some of Devon's finest rivers are born. The area is a National Park with great mires, rough ground rising to two thousand feet, drystone walls, cattle grids and small, isolated communities. It has a lot to offer wilderness romantics and loners who want to 'get away from it all'. Here weather becomes poetry but the hot-dog stand in the car park by the beauty spot caters for more basic needs.

Dartmoor is sky, rock and great distances often free of dwellings. It can be grey and unfriendly or bright, sunny and ringing with larksong.

WALK ELEVEN
Crockern Tor, Higher White Tor, the West Dart and Two Bridges.

Length: 5 miles
Grade Ⓐ

Along the edge of real wilderness.

I parked the car in the small, tucked away car park at Two Bridges, loving the sunlight of late spring and the radiance it

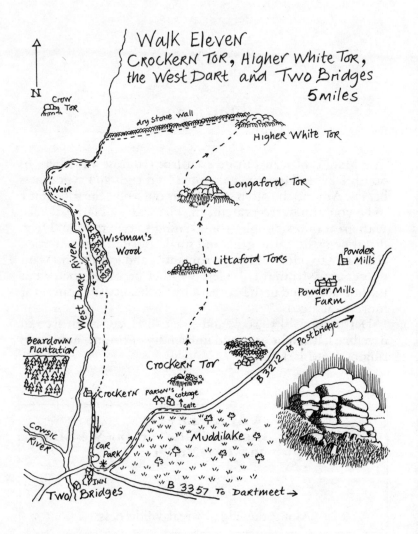

Walk Eleven
Crockern Tor, Higher White Tor, the West Dart and Two Bridges
5 miles

N

Crow Tor

dry stone wall

Higher White Tor

Weir

Longaford Tor

Wistman's Wood

West Dart River

Littaford Tors

Powder Mills

Powder Mills Farm

Beardown Plantation

B 3212 to Postbridge

Crockern Tor

Crockern

Parson's cottage

gate

Cowsic River

Car Park

Muddilake

INN

Two Bridges

B 3357 To Dartmeet →

lent the North Moor. Then I took the Postbridge Road, the B3212, and walked into the curlew cries. The birds had nested on the mires of Muddilake. Their calls of two syllables floated across the morning and every so often birds rose from the boggy ground between the willow scrub and flew off to feed.

A little beyond Parson's Cottage, the distinctive house on the left, the gate opened onto the moor and a gentle, rock-littered ascent brought me to Crockern Tor. This isn't one of those spectacular lumps of granite which draw the masses but in human terms it has a distinguished past. Tin miners from the four Stannary towns of Ashburton, Chagford, Tavistock and Plympton once held their parliament and court here (a Stannary is a place or region where tin is mined or worked). There's a wealth of literature on the subject with references to the Judge's Chair and Lydford Law. The shelves of local bookshops groan under the weight of knowledge and speculation unloaded by the expert and the not-so-expert! But the curlews were calling across the marshes of Muddilake Brook, and to the south east Bellever and Laughter Tor were refusing to be ignored.

Granite sculpted by time and weather can be glorious. Exeter Cathedral and Hay Tor have something in common: they are both statements of the sublime. Crockern Tor, on the other hand, is just a nice jumble of rocks varnished with human history.

I walked north over spongy turf, wary of the Galloway cows which could be a bit wild when they were calving. They certainly aren't at their best if approached furtively from behind. But should you find yourself confronted by a bad-tempered cow that looks ready to charge, don't run unless you are close to safety. I have stood my ground on several occasions, growling, arms spread like a wrestler. Once or twice it has been necessary to give really aggressive creatures a tap on the nose with my fist. Despite the success of this tactic I refuse to accept any responsibility if you attempt something similar and fail. Individual cows may respond differently but the Dartmoor cows have always backed off after the 'growl and tap' treatment. Maybe my phony confidence has puzzled them.

I strode on considering the implications of this line of thought. An unarmed man against a lion or tiger would have made big game hunting interesting, even sporting; and three or four men on foot chasing after a fox or a stag wouldn't be all that bad for civilisation. Dartmoor has a way of nurturing eccentric notions, but I found the ladder stile over the drystone wall of Longaford newtake and struck across rough ground for Littaford Tors to the north. En route I put up some lapwings which rose and fell in tumbling flight, uttering their high, sad cries. Larksong, the chorus of peewits and sunlight in a wilderness place! My blessings were many and I was in the prime of life (aren't we always, whatever the age?).

Littaford Tors were three main masses of granite walled in with sky and scent. From any one of the outcrops the views opened up but I couldn't take my eyes off Longaford Tor which was waiting not far off, directly ahead. Wobbling in the heat it had the mystery and appeal of those mountains that are part of the grandeur of Scotland's Northern Highlands. When I was a boy I slept on one of Longaford Tor's grass and whortleberry terraces and was woken by a wheezy old sheep breathing on my face.

I jogged on in my anxiety to climb the tor and sit on the edge of the eighty foot crag that faces east. From there I could look over the boggy flats of Powder Mills and the upper Cherry Brook to Bellever Forest and the moorland beyond. Longaford provides a superb panorama of tors standing in distances that crumble to haze on certain days.

The sky was clear and vast. Great curves of down surged from the far off vagueness and I felt that I had truly said goodbye to the worst aspects of urban life. I didn't suppress the urge to sing.

Looking in the opposite direction, down into the valley of the upper West Dart, I could see the tree tops of Wistman's Wood. Above the little oaks was Beardown and its large tors. Further to the north Crow Tor was perched on the hillside like a giant boulder. Even further north Rough Tor stood on the edge of bleaker remoteness.

For me most tors have a magnetism I can't resist. They are focal points in an open, undulating landscape. I wonder why so many human beings have the urge to get up in the sky. Reluctantly I forced myself to leave Longaford Tor and came awkwardly over tussocky grass to Higher White Tor where it stood slightly to the north east a short distance away. At 1,712 feet and crowned with a cairn this outcrop is as high as a lot of Welsh mountains.

Making myself comfortable on the sun-warmed granite I took out the cheese, the bread rolls and the thermos flask. I realise I'm forever singing the praises of ripe Stilton – and why not? If I'm in love with a cheese why shouldn't I catalogue its virtues? The rolls were fresh and the Stilton gooey with age. It smelt like grandad's feet used to smell, but all the cheese of Heaven could not conjure up a more cryptic flavour. Then I unscrewed the top of the flask and filled the plastic cup with a measure of cool, Churchward's cider – the real farmhouse rough. The marriage of scrumpy and Stilton was miraculously successful and I narrowed my eyes with pleasure while the larks sang and I sweated.

The day was a scorcher and I spent two of its hottest hours sunbathing on Higher White Tor. Then I followed the drystone wall down into the valley of the West Dart and selected a place deep enough for me to wallow in the raw. A group of pony mares and their foals watched from under long lashes as I emerged rejuvenated to towel down and put on a dry T-shirt from my rucksack.

Walking beside a Dartmoor river can be fun at anytime of the year but on a glorious spring day it takes some beating. The flow is hypnotic. It dances along and carries you with it. By now morning had become afternoon. I stopped and peered into the slack reaches between torrents where brown trout hung nose to current. I would liked to have seen a dipper walking underwater in search of aquatic insects, but none of these handsome little birds was around. Perhaps they were all underwater. The dipper is a moorland character. Head down, it walks along the stream bed into the current with the force of the water gliding over its slanting back preventing it from bobbing to the surface. Evolution is remarkable, and behind Nature and its myriad equations there is a gentle logic.

Keeping to the left-hand bank I came down to Wistman's

Wood which is another Dartmoor oddity. It is a narrow band of trees lying alongside the West Dart. Dwarf oaks grow in the gaps between boulders and the gnarled and stunted trees are covered in epiphytic ferns. These plants are harmless lodgers and lend the trunks and branches a shagginess. Wistman's origins are prehistoric. I've watched foxes come and go from the boulder clitter on the hillside, threading among the funny little trees and taking the cushions of lichen and mosses in their stride. Once, during my boyhood, I saw a vixen playing with her cubs on the turf beside the wood and later in my life included the event in one of my novels.

Easier walking was to be found above Wistman's but I didn't mind the odd boggy patch at the riverside. Wilderness walking implies a certain amount of discomfort but everything is relative, and the occasional bootful of water is part of the experience.

Where the trees ended I swung up to the left and found the path that carefully negotiated drystone walls with respect for the farmer. People who haul themselves over these walls in selfish disregard for others annoy me. They're the sort who would eat fish and chips with their fingers while reading the Book of Kells. I recall occasions when I've been forced to have words with thoughtless walkers but whenever possible hill silence is best met with your silence. The cries of curlews and the larksong are the marginal doodles which make a moorland day in spring so memorable. I fairly flew along the hillside to the junction to meet the rough stone track above the buildings of Crockern. The river was broader now on my right as it swirled and bubbled among the rocks on its way to Two Bridges.

I completed the walk under banks of gorse and found my companion waiting at a table outside the Two Bridges Hotel. The sleever of lager had the dew of coolness on its glass.

WALK TWELVE
Hay Tor to Hound Tor and back along the road.

Length: 6 miles
Grade Ⓑ

From tor to tor and a moorland road to bring you back.

Hay Tor lords it over the South Devon countryside. It is one of Dartmoor's God-made cathedrals of granite rising from a hilltop 1,490 feet above the sea. The word 'tor' probably comes from the Welsh 'twr', meaning 'tower'. If this is so then Hay Tor is aptly named and another Celtic connection is established.

The outcrop is a blunt grey mass visible from almost every corner of the South Devon lowlands. It is very popular and very close to the road but when I left the car park just below it the bulk of the tourists were still at the breakfast table and the tor was deserted. I scrambled to the top of the granite dome to look back across the countryside which I know better than any other landscape in Britain. There was the silver Teign and the English Channel, and to the south a glimpse of Berry Head. This view never fails to fill me with optimism for the human race. Despite everything the world remains a beautiful place.

Returning to the ground on the east side (the side facing the sea) I picked up the broad path north to the disused quarry and old granite tramway. I was warm and the sky was blue and larks were singing as they usually do throughout the year. Only in August are they less active.

In the quarry the low grey walls were all dressed up in heather, rowan and ferns. The larger and deeper of the two pools was patrolled by dragonflies that whizzed and rattled over the lily pads. House martins swooped to drink on the wing. I was contemplating a dip when half a dozen ramblers arrived and took up residence to eat sandwiches and enjoy the peace.

A little to the left beyond the entrance to the quarry the

61

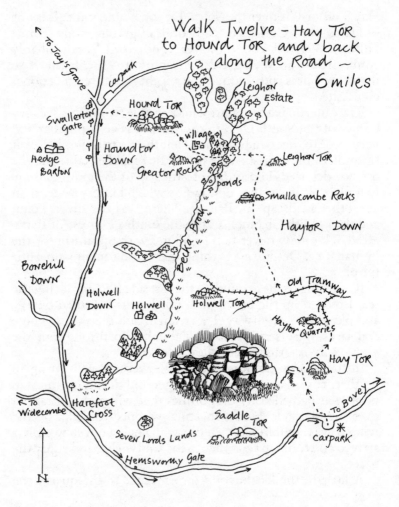

Walk Twelve - Hay Tor
to Hound Tor and back
along the Road -
6 miles

To Jay's Grave

Carpark

Hound Tor

Leighon
Estate

Swallerton
Gate

Houndtor
Down

village

Hedge
Barton

Greator Rocks

Leighon Tor

ponds

Smallacombe Rocks

Haytor Down

Becka Brook

Bonehill
Down

Holwell
Down

Holwell

Holwell Tor

Old Tramway

Haytor Quarries

Hay Tor

To Widecombe

Harefoot
Cross

To Bovey

Saddle Tor

Seven Lords Lands

carpark

Hemsworthy Gate

N

tramway divided and I followed the sharp left-hand fork. In the nineteenth century the quarrymen trundled their wagons full of stone over granite rails to the Stover Canal where barges took it to the schooners at Teignmouth dock. Granite from Haytor quarries was used to rebuild London Bridge. But I wasn't too concerned about the industrial past. Galloway cattle were enjoying a peat wallow among the whortleberries and ponies lifted their heads as I passed. The path to Smallacombe Rocks was clearly defined to the right and I strode along it with Hay Tor behind me.

The beauty of the downs was startling. By the time I had reached Smallacombe Rocks, which is an authentic little tor offering superb views west over Houndtor Valley, I was halfway back to childhood summers. Down below me was the tree-choked lap of the valley where the Becka Brook flowed into the Leighon Ponds before gushing on into the woods. Before me was Holwell Farm and the far reaches of the childhood countryside I had once explored as eagerly as any animal. To the north west were Greator Rocks and Hound Tor with Hayne Down beyond.

The path left Smallacombe Rocks as no more than a pony creep snaking between stands of bracken. As I walked I could look left into the lovely valley. The trees of the Leighon estate filled the approaches to Manaton. A buzzard was quartering the bog of sphagnum and grass, gliding over the scrub willow and alder. Flies rose from the bracken but they couldn't blight the glory of the morning. A little later under Leighon Tor which isn't named on the Ordnance Survey map, I branched left and came down the grassy ride which has been eroded by generations of walkers. It was cooler under the trees and soon I was standing on the stone bridge over the Becka Brook. I couldn't see any trout in the water.

The Becka Brook ran under green summer leaves. I smiled and loped on up the steep hillside past the larch plantation to the holly tree and first boulders of Greator Rocks. Latching the gate behind me I crossed the turf to the main rocks and climbed onto them. The ponds were there below in the valley, surrounded by trees. Canada geese nested on the island in the middle of the first pond and I saw otters there during my boyhood. Now the mink have taken over which is a shame although the little mustelids never asked to be brought here from abroad and farmed for their fur.

At length I returned to the path and followed it above the remains of the mediaeval village and on up the bracken clad flanks of Houndtor Down to Hound Tor. Here Celtic mythology took over. The story goes like this. When Bowerman the hunter was turned to stone on Hayne Down by a gang of local witches, his hounds ran on only to be overtaken by the spell and suffer the same fate as their master. They are the granite shapes which dominate Hound Tor's stacks and towers. These dark grey rocks are said to have inspired Conan Doyle during the conception of his Sherlock Holmes adventure, *The Hound of the Baskervilles*. For me the blocks and towers seem friendly enough because I've climbed them in all weathers and have a great deal of affection for this bit of Britain.

Then I heard voices and saw the young couple lying together on the turf, wrapped up in a love it would be difficult to ignore. So I crept away and aimed for the road at Swallerton Gate. But instead of swinging left I took the narrower road opposite the cottage and walked to Bowerman's Nose.

This extraordinary granite stack, standing about twenty-five feet high is supposed to be the petrified remains of poor old Bowerman who upset the witches.

After a walk around the many unnamed outcrops of Hayne Down I returned to Swallerton and set off along the road back to Hay Tor under the beeches of Hedge Barton. It wasn't necessary to keep to the hard surface. The wayside turf offered good walking until I came up against the first drystone wall of Holwell Lawn and strode downhill on the road again to the tall, handsome beeches by the cattle grid.

Beyond the grid, which I examined for trapped hedgehogs, I took to the moor again. On my right was the ridge crowned with Chinkwell and Honeybag Tors. Agitated lapwings rose and fell in crazy flight as they voiced their alarm. Ponies and sheep were at the roadside. The Scottish Black Faces were taking advantage of the grazing but they were animals which always seem close to distress.

I walked past Holwell Down to the mire the other side of

the last drystone wall where more lapwings were calling above their nesting sites. The hawthorn was in blossom almost a month later than the trees of South Devon and I was enjoying a second spring. To the east, Rippon Tor, Saddle Tor and Hay Tor looked enormous on the skyline.

So I arrived at the main Bovey Tracey–Widecombe Road, and walked left beside it among heather and furze. To the south were Foale's Arrishes, Grey Goose Nest and Blackslade Mire. Foale's Arrishes are the little 'Celtic' fields of an Early Iron Age settlement. On the other side of the road were Seven Lords Lands and Houndtor Valley. My stride lengthened as I approached Hemsworthy Gate and hopped across the cattle grid after a hedgehog search, although the altitude would probably deter the hardiest of those likeable little animals. To my right rose Rippon Tor, its approach-slopes braided with drystone walls. Ahead Saddle Tor beckoned and the view across South Devon to the sea lay under sunshine and bird calls.

When I reached Haytor carpark Allan's hotdog van was waiting and I asked for a generous squirt of mustard on the onions before putting my lips to a mug of hot tea. Coaches rolled in and the tor was covered with tiny figures.

WALK THIRTEEN
Two Bridges to Bear Down Man, Rough Tor and back.

Length: 9 miles
Grade Ⓒ

An autumn trek for a trio of friends or ageing loners.

Thunder was rumbling over the north moor when I put Two Bridges behind me and walked the Tavistock Road to pick up the public footpath a few yards along on the right. The atmosphere was warm and sticky and the summer sky overcast, darkening by the moment; so I got into my cagoule and prepared for the worst.

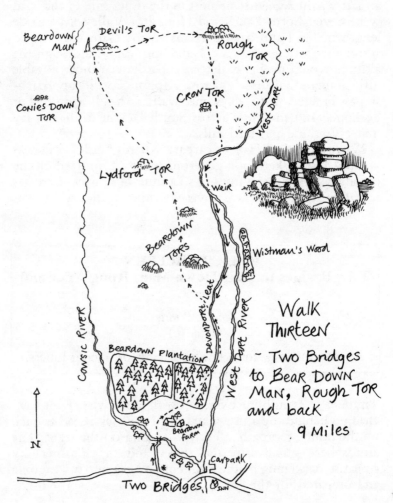

Beardown Man

Devil's Tor

Rough Tor

Conies Down Tor

Crow Tor

West Dart

Lydford Tor

Weir

Beardown Tors

Wistman's Wood

Cowsic River

Devonport Leat

West Dart River

Beardown Plantation

Walk Thirteen

- Two Bridges to Bear Down Man, Rough Tor and back

9 Miles

Beardown Farm

Carpark

N

Two Bridges

The path crossed the River Cowsic and swung to skirt Bear Down Farm before cutting through the conifer plantation of Beardown Hill. The fir tree gloom was gothic and I quickened my pace to escape it and walk beside the Devonport Leat. This is one of the moor's most famous man-made waterways. Originally it carried drinking water to Devonport but now it finishes up in Burrator Reservoir.

Suddenly the air grew cooler and thunder growled across the tors and coombes, pursued by a cracking roar. Lightning played on the horizon to my right and the thunder became an almost regular pulse. Then as the din mounted it began to rain.

I climbed the slopes of Beardown with big drops smacking against my cagoule and through my trousers which were tucked into woollen stockings, tied below the knees. The thunder crashed and a series of terrific detonations ripped through the darkness. The sky was navy blue, lit by the lightning. I bowed my head and said a prayer, but the downpour became a deluge and I kept walking. To have sheltered among the rocks of Beardown Tors would have been suicidal with the flashes fizzing and crackling all around me. After each boom and slow rumble away the rain drummed on the turf and the lightning blazed. Trying to remain calm I lengthened my stride but couldn't help wondering if one of the bolts had my name on it.

The sheep and cattle seemed unperturbed by the noise and the lethal electricity flaring in the murk. The lightning made the tors leap out of the darkness with a garishness the Victorian melodramatists would have appreciated. The landscape smelt of wet grass and stone and I was breathing rain. Forked lightning and sheet lightning competed to steal the show. It was an amazing gloom, deepening around the three separate outcrops of the tors. Maybe, I thought, the military hut on the eastern rock would get a direct hit and vanish in an explosion. That would have been poetic.

Gradually the rain abated and the gloom retreated beyond Lydford Tor; but the wind was cold and although it was July it was as dark as a winter dusk. But the interlude didn't last long. The horizons were masked and the rain lashed down, hammering into the hood of my cagoule. I sloshed on the short distance to Lydford Tor, following a line to the north west of Beardown's final tor.

The afternoon brightened and the rain swept away in misty columns. A grumble of thunder spelt the end of the storm and very shortly the sun was slanting across the Cowsic valley – as if nothing unsummery had occurred! I took off my cagoule and shook it before tucking it away in the rucksack. I regretted leaving my gaiters at home for the water had run down my legs into my boots.

Behind Lydford Tor was a drystone wall and a stile. I looked back towards Bellever. A great ocean of blue sky was spreading westward but behind it over South Devon was another bank of cloud. Leaving the future to take care of itself I climbed the gentle hillside above the Cowsic with little Conies Down Tor a handful of grey crumbs on the other side of the valley.

Ahead, in an almost straight line from Lydford Tor is Devil's Tor, one of those charming yet totally unimpressive outcrops. So why 'Devil's' Tor? Well, why can't evil be titchy and unimpressive? Why can't the Devil be a midget in a Co-op off-the-peg kid's suit? Why must he be forever portrayed as a kind of King Kong with horns? Why can't he be the four-foot-nothing, dapper insurance agent and spare-time mass poisoner? But Bear Down Man is tall even as standing stones go. It is an eleven foot menhir of weathered granite a little to the west of the outcrop that is called Devil's Tor on the map. According to the great Victorian walker and Dartmoor authority, William Crossing, the 'Man' is a corruption of the Welsh, 'maen', meaning 'stone'. Another suggestion of the region's Celtic pedigree, I mused.

The sky above was blue and the clarity alarming but the next wave of clouds was breaking around Bellever and rain had blotted out the countryside to the south east. Bear Down Man was also darkening and for the first time its great antiquity touched me. I had visited it throughout my life although the prehistoric remains on Dartmoor have always been peripheral elements of the total outdoor experience. But standing before the Bear Down Man, which might have been a marker stone on some ancient route or a religious symbol, I actually felt the weight of all those yesterdays press down on my spirit. Then the larks sang out and I looked up at the sky. Blueness was running before the next storm and light was fading. A moment or a thousand years – it didn't matter, not on Dartmoor.

It thundered. Gazing east from Devil's Tor I saw Rough Tor waiting and the cotton grass very white in the advancing shadow. This was uncompromising wilderness with a lonely ache to it. I tried to plot a route as I got into the cagoule and knotted the drawstring of the hood under my chin. The storm broke and lightning flickered and I walked east into the rain. Between grass covered peat hags were deep channers and hollows full of flood water, so my progress was a series of leaps and bounds with wobbling pauses on tussocks.

The rain hissed into the grass and one enormous explosion of thunder rumbled across the sky that had engulfed the wastes. Avoiding the worst sogs and the odd mass of cotton grass I came in the teeth of the storm to Rough Tor and its symbol of the military presence. The little hut with its green roof was an absurdity, a blatant act of vandalism, an outside lavatory planted on the centre court of Wimbledon. Over the north moor the sky was black and rain had closed down the landscape. The occasional growl of thunder spilled into my mood of defiance. Few parts of the world are weighed for their own worth.

I sat under some rocks and forgot about the occasional flash of lightning. The rain was easing and I wondered what the sky was doing behind me. The last drops pattered down and after a while sunlight swept into the gloom.

I pushed back the cagoule hood and glanced up. The fringe of cloud was silver and behind it was blue sky – acres of it. Getting to my feet I couldn't see any more cloud in the west. The afternoon was nearly spent and I was going to enjoy one of those sparkling Dartmoor evenings which sometimes burst from the heels of bad weather to make you feel guilty for cursing the Westcountry summer.

I had no appetite for the upland mires that lie between Rough Tor and the great shattered mecca of moor walkers, Fur Tor. I left the place to the sundews, frogs and occasional travelling fox.

I came south with the Princetown radio mast as a

landmark, and dropped into the valley of the West Dart to the left of Crow Tor and the enclosure where the river looped and Longaford Tor was prominent on the eastern horizon. The way back southwards wasn't difficult but the water in my boots made the walking comical. In all honesty, I confess that personal discomfort has rarely soured my enjoyment of the wilderness. A motorbike snarling along some upland road on a quiet day can make me homicidal but cold, wet feet or numb fingertips are often part of hill walking for most of the year. The sun was low and the valley in shadow which was luminous compared to the storm murk. Ridges and grassy hillsides glittered. The going was rough but never hard.

At the weir below Longaford Tor I took to the Devonport Leat and found easy walking along the lower slopes of Bear Down. Striding above Wistman's Wood and the river was a peculiar sensation for the water of the leat beside me appeared to be flowing uphill. No one was about but I spoke to the sheep and the ponies as the waterway brought me down the West Dart valley with the gnats dancing around my head and the larks shrilling close to hysteria. Never fond of conifers I hurried through Beardown plantation and its dripping shadows trying to understand the mentality that can ruin the character of a place like Dartmoor for a few quid. The maxim: 'One man's profit can be a nation's loss' is applicable on a wide scale.

Then I was clear of the trees and my own gloom crossing the sunlit pasture of Bear Down Farm and the return to my starting place on the road above Two Bridges. It was a lovely evening.

WALK FOURTEEN
Saddle Tor, Jay's Grave, Heatree Cross,
Widecombe, Saddle Tor.

Length: 12 miles
Grade Ⓑ

Perfect summer Sunday afternoon for a family of
adults and teenage children.

Saddle Tor was deserted. The big grey 'loaf' of granite was
washed by autumn sunlight as I set off for Hemsworthy Gate,
following the pony path beside the road to Widecombe.
Thrushes sat in the hawthorn trees snipping off the red berries
with their beaks. A raven loosed a cry that honed the solitude
to a fine edge. The drifts and sales had emptied the moor of
most of the ponies although a couple of mares and filly foals
were grazing at Seven Lords Lands. At Harefoot Cross I took
the road to Hound Tor, keeping to the wayside turf as I
passed above boggy ground that swept down into Houndtor
Valley. To my left were Bonehill Rocks, Chinkwell and
Honeybag Tors and heather moor puddled with mires.
Beyond Holwell Lawn and its nameless little granite outcrop
was the cattle grid, the line of old beeches and the hill which
ended in a sudden vision of Hound Tor on the skyline ahead.
Leaves were heaped under Hedge Barton's beech trees and
the sun lent the leaves still hanging on the boughs above me a
golden flush. The sky was a cloudless pale blue and apart
from the occasional car I had the moor and the morning to
myself.

At times I glimpse merlins here but on that walk they were
absent. Where the beechmast lay at the roadside pigeons were
feeding. They clattered away as I approached and returned
when I had gone. Hound Tor stood in sharp relief, holding
the translucent light of the season. Even spring cannot rival
that clarity.

I've seen stoats in the drystone walls by Swallerton Gate
but there were only finches that morning as I strode on with
Swine Down to my right. Coming up the incline at a good

71

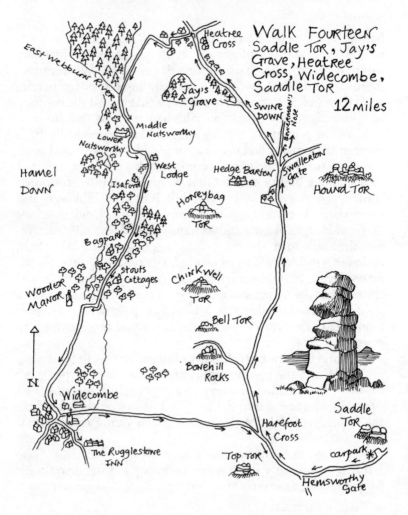

Walk Fourteen
Saddle Tor, Jay's Grave, Heatree Cross, Widecombe, Saddle Tor

12 miles

East Webburn River

Heatree Cross

Jay's Grave

SWINE DOWN

"To Bowerman's Nose"

Middle Nutsworthy

Lower Nutsworthy

West Lodge

Hedge Barton

Swallerton Gate

Hamel Down

Isaford

Honeybag Tor

Hound Tor

Bagpark

Stouts Cottages

Chirk Well Tor

Wooder Manor

N

Bell Tor

Bonehill Rocks

Saddle Tor

Widecombe

Harefoot Cross

carpark

The Rugglestone INN

Top Tor

Hemsworthy Gate

pace I paused at Jay's Grave. The little mound at what was once the crossroads had a simple, blank granite headstone and a jar of flowers which looked quite fresh. This was the burial place of the tragic young suicide, Kitty Jay, who in the last century hanged herself after being made pregnant by some local tearaway. The poor girl suffered according to the taboos of the age while the man escaped free of blame. In those days suicides were buried in unconsecrated ground at crossroads so the devil wouldn't get their souls. Such was Christian charity in Victorian times!

I walked on, thinking dark thoughts about 'respectable' society, but by the time I had reached Heatree Cross and taken the left hand lane I was back in the beauty of the morning. Stopping briefly to extract a banana from my rucksack I took the opportunity to read a passage from the *Journals of Dorothy Wordsworth* which usually travel with me. Refreshed, I climbed the hill past Heatree House, out of the trees, and swung left on the lane across open countryside. The wooded valley of the East Webburn River was to the right with Heatree Down on the opposite side.

The lovely colours of the season spilled into the day's serenity and I swung along in utmost cheerfulness. Place and fine weather have the power to raise us to heights of good humour. My senses grabbed at things. Sometimes the sky was dark with flocking birds and cattle belved from the distance. And brooding over the Webburn valley was the immense bulk of Hamel Down. King Tor stood at the north end with Hamel Down Tor almost opposite Natsworthy Manor. Leaves fell, adding to the air of melancholy surrounding the old, neglected manor which stood in overgrown gardens. The trees crowding together above me had created splendid brown and gold shadows that stirred and whispered.

The lane made a right-angled turn beyond Middle and Lower Natsworthy and there was a field with a house in it and a glimpse of Widecombe Church tower in the distance. Then the way dropped to West Lodge and Isaford and climbed a hill between tall hedges. I could not recall seeing anything lovelier than the sunlight on bramble leaves. So I stood and enjoyed the sight for a long moment.

Presently I came to a little track on the left of the lane which led up to the ridge that was dominated by Honeybag and Chinkwell Tors. A traveller in a hurry could be forgiven for ignoring it. Tightening a bootlace I continued down to Bagpark with its houses and copse, and I found a donkey rubbing its head against the bole of what looked like a giant Lawson Cypress. It was a gentle animal and allowed me to scratch its muzzle.

We parted company reluctantly and I sauntered through the autumn smells, picking up more fleeting glimpses of Widecombe Church tower until I passed Stouts Cottages. These little old buildings were set back from the lane in leafy seclusion. Leaves unhooked themselves from twigs overhead and floated down to swell the carpet underfoot. Jackdaws chakked and the hush was ruffled by the patter of the falling leaves and the muffled clatter of running water.

Purists may be wondering why I bother with the lanes when there is so much heather and grass moor to accommodate the walker's requirements. I've spent the greater part of my time as a walker and climber in wilderness country, usually alone, but the romantic in me is fascinated by the lane that winds on and on with the chance of something interesting hiding round the next corner or over the next hill. Give me four days in unspoilt hill country and the fifth doing an Edward Thomas stroll away from the 20th century.

I crossed the little stone bridge spanning the East Webburn at one of those bends I've just mentioned. Here the river was a confident trout stream flowing under false pretences, although all rivers I suppose can't claim to be much in their upper reaches.

I was in the valley now, passing Wooder Manor Hotel and striding purposefully towards Widecombe and the grey tower of the church. Left of me a hillside patched with small fields soared to Bonehill Rocks. It was mid-morning but few tourists were in the village. The green was deserted and the shops looked ready to pack in for another six or seven months, discounting weekends. This was the place Uncle Tom Cobley and the grey mare never reached although their failure hasn't handicapped the celebrated end-of-season fair.

The church is known as the Cathedral of the Moors. It's a

shapely granite building with a friendly minister in the Reverend Bill Bulley. I exchanged 'good-days' with a lady walking several spaniels, swung past the National Trust Shop and the old church houses to take the narrow road to Audrey's pub. Few visitors use this most pleasant and unpretentious of ale houses. The Rugglestone and its landlady, Audrey, are an institution far more authentic than Uncle Tom and the fair. I walked the quarter of a mile or so to the pub south of Venton Bridge. It has no sign and could be mistaken for an ordinary house. Here I found Audrey standing, arms folded, in the doorway a few yards from the stream that flows in front of The Rugglestone. Up the passage was a tap room with barrels and bottles, and the parlour on the right.

Audrey's parlour is pure 1920s with its wooden furniture and modest fireplace. That morning it was dark and unadulterated A.E. Coppard. I sat in the window piece and drank cider that was rough enough to leave my gums dry. Audrey's Devon accent is broader than my own and reminded me of my dad and his parents. They said 'stoo' for stew, 'dug' for dog and called bramble, 'brimble'. The language was butter on their lips and Audrey had the burr.

I left feeling good, returned to Widecombe and set off up the hill after turning right at the National Trust Shop. Once the last café was behind me and I had crossed the East Webburn again I could settle into the walking and achieve a nice rhythm. Rhythm was necessary because the hill climbing east out of the village was long and steep. Those who pause frequently on the ascent, protesting that they've only stopped to look back at the view, should get down to the gym or start serious jogging. Compared to the haul up Crib Goch and other mountain scrambles this is really a stroll.

The fields became open moor as I got higher. A coach brushed past me. I wonder why walking provokes self-righteousness and the need to sermonise? Fortunately the indifference of the hills put me firmly in my place. I climbed higher still, above that spartan elitist thing which can render outdoor types unbearable. To the right was Top Tor and across the way Bonehill Rocks lay under upland over which Chinkwell Tor presided.

I came to the brow of the hill and saw Saddle Tor waiting beside the road not too far away.

WALK FIFTEEN
Postbridge, up the East Dart to its source and back.

Length: 15 miles
Grade ©

A loner's classic — especially in the winter.

Postbridge isn't far from one of the four Walla Brooks on Dartmoor, and there you have another Celtic link. Walla is a derivation of the Saxon Weala which meant 'foreigners' — hence Wales. The prefix Walla indicates areas of Celtic occupation while Yolland, corrupted to names like Yelland, Yellam, Yalland and Yeoland, speaks eloquently of 'old land' which the Celts had cultivated before the Saxon occupation. The old field systems which influenced the invaders' own approach to the creation of meadow and pasture remain as the 'literature' of a distant past. But there was little evidence of former agriculture on the winter's day when I prepared to walk up the East Dart to its source high on the North Moor.

Before setting out I went and looked at the largest clapper bridge in the National Park and ate a peanut butter roll.

A white wind had swept away the last vestiges of the tourist season and, although the roads were open, snow had underlined the remoteness of that particular stretch of wilderness. Before leaving home I had written a note describing my proposed route from departure point to goal. Then I had stuck it on the mantelpiece next to the clock where it couldn't be ignored or knocked off by one of my cats. In the rucksack were all the extras I'd need in an emergency – plastic survival bag, food, spare clothing, torch, compass, whistle, garden trowel, medical kit, flask. The moors under arctic conditions demand the respect I pay high mountains but winter treks shouldn't be undertaken by the

Taw Head
Cranmere
East Dart Head
Whitehorse Hill
Black Hill
Tinner's Hut
Kit Rocks
Winney's Down
Broad Marsh
Sandy Hole Pass
waterfall
Hut circles
Broad Down
East Dart
Alternative Route
Hartland Tor
Roundy Park
Hartyland
Car Park
Postbridge
Clopper bridge
Bellever Forest
To Two Bridges B3212

Walk Fifteen
Postbridge up the
East Dart to Cranmere
and back - 15 miles

Note: The route follows
the river but the
crossings from bank
to bank aren't
shown.

N

inexperienced or unfit. Dartmoor can, and does, kill the foolish and unwary, and even hardy regulars are reminded now and then of their human frailty. The garden trowel, by the way, was to dig a snow hole to shelter in if I was overtaken by misfortune.

I usually walk up the right hand bank of the river from the bridge keeping as close to the water as possible, but maybe I've been trespassing all these years without knowing it. The 2½ inch Ordnance Survey map shows a public footpath a little further up the B3212, the Moretonhampstead side of the East Dart. This takes you past Ringhill before a sharp turn left brings you down to the river below Hartyland. From here the route north is well defined. The East Dart is your guide and it had a wild beauty that day.

Once beyond the house and its trees I could have been heading up a Siberian river into the sort of bleakness which many people find depressing and somewhat frightening. In spite of everything I still believe 'Nature never did betray the heart that loved her', although she occasionally swats those who treat her with contempt or arrogance.

I went happily into the wilderness. The sky was grey and another snowfall or two seemed likely but I knew I could turn around and retrace my steps whenever I chose. Nothing was further from my mind, though, as I crossed the river and crunched over the snow by the Bronze Age Settlements of Roundy Park. Ponies were casting about for grazing on the flanks of Broad Down opposite Hartland Tor. I worked up a bit of a glow which made my woollen hat unnecessary. Weaving in and out of the reeds and tussocky grass I made good progress.

Snowflakes fluttered down but came to nothing and I reached the pronounced loop in the river under Stannon Tor. The valley was littered with the hut circles of the Bronze Age and the East Dart was full of rocks and boulders where the flow narrowed and the sides of the valley steepened and pressed closer together. Then I was clambering up a bank of snow-encrusted heather to stand above one of my favourite moorland falls – Winney's Trough. The sides were hung with organ pipe icicles but the gush of scrumpy-coloured water over the slabs into the pool below was delightful.

I put on my hat, pulled it down over my ears and got out the flask. The coffee was hot and sweet, the water alive and the prospect of what lay beyond the falls was exciting. From there on I felt I was in 'proper' wilderness although the hand of man has fallen on much of the moor, and Sandy Hole Pass provided more evidence of past activities.

Not far from Winney's Trough the tin miners had narrowed the flow with banks to 'stream' for the mineral. I'm not qualified to go into the ins and outs of the business but I'm glad Nature comes along behind Man to dress things up with vegetation and reclaim the mess so that it looks natural to the untutored eye.

When I first walked the East Dart as a boy in search of Henry Williamson's Tarka I had no idea why the river was narrower and faster at Sandy Hole Pass. Striding above it through the snowlight industrial archaeology was still low on my list of interests. Clouds were massing over Winney's Down to the north, dark grey on cigarette ash grey, and the wind was sending snow hissing through the grass haulms.

Winter-walking the source of a hill river you cannot avoid wet feet but on that occasion many of the seepage bogs on the slopes were frozen and the streamlets could be jumped. It was good to crunch across an iron hard mire remembering previous dunkings. Memories surfaced as they will when you are alone in a lonely place. There is a haunting magic about countryside that can free us from the Now of existence and raise visions of former seasons. And the high country of the East Dart works that way for me. The white hills swept on every side to clean horizons. The bog cotton grass was also white now with snow. The silky tufts of summer were long gone but those moments when I had first waded among them in my shorts forty years ago were vividly alive again as I stood for a moment swallowing the emotion. I was the little brown guttersnipe and Tarka wasn't dead. The bubbles rise and burst but the otter isn't floating lifeless out to sea. I can turn the pages of Henry Williamson's prose and Tarka is there, calling across the insect-humming desolation of Cranmere.

Snow drove into my face and a white-scribbled greyness descended. I walked on.

The walls of the tinner's hut, another of yesterday's shells, confirmed that I was on the right track. The ruin was there beside the river up from Broad Marsh and Cut Hill stream. Cut Hill was a lowering gloom to the west, among cloud with the snow dying away.

The course of the East Dart is never dramatic. There is no broad torrent gushing through the sort of deep valleys you find in Wales and Scotland. It is the quintessential West-country hillstream and on a winter's day of snow and leaden skies, with no birds on the wing and the landscape stiff and apparently lifeless, it was alive like a current of raw energy. Wherever a brook joined the river from the hillside there were reeds and bogs and water to cross. Once or twice this meant a detour because not all the wayside mires were frozen solid. The great hanks of grass, like washed-out mop heads, had crisped under the frost and snow to something less unpleasant than usual to walk over. A few of the marshes were problems but they could be avoided by changing banks.

The tin streamer's hut on the right of the river, a little before an exaggerated kink in the course, housed a couple of crows that departed as I arrived. To the left ahead was Black Hill. The snow phantoms were running with the wind and all those empty white acres caused me some unease. The valley was broad and shallow and I was about 1,750 feet above sea level. Alas, the Ordnance Survey maps of today have reduced everything to metres and those three figure heights of hills and tors are meaningless. As I've said elsewhere feet lend British hills a British quality. 3,000 feet is high; 1,500 feet, respectable; the figure 506 on some hill is irritating.

I continued to climb, with great swells of whiteness to the left and right and the rocks on Hangingstone Hill printed on cloud. Each side of the river there were spreads of snow-encrusted morass. After heavy rain these mires and those above can be a problem. You have to jump from peat hag to peat hag to avoid a wetting, and after a long trek this isn't an ideal conclusion especially if you are out of condition. Also, it might be unwise to forget that, unless you have arranged for transport to be waiting for you on the military loop road to the north of the East Dart head, you have to go back the way you came. I hadn't laid on a lift. It ws my intention to visit Cranmere Pool and come down the East Dart again at speed and sample the ale and fireside of the East Dart Hotel.

Beyond the wellhead of the East Dart, at over 1,800 feet, the tundra landscape was hissing and whispering as grains of fallen snow were sent flying through the vegetation by the wind. Then flakes danced around me in a flurry but the squall passed and I took my bearings.

Five rivers begin on the blanket bog of the north moor: the Taw, Teign, Tavy, West Okement and the East Dart. It is one of those superb wildernesses that guarantee solitude even in August. Then I can walk among sundews, cotton grass, liverworts, sphagnum, heather, frogs and lizards. Spring isn't the glory here that it is away from height and bleakness but the light is wonderful. Autumn's clarity and the yellowing of the landscape under a blue sky can also bewitch – and bewitch isn't an extravagant word.

But there I was in the first week of February, like the last human being on earth. I checked the compass. Directly before me to the north was Taw Head with Hangingstone Hill about half a mile west of it. I had to take a line up the hillside north west for probably the same distance, but anyone unfamiliar with the mires might do well to walk to the Taw Head and then in a line almost directly west – making a right-angled turn to the left, so to speak. The jumping of frozen surface flood water, from tussocky hag to the next was the final obstacle course; but it can be managed without too much exertion. A false step would have left me thrashing about in the peat gruel for although the pools were frozen I was reluctant to find out if the ice would hold my weight.

I had followed my north-west route out of the great bowl of boggy ground where the East Dart began on to the wobbling plateau of hags. Before me were the tors of the north moor including High Willhays, which, at 2,000 feet, is the highest point on Dartmoor. Westward was another vision of Siberia with Great Links Tor prominent and a Lord of the Rings atmosphere. To the east Hangingstone Hill was vanishing in another white-out.

I walked on towards Cranmere Pool. Why Cranmere

Pool when there was just a white depression and some ice-coated peat? Obviously there was a mere or pool here once because our ancestors weren't daft enough to give places like this names which they didn't warrant. Was it, as some writers insist, Crow's Mere or Crane's Mere? Crane was the old Devon word for heron.

I found the 'pool' and the granite letter box which brings thousands of Dartmoor letterboxers to this remote place. It was a strange-looking object – like a squat stove. I rate it among the most curious artifacts in the National Park. But the wind was rising and my body was cooling so I got down under the bank, pulled up my hood and opened the rucksack.

I rarely carry stuff like Kendal Mint Cake or glucose tablets. My love of strong cheeses hasn't diminished over the years despite the tut-tutting of the cholesterol conscious. Ripe Stilton or a mature Campazola accompany me along the Celtic ways. So I sat on my bivvy bag and ate a chunk of the strong stuff between wholemeal bread and drank coffee from the thermos. For dessert I managed a peanut butter and strawberry jam roll! Then I pulled down my mit and consulted my watch. If I walked hard I would arrive back at Postbridge as the pub doors opened. It would be dark long before then but the snowlight would make dusk thrilling and the river wouldn't let me stray.

WALK SIXTEEN
**The Warren House Inn to Hameldown Beacon
and back.**

Length: 12 miles
Grade Ⓑ

A walk any reasonably fit terrier could tackle!

Timing is of the essence if you wish to incorporate the delights of the pub with the pleasures of walking. It is no good finishing up at a place that is closed. No matter how

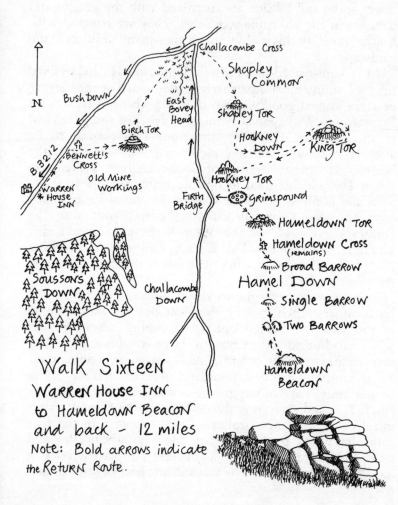

Challacombe Cross

Shapley Common

Bush Down

East Bovey Head

Shapley Tor

Hookney Down

King Tor

↑ N

B 3212

Birch Tor

Bennett's Cross

Old Mine Workings

Hookney Tor

Warren House Inn

Firth Bridge

Grimspound

Hameldown Tor

Hameldown Cross (remains)

Broad Barrow

Soussons Down

Challacombe Down

Hamel Down

Single Barrow

Two Barrows

Hameldown Beacon

Walk Sixteen
Warren House Inn
to Hameldown Beacon
and back - 12 miles
Note: Bold arrows indicate
the Return Route.

attractive the exterior may be, it doesn't do much for your interior just standing there with a rumbling stomach and dry throat. If you choose to walk to a pub you should be received by a fire roaring up the chimney and food worthy of the occasion. In the summer a beer garden is ideal, preferably by a river, where you can read extracts from *Mr Polly*.

The Warren House Inn stands at 1,400 ft on the B3212 road between Moretonhampstead and Postbridge. It is one of those squat pubs built to scorn Dartmoor winters. Tin mining associations are conspicuous here. Just across the road the coombe and hillside are furrowed with the gulleys and trenches of the old mine workings. They are covered with heather now but this is obviously a man-made addition to the landscape.

My rough-haired Jack Russell, Jamie, liked it, and he liked the cool, sunny morning of early spring which opened before us as we waved goodbye to our driver who was off to visit Princetown. We began at Bennett's Cross just along the road in the Moretonhampstead direction. This proved to be another of those distinctive pieces of granite set above the heather-clad mine workings of Golden Dagger, Vitifers and Birch Tor which ceased to operate many decades ago.

While Jamie watered the foot of the cross I looked back over Soussons Down towards Soussons Plantation. The landscape each side of the West Webburn River had a bleached wintry look. This is one of those bird-watching Klondikes which bring in the birdy folk with RSPB badges on their bobble hats.

Winter is the best time to visit Soussons. Great flocks of birds gather at their roosts in the plantation in the early dusks of the season. I looked out for incoming wheatears and whinchats but not much was on the move although curlew were calling from the coombe and lapwings were doing their aerial tumbling beyond Headland Warren. Maybe Jamie would flush a pack of red grouse as we crossed the hillside to Birch Tor, and there was always the chance of seeing a ring ouzel in the old mine gulleys. Once or twice in the past Jamie has put up foxes from their couches in the heather and on one memorable occasion he disturbed a sparrowhawk at its kill. For a ten year old he was still an alert, fit little animal but he wasn't too fond of distance walking.

We mooched around the gulleys and trenches amongst the deep brown heather with no signs of spring to brighten the scene. Soon we were climbing the hillside away from 'Twitcherland' and the scars of industry to meet the wind on Birch Tor. A conifer seedling grew among the rocks and whortleberry bushes but the views swimming away on all sides were too magnificent for the eye to dwell on minutiae. Great anvil-head clouds were sailing in from the north across the sunshine. Jamie sniffed at the wind that bumped against him like a big invisible creature. Then he cocked his leg and we headed east towards Challacombe Cross and the meeting of two roads. To the north was Fernworthy Plantation, and east of the dark conifers Chagford Common opened onto some beautiful in-country.

We jumped the head waters of the East Bovey and nipped across the road onto Shapley Common. For those who are uncomfortable in wilderness solitude this walk provides a taste of the wilds tempered by flourishes of pastoral country-side with the road at hand as an escape route back to human company. And Shapley Common is a handsome corner of the world. Among the drystone walls of its enclosures we found an exquisite little outcrop, nameless, and barely discernable on the map. I called it Coombe Down Tor although others have probably given it different names.

From the rocks we walked south with the drystone walls, up a grassy slope to Shapley Tor and crossed the Two Moors Way. The air was cold but I searched the grass for celandines, needing a glint of spring gold to confirm the arrival of the season. I found only sheep droppings and the pull-rings of drink cans. But a pair of ravens passed over the down in courtship flight and Jamie glanced up. Then the sun went out and hail beat down; and after it had passed the morning held that high-country freshness and glitter. The dog sneezed and shook himself and looked at me. So I let him lead the way south-east over Hookney Down to King Tor and King's Barrow. The tor was impressive and so were the views. Immediately below was Heathercombe Brake and the field patterns of the East Webburn Valley with the panorama of moor and in-country sweeping to the sky beyond Easdon

Tor. The tor–dotted distances were magnified by the astonishing clarity.

Jamie and I came through it due west to Hookney Tor and the chance to gaze up the valley and over Headland Warren Farm to Challacombe. From there the far-off horizons were blue and mysterious.

Down in the goyal between Hookney Tor and Hameldown Tor was Grimspound, a much-visited Bronze Age village of hut circles enclosed by a pound. The massive surrounding wall of drystone had once kept out marauding wolves and kept in the clan's cattle. Jamie wandered among the hut circles and marked some new territory with raised hindleg. We sheltered under the wall as the next shower machine-gunned the pound. Hail danced on the granite like rice and beat a tattoo on my cagoule. Then it stopped and we walked up the steeps onto Hameldown Tor which wasn't spectacular. But we were now on a continuation of the Two Moors Way with enough of Dartmoor visible on both sides to lift the meanest spirit. Many a British mountain has less to offer.

Jamie raised his muzzle, narrowed his eyes and his nostrils dilated and contracted; and watching him I regretted how modern living had blunted my senses. The ravens were overhead again, cronking and obviously well-mated. They were part of the sky, holding its light in the blue sheen of their feathers. Your heart would have to be stone to ignore the celebration of life encompassed by that moment.

My dog looked at me, wondering why I had stopped. I crouched and roughed him up in a manner he likes and expects. Then we strolled on to the remains of Hamel Down Cross and Broad Barrow for more of those heady panoramas; and we were confronted by a seemingly limitless sea of hills.

The Jack Russell was determined to push on and our pace quickened to bring us to Single Barrow and Two Barrows which I assume are ancient burial places as close to heaven as the animal-men of yesterday could manage. At Hameldown Beacon and the cairn we looked towards Honeybag Tor and Chinkwell Tor and beyond. The chimney smoke of Widecombe, down in the valley to the south, was rising like what my dad used to call 'the breath of humanity' when he was in an expansive mood. The smoke was the limit of something that hadn't been brought entirely under Man's thumb. From the Beacon the views were everything.

Another shower chased us back along the ridge to Grimspound, and when the hail was spent we came down the stream to Firth Bridge to turn right and walk the narrow road to Challacombe Cross again for the return to the Warren House Inn along the B3212. At the pub door I took off my cagoule before leading Jamie to the fire and rubbing him down with his towel. It was early and we had the bar to ourselves except for the young couple who were totally absorbed in each other. I gave Jamie his biscuits and a bowl of water and fetched my ale and pasty from the bar.

Soon we were joined at the fireside by a group of lads who had been out training for the Ten Tors event. The chat and laughter created an atmosphere of comradeship which embraced all generations. You find it in other hill country inns – The Pen y Gwryd in Snowdonia, the back bar of The Talbot Hotel in Tregaron, Frank's Bar on the Hebridean Isle of Mull. Maybe this was another of those Celtic links – the fireside, the beer and small talk after a morning in the hills. Maybe wilderness romantics can find it anywhere providing they are on the sunset side of Britain.

WALK SEVENTEEN
Great Mis Tor, Great Staple Tor, Vixen Tor and Merrivale.

Length: 7 miles
Grade Ⓑ

An ideal amble over rough ground within easy striking distance of the road.

A short distance from Rundelstone, west of Two Bridges on the B3357 road to Tavistock, is an unobtrusive little car park blessed with trees. It was deserted when I set off north for

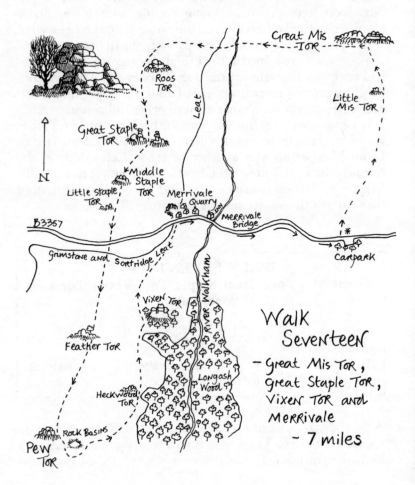

Great Mis Tor

Roos Tor

Little Mis Tor

Leat

Great Staple Tor

Middle Staple Tor

Little Staple Tor

N

Merrivale Quarry

Merrivale Bridge

B3357

Carpark

Grimstone and Sortridge Leat

Vixen Tor

River Walkham

Feather Tor

Longash Wood

Heckwood Tor

Rock Basins

Pew Tor

Walk Seventeen

- Great Mis Tor,
Great Staple Tor,
Vixen Tor and
Merrivale
- 7 miles

Great Mis Tor over the road on a route that wasn't too clear. But what need was there of a path with the moor kept open by grazing farmstock and the tor waiting on the hilltop? We live in a signposted age of paths running officiously from A to Z, and nearly all the unexpected eradicated. The incalculable dimension has been stolen from today's kids and maybe this book is contributing to that loss. I confess this is as much a celebration of landscape as a guide; but should you feel inclined to wander off the beaten track without fear of adding to the erosion problems of many popular places, do so. I explored a lot of open country with little help from books. On the other hand, today's loners may feel they're running out of wilderness and time and need all the compass bearings they can get. See how easy self-justification becomes when conscience pricks?

On the way up through the misty autumn I encountered Little Mis Tor whose name is printed in small letters on Ordnance Survey Map 28 just to let you know the outcrop is really small. Here the larksong was muted and the tor had three distinct little towers. Among the fading colours of the season it possessed a remarkable solidity. For me it was one of those symbols of the spirit of the place.

The whole of the moor was the colour of a hen kestrel. Mist hung in the Walkham Valley to the west and the sky was the palest of blues over the Tamar and Cornwall. I came up the slope of dewy turf and spider spin to Great Mis Tor which proved to be a sprawling assemblage of rocks on the hilltop. The largest lump to the west had a flagpole. Then there were two modest outcrops, a stack and another sizeable 'tor'. A couple of huts advertised military interest. Despite the turf on their corrugated roofs they were intrusive, but the vision of open moorland Great Mis Tor presented to the eye made me bite my tongue.

I could look north and east over gently rolling wilderness to hills crowned with other tors and separated by broad, shallow valleys veiled in mist. Westward mist blurred everything but enough was visible to make me ache to walk there. Dartmoor caters for the desire to approach the unknown if only in the imagination. It panders to the spiritual itch that no amount of scratching can dispel.

I climbed all the main outcrops just to have tactile knowledge of Great Mis Tor and prove to myself that middle age hadn't blunted my ability. But it had! I was not the kamikaze squirrel of my boyhood and youth that could flow up vertical rock. Anno domini smiles on the walker as it slaps the climber's wrists. But I was happy. Spring and autumn are the positive seasons, representing as they do beginnings and endings. The slopes to the west were rock-littered. Strands of spider spin hung between grasses and stabs of whortleberry. They rose in the light breeze and settled slowly again, one after another all the way down to the upper Walkham. The larksong was barely audible. It seemed to come from another room.

I descended the slope in one awful act of desecration, breaking those strands of gossamer and slithering and stumbling whenever I trod on the rabbit droppings which littered the turf. Dartmoor is a wonderful deflater of egos. It brings you down to size yet never makes you feel puny.

The sun had less warmth than a sparrowhawk's eye. Sheep and cattle raised their heads as I passed but the banks of the Walkham were deserted. The river was beautiful and lonely. Above it I found the Grimstone and Sortridge Leat and crossed that as well to climb onto the broad ridge. A solitary crow pursued me and said 'Caw!' three times before flying off, presumably to tuck into a dead sheep or something. The breeze blowing from the east was hardly strong enough to lift the dust off a butterfly's wings. A pony whinneyed and was answered by another, but there were few about.

Now the walking was ideal on the sort of turf you dream about. Landmarks were easy to identify. Ahead, to my left, was Roos Tor with its splendid rocks and military flagpole. It was surrounded by a dozen granite posts. During an arctic spell in one of Dartmoor's winters I came here and found it encased in ice over eighteen inches thick in places. The drifts surrounding Roos were frozen into sharp-edged geometric shapes like modern sculptures. The sun was shining and the whiteness of everything hurt my eyes.

Walking a ridge above a still, West country autumn, with a tor growing in size as I approached it is very satisfactory. The larksong remained hushed and a calm lay on the landscape. I looked to the north west across the in-country, with fields and woods reaching to the volcanic outcrop of Brent Tor. Perched on top of the rock was Brentor Church and I don't suppose many British churches can boast such an eminence.

Great Staple Tor is probably a corruption of 'steeple'. It turned out to be an imposing collection of granite blocks arranged in piles in a commanding position. The rock formations were lovely and the stacks or 'staples' invited climbing. I sat on top of one and stared through the mist over the Tamar Valley towards Bodmin Moor. Then I was conscious of the splendour of the Dartmoor plateau. The westward panorama was vast. Across the mist drifted flocks of starlings, daws and rooks but there were few birds close at hand. Seated on my steeple of granite I felt at home. Like all animals I was happy in fine weather and leaving the Tor I lengthened my stride to suit my buoyant mood.

Halfway down the hillside to the Tavistock Road was Middle Staple Tor. Its situation lent it magic but Little Staple Tor further on was just a jumble of boulders it would be easy to miss as you came down to the road east of Pork Hill car park. Ahead was Whitchurch Common with Barn Hill concealing Feather Tor and Pew Tor. In the south east, the majestic Vixen Tor was waiting against the golden brown woods of the Walkham Valley.

A convoy of army vehicles passed with headlights on. Squaddies stared down at me from the backs of open trucks. I crossed the road and walked south up Barn Hill and on to Feather Tor beyond the granite cross. Whitchurch Common wore its autumn hues well. I was alone. No other walker or letterboxer was afoot on that normally popular part of the moor.

Feather Tor was a fine little spread of outcrops and slabs set in the turf. Two hawthorn trees stood amongst the rock litter, covered in wine-red haws. Pew Tor was more impressive but less attractive at the top of a gentle sweep of bracken the colour of a fox. The main outcrop of great, blunt-edged blocks gave me the chance to collect another series of autumn visions before taking the footpath around the Rock Basins and following it north east above the disused quarry, the fields, drystone walls and oaks of the Walkham

Valley. On my left was Heckwood Tor, small and beautiful in the rust-brown bracken. By now Vixen Tor was looming although I wasn't in the best position to catch one of its many famous faces.

The Vixen is among the most distinctive tors and it is only a short stroll away from the road. It shares a paddock of turf and bracken with some hawthorn trees, all of which were red with berries as I approached the gate. The tor rose vertically in a high crag that has defeated many climbers. The vixen shape which some claim to see has never struck me as obvious; but the sneering profile of a man or woman, troll or witch, is unmistakable. It depends on where you are standing; but one aspect is definitely sphinx-like.

I went and stood under the south western crag. Eighty feet of rock towered above me and I recalled the time I had clambered up the chimney between the main outcrops. The occasion was buried in another autumn, but with wood pigeons flighting in to the oaks of the valley the past came alive again.

I ambled across the common, remembering companions who had dropped out of my life. Autumn is the season of nostalgia. Sunlight was strengthening and the colours of the moors were taking on a radiance. Then the road was there and a car roared by followed by others. I walked to the right, eastward, down into the dip at Merrivale with the stone quarry up to the left and the Dartmoor Inn a little further on from the despoiled landscape. One of the pony drifts (round ups) had ended in the pound below the inn and I recalled the scene – the jostling animals being separated by their owners, the shouting and laughter and the cries of the ponies. The pound was empty and silent as I crossed Merrivale Bridge over the Walkham and followed the road up the hill. The car park wasn't far beyond the Merrivale Hut Circles and I wasn't weary or footsore.

An old man in long shorts free-wheeled by on a bicycle loaded with bulging pannier bags. He had white hair and very thin brown legs. Seeing me he lifted a hand, smiled, and whizzed on down the hill into his own adventure.

WALK EIGHTEEN
Yar Tor to Leigh Tor, Bel Tor and back.

Length: 8 miles
Grade Ⓑ

Where in-country and wild moorland meet.

The landscape where the in-country blended with open moor was at peace with itself when I set foot on the summit of Yar Tor. It was a morning in early June and work and urban life had got into me so I had driven up onto Dartmoor without anything planned. I just wanted to walk and receive whatever each moment had to offer. I had parked at Dartmeet and come up the Ponsworthy Road to leave it at the first opportunity and climb the hill to my left for Yar Tor. Pushing up by the hut circles a pleasant route had taken shape in my mind.

Yar Tor is a group of low-lying rocks on a rounded hilltop but it gave access to views of fine moorland countryside wearing the greens of the season. Instead of rushing on as I would have done in my youth, I sat down and got out the grubby little paperback of Wordsworth's poetry and opened it at *Tintern Abbey*. On the downs all about me larks were singing and a cuckoo called from the woods at the meeting place of the two Darts. I read the verse and it seemed to be addressed to me personally. Maybe it was the June weather and the blue sky which belonged to childhood summers. I was at ease. The sheep and lambs were at ease. The air was calm. But before long I became restless and shouldered the rucksack and headed due east for Corndon Tor.

The walking was totally undemanding. I crossed a shallow col and the Babeny Road and wandered up to Corndon to be greeted by the panorama beyond the West Webburn where familiar hills marked the beginning of my own special part of Dartmoor.

Corndon might be dismissed by the unimaginative as just another hump of weathered granite in a wild setting. Maybe people lacking in vision shouldn't venture off the beaten

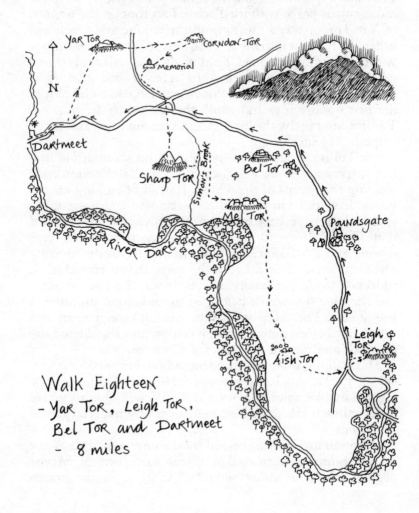

Walk Eighteen
- Yar Tor, Leigh Tor,
Bel Tor and Dartmeet
  - 8 miles

track alone into any wilderness. Corndon like most tors allows the imagination to be exercised as well as the body. If you scoff at this then forget these walks and get on the 'power jogger' at your local leisure centre.

South of Corndon was Sharp Tor but Corndon doesn't supply the view this outcrop deserves. There are ten Sharp Tors on Dartmoor but for me this one just off the Ashburton–Dartmeet Road is the most attractive. Choose the moment you can have it to yourself although the company of a few kindred spirits rarely jars.

I loped down the side of Corndon Down towards Sharp Tor glad to be there in the sun. Beyond the twin 'peaks' of the Tor were the golden-green oakwoods of the Dart Valley with Bench Tor on the other side of the ravine and the vast in-country to the south-east. It was incredible the way the wilds seemed to go on forever until sky and land blurred to a haze. When I was young I couldn't confront these distances without the urge to run into them. Little had changed. But I tripped over my own feet and landed heavily on my heels to snap out a very unphilosophical little word. What paradoxes we are! It's such a short trip from Elgar's *Cello Concerto* and John Sell Cotman's *Greta Bridge* to the chip shop and the dirty joke and the scraping together of the price of the M.O.T.

On the hillside overlooking the road and Sharp Tor was a stone cross that had been erected in memory of an army officer, Lieutenant Evelyn Cave Penney, killed in the Great War at the age of nineteen. I tried to remember what I had got up to at that age when optimism sparked from every fibre of my being. Life is the thing but I'll never be able to fathom out my species and its long courtship of violent extinction.

Over the roads I avoided the boggy ground and the stream and ascended the gentle slope to the tor and the larger of the two rock masses. A buzzard startled me with its mewling cry. It was riding one of those roundabouts of wind high above the Dart Valley. Do buzzards sport thermal underwear beneath their plumage in winter? I used to ask my kids daft questions like that and wonder why they groaned at the awful jokes.

Before long I was on top of the tor beside a small hawthorn. The oak-filled valley was at my feet and above the ravine Bench Tor was a stammer of seven outcrops poking from the turf. The buzzard circled between my tor and Bench Tor.

Sharp Tor is really a wave with two peaks, a sort of toy size Tryfan, which often puts me in mind of that lovely Welsh mountain. The river valley carried the eye to the in-country and the small fields lying within their drystone walls. I sat and turned my binoculars on the buzzard. Beautiful old coney hawk loosing one of the authentic voices of Devon! The sun was burning my arms. I ate an orange and set off again.

The path brought me down to the south-east over Simons's Lake Brook and along beside the drystone wall. On my right the bracken steeps fell to the oaks of Meltor Wood and the invisible river. It was a short distance to Mel Tor which is one of the finest outcrops overlooking the Dart. And it was the perfect counterpoint to Bench Tor. From the summit I experienced that sensation of height presiding over distance.

An elderly couple exercising an elderly dog joined me. We exchanged pleasantries and they went off in the direction of Sharp Tor. The buzzard had gone and the sky was blue from horizon to horizon.

I liked the way Mel Tor stood with the wild valley on one side and the fields and walls on the other. It was a microcosm of Dartmoor – woods, river, heath, pasture, walls, tor, sky, larksong.

Walking on, I dredged up some lines I had written about the moors when I was young and needed to write love letters to places and girls:

We walked the green bracken aisles
And saw the moor's darkest face,
While shadows blurred the rolling miles
From Haytor Down to far Teign Grace.

Beginnings came easy but development was hard.

The path crossed the hillside past many of the wallbound pastures that ran down to Poundsgate. At Brake Corner you might be forgiven for expecting to see Aish Tor surfacing from the hill before you. Instead you will be confronted by bare slopes and a scattering of rocks. These granite bits and pieces are the tor and the conceit of it all brought a grin to my face. But there were refreshing views of the Newbridge Valley and Holne Woods to the south and the trees of Holne Chase due east. Also in that direction was the magnificent Leigh Tor – a craggy outcrop Wordsworth would have admired.

I crossed the Ashburton Road and went through the official gap in the drystone wall and walked up the slope of bracken and bluebells towards it. The symmetry of the rocks was delightful. They were set among scrub oak and silver birch which were in tiny leaf. Sunlight did the rest and I searched for something in Wordsworth to seal the moment. Why Wordsworth? Well, I'm addicted to the crashing organ music of his words and his genius for leading the reader into an astonishing serenity. But for once he failed to produce the lines to transfix the occasion, so I climbed Leigh Tor, letting the beauty of the place take care of itself.

A milk tanker went up the steep hill with a grinding of gears. I left the rocks and followed it less noisily although the cartilage in my left knee was crackling.

The road to Poundsgate was pleasant enough and the hamlet itself was not fully awake. The Tavistock Inn at the wayside awakened memories of a drinking session back in my twenties after a moorland marathon in the company of friends. According to legend the Devil also dropped in for a pint en route to snatch some local tearaway, but that was long before my time. While he drank steam jetted from his nostrils. A sobering tale and one which my dad told me with all the gusto of a ham actor. It never put him off the booze though, and he was still knocking back scrumpy a few days before he died in his eighties.

I walked past Higher Lodge and Uppacott Farm with Leusdon Common to my right and the in-country character of the landscape sweet to behold. Around the next bend was Bel Tor. From the roadside it wasn't conspicuous. I looked over the drystone wall and there it was, a field away, demanding close inspection. The farmland lent this 'cake' of a tor a supernatural quality. It was like a large stage prop discarded from a Victorian melodrama. The stacs were small Bowerman's Noses rising from deep green grass and bluebells. Sheep crept forward to stare at me as I sat down. A ewe said baa and I glanced at her. She had the lovely expressionless face of her kind. Then a cuckoo began to repeat its name over and over and the ewe stood motionless among the bluebells.

More sheep were grazing Sherberton Common and the traffic had begun to build up on the road. Several cars were parked at Dartmeet when I at last reached the carpark.

WALK NINETEEN
Black Tor, Fox Tor, Hexworthy, Princetown and Black Tor again.

Length: 19 miles
Grade ©

A wilderness marathon best enjoyed by the fit in the autumn.

As I've already said one of the advantages of moorland walking is you don't always have to stick to any given path. Animals can provide narrow trails to suit your purpose, and an exact step-by-step guide in these circumstances can be irritating if you are by nature a free spirit. If you are a loner you will be content to set off after checking the map and just walk in the general direction until you eventually arrive at a suitable place as I did one bright day in September many years ago.

I left the B3212 Yelverton–Princetown Road east of Black Tor, walked to the tor and on to pick up the Devonport Leat at the aqueduct over the River Meavy. The aqueduct is an old tin mining launder and it was awash after a week of heavy rain. The leat tumbled white off Raddick Hill and I climbed the steeps beside it over plashy turf hackled with heather. The sky was blue and I was young and in love and had the heightened sensibility of a wild animal.

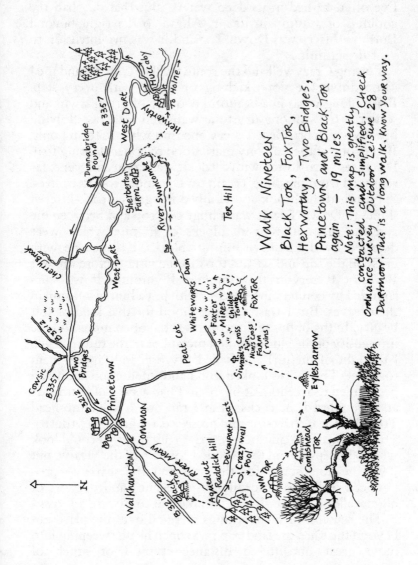

Walk Nineteen

Black Tor, Fox Tor,
Hexworthy, Two Bridges,
Princetown and Black Tor
again — 19 miles

Note: This map is greatly
contracted and simplified. Check
Ordnance Survey Outdoor Leisure 28
Dartmoor. This is a long walk. Know your way.

N

Huccaby
West Dart
B 3357
Dunnabridge Pound
To Holne
Hexworthy
Sherberton Farm. ruin
River Swincombe
West Dart
Cherrybrook
B 3212
Tor Hill
Two Bridges
COWSIC
B 3357
B 3212
Whiteworks
Dam
Peat Cot
Fox Tor
Mires
Childes
Tomb
Fox Tor
Princetown
Simon's Cross
Nun's Cross
Farm (ruins)
Devonport Leat
Walkhampton Common
River Meavy
Aqueduct
Raddick Hill
Crazywell
Pool
Black Tor
B 3212
Down Tor
Eylesbarrow
Combeshead
Tor

I raced up the hill and came along the leat to Crazywell Pool. This is the flooded remains of an old tin mining pit and I've often bathed in its deep waters. But that day had the coolness of autumn in its air. Ahead to the right beyond Burrator's trees was Down Tor and it was my intention to visit its summit.

Putting Crazywell and the route marker cross behind me I came down the slope kicking up spray with every step. Before long I was in a beautiful coombe of green lawns and scattered trees among drystone walls and little fast-flowing brooks which broadened every once in a while to form pools. Beside one of these a pony mare stood over her sleeping foal. Distances were dotted with cattle. It was a peaceful scene, far removed from the pixie, cream tea Dartmoor tourist centres.

I jumped the brook and climbed the grassy, rock-littered slopes to Down Tor. It was a huge outcrop and between me and the main mass were blocks of granite which were dwarfed by the massive summit blocks. I chose one with grass on the top and sat and took in the vista. Before me was Burrator Reservoir that supplied Plymouth. It was surrounded by conifers and beeches with just a hint of autumn in their leaves. But I wasn't in the mood for that kind of soft beauty. In the opposite direction was the open moor and the immensity of the blue sky like a metaphor of the future. Then I thought of the girl and balled my fists and tapped them together. The world looked good and smelt good and I had been given its freedom at birth. So I had a swig of lemonade and shouldered the rucksack and ran down to Combshead Tor which was charming and possessed a solitary hawthorn – a tree common to quite a few tors. From the top I could look west to Sheepstor and the wooded country of the Meavy, but I was heading south for the hills and Eylesbarrow (pronounced Yelsboro according to Crossing) and the sort of high walking I love. It would take me to Siward's Cross.

The remains of tin workings were all over the place but beyond the cairn the landscape was open heath sweeping into those great uncluttered distances typical of much of Dartmoor.

Southward were some fine tors and the Erme Plains, and to the north west across the broad coombe was Raddick Hill and swells of upland. The flow of the far horizon beyond Walkhampton Common was spoilt by the tall radio mast on North Hessary Tor.

It was just over a mile to Siward's Cross and as I approached this granite antiquity an animal sprang up from the undergrowth ahead of me and ran off. It was one of those rangy, greyish hill foxes leaving its kennel with catlike nimbleness. And the creature meant more to me than the cross. The Bronze Age hunters treading that ground must have been startled by foxes on many occasions. The animal was one of those living links between my world and their gone-forever world. Dartmoor, for all its timelessness, can raise the past in the croak of a raven or the blur of a departing fox.

Siward's Cross, which is also known as Nun's Cross, is a Dartmoor Forest boundary mark standing on a branch of the so-called Abbot's Way – an ancient path popular with ramblers.

The landscape of low, rolling hills and great stretches of bog spilled away on every side.

I turned east at the cross past Nun's Farm towards Fox Tor, my intended goal discarded and my legs full of walking. Down to the left was Foxtor Mire which Conan Doyle called Great Grimpen Mire in his Sherlock Holmes adventure, *The Hound of the Baskervilles*. He killed off the villain here but I've crossed it a few times and suffered nothing more than wet feet although in places it does make you uneasy. It is best avoided although Whiteworks on the edge of the mire at the end of the rough road south from Princetown will interest walkers who like industrial history.

I came along the contour line to Fox Tor and discovered a small outcrop perfectly suited to its remote location at the top of the Swincombe Valley overlooking the mire. Not so many springs ago, I recalled as I sat and ate one of my mother's pasties, I had seen merlins quartering the bogs where the Swincombe began. The quietude might have kept me there for most of the day but laughter gusted across the hush and I turned to see a crocodile of boy scouts approaching. During my departure I didn't bother to visit Childe's Tomb which stands to the north of Fox Tor.

The 19th century cross on its lop-sided granite plinth is a memorial to the hunter who could have been Ordulf, son of the 11th century Earl of Devon. Caught in a blizzard he killed his horse, cut open the carcass and crawled inside to keep warm, but he still froze to death. Despite his condition he dipped a finger in blood and wrote his will on the nearby stones: 'They fyrste that fyndes and brings me to my grave, the Priorie of Plymstock they shall have.' A band of monks from Tavistock brought the body to the abbey and duly inherited some of Childe's lands.

Originally I had planned to walk to Fox Tor and back via Whiteworks to Princetown, but the desire to push on eastwards grew as I skirted the mire and walked the lower west-facing slopes of Ter Hill into the Swincombe Valley. Soon the stream lured me to its banks and I delighted in the way it tumbled among the rocks and squirted between boulders down to the separation works. The weir and sluice were odd additions to the wild scene.

People came to the Swincombe merely to visit John Bishop's House – and there it was, a ruin in the ruins of summer with trees sprouting from the drystone walls and hedgebanks. But the river was alive and beyond man's things the natural world took its life from the plants and animals, the weather and the seasons. It was comforting to be beside white water and the rowan trees.

In the lower part of the valley the monks of Buckfast Abbey had beehives in one of the riverside fields. Further downstream the old buildings of Sherberton Farm crowded together on the hillside overlooking the West Dart. At Sherberton compassionate animal husbandry is central to the farming. Returning to the place in the winter of 1986 I saw Mrs Coker feeding hay to her stock from tractor and trailer. An elderly cow wearing a coat sauntered through the yard.

Sherberton presents the walker with a choice. If your car is at Black Tor on the B3212 you can walk a different route back via Princetown. The footpath over Royal Hill westwards is clearly marked on the $2\frac{1}{2}$ inch Outdoor Leisure Map No. 28.

Those with a preference for long distance treks will continue as I did to Hexworthy and the Forest Inn (to refuel!). The West Dart at Huccaby, below the pub and zig-zagging road, winds across a touristy part of the moors although it wasn't such a honeypot in the early 1950s. I went over the bridge and on to the junction with the B3357 Dartmeet–Two Bridges Road. Here I turned left and walked to Dunnabridge, finding the legwork easy after the up and down and boggy stretches of the wilderness. Dunnabridge Pound, just before you reach the bridge spanning the Cherry Brook, is another of those meccas for history buffs which casual tourists miss even though it lies beside the road. Here, in the Middle Ages, cattle and ponies that had strayed onto the forest were impounded until their owners paid the fines. The granite 'seat' just to the left of the entrance is known as the Judge's Chair and was once part of the natural furniture on Crockern Tor where the tin miners held their parliaments. I think if I'd known this then I would have still loped on, unwilling to break my rhythm.

I had a sense of history, but being in love and loving the life all around me I had no time for the symbols and relics of the past. I came along the straights to Two Bridges and took the Princetown turning to walk past the prison and through the village onto the B3212, the Yelverton Road. Before me was Black Tor and Burrator again. There wasn't a cloud in the sky. I was in one of those stationary anti-cyclones on the top of Devon with my life stretching before me like the Road to Wembley.

WALK TWENTY
Leeden Tor, Ingra Tor, Leather Tor and back.

Length: 6 miles
Grade (A)

The four seasons have much to offer in this most beautiful corner of the moors.

Many of the celebrated tors have 'beauty spot' status in the summer and if I visit them during the holiday season it's

Walk Twenty - Leeden Tor, Ingra Tor and Leather Tor from Princetown – a rough circuit of 6 miles

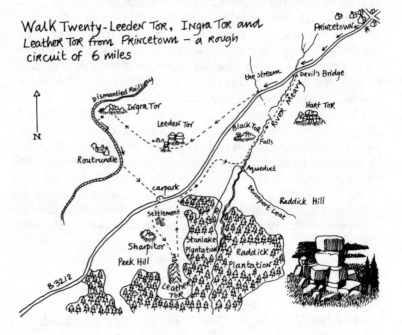

Princetown

the stream

Dismantled Railway

Ingra Tor

Leeden Tor

Devil's Bridge

River Meavy

Hart Tor

Black Tor

Falls

An

Routrundle

N

carpark

Aqueduct

Devonport Leat

Raddick Hill

settlement

Sharpitor

Stanlake Plantation

Raddick Plantation

Peek Hill

B 3212

Leather Tor

usually around breakfast time or at dusk. I'm a beginnings and endings person, in love with dawns and sunsets. I also respond like a kid to 'handsome' weather – blizzards, droughts, cloud-bursts and storm-force winds.

During the long hot summer of 1976 I was still the sunny side of forty and only had a few small cracks and creases in my face. It was the summer of drought, of reservoirs reduced to puddles and Dartmoor scorched to the biscuity colours of the African veldt. Ponies and cattle crossed the great spreads of blond grass in search of peat wallows which had become hard-baked and useless. Wherever there was accessible water, farmstock was standing in it. The heat-dance was mesmeric; the humidity incredible. I lived in shorts like the beachbum I had been as a teenager.

Late one morning in that incredible summer I hitch-hiked to Walkhampton Common, west of Princetown, and set off from the roadside to walk the long slopes for Leeden Tor. I began at the stream which had been reduced to a mere whisper of water and came through the parched grass to the outcrop that stood in haze on the near horizon. An airliner flying at some unimaginable altitude left twin white vapour trails on the blue sky.

Leeden proved to be a generous jumble of outcrops with a beautiful and conspicuous central mass and a delicately balanced boulder. From the top of the central outcrop there were splendid views of both North and South Hessary Tors, mirage-like in the 'wet-look' of heat. To the south the grooved bed of the Devonport Leat was visible on Raddick Hill without its customary white water. Also, close at hand beyond the dark conifers of Stanlake Plantation, were Sharpitor and Leather Tor. Much further off Cornwall dozed under the haze of Mediterranean weather. Swifts were flying high and leaving the tor to walk to a small shapely stac a few yards to the west, I made the reeds crackle. It was fine to be bronzed and fit in that thirsty upland with the tors like bits of Greek mythology.

Swinging lazily northward I came by small pastures within drystone walls to Ingra Tor which was considerably lower than Leeden. It rose with a heave of grassy shoulders to a shattered summit which overlooked the farmland of the

Walkham Valley. The greenness of the trees, after acres of sun-scorched moor, was delicious. All about the rocks sheep and their lambs were grazing. The ewes were skinny and white after the shearing.

I hadn't been on foot long but I was already craving fresh water to splash about in. Maybe I'd head for Burrator Reservoir or try Crazywell Pool although I suspected it would be dry. I wasn't in a hurry so I took off my rucksack, got out a can and drank, then I lay back and caught some rays for half an hour. Upon the hill to the north was King's Tor and further west across the coombe with its little fields and the remains of ancient settlements were Sweltor and Foggin Tor quarries which were closed years ago. The glare was painful on the eyes and the heat-dance hypnotic; but the larks were silent.

Westward, just below Ingra, I found the footpath which would lead me back to the Yelverton Road over the old dismantled railway the other side of Routrundle Farm. Here the rabbit and sheep droppings had been baked to little fibrous balls by the sun, and the grass was yellow. I let the path take me past some unnamed rocks to the road and the carpark. These moorland carparks, by the way, are small paddocks bounded by turf-clad banks. Up on the hillside almost due south was Sharpitor which should have been Sharper to warrant the name.

I strolled between the outcrop and the remains of Bronze Age dwellings towards Leather Tor to confront another link in the Celtic chain. It was once spelt 'Ledder' and means 'sharp'. The double 'd' was pronounced as the heavy 'th' in 'thee'. Ledder is a derivation of the Welsh word 'llethr', meaning slope. And there it was, on the hill within two horns of conifer plantations.

Now this was a sharp tor! Broken rock leapt to superb summits of no great height but sufficient to demand some scrambling. I ascended it and walked a narrow ridge of pillars and blocks with Burrator Reservoir in the south immediately below me and enough broad leaved trees to break the conifer monotony. The water was very low and a lot of shore was showing under the beeches. Beyond the reservoir was Sheeps Tor and downland the colour of a lion.

Burrator isn't really Dartmoor but the sight of sunlight glinting on fresh water had my body crying out for immersion. I didn't fancy creeping over all the mud to get into the coolness so I turned my back on it and walked above Stanlake Plantation to the road. Then I kept to the turf until I was level with the Devonport Leat and Raddick Hill. Down by the aqueduct the River Meavy was almost bankrupt and the leat was less than a token trickle.

I walked upstream to the little falls below Black Tor and discovered a natural rock 'bath' with just enough water to cover my body. God it was bliss! I thrashed about and wallowed and ducked my head, taking the coolness into every pore. A party of ewes watched me from the sward by the old blowing house that stood beside the river as a monument to the tin mining industry. What odd creatures we must appear to be to the animals living under our mercy! There I was, like a two-legged piebald with my brown body and limbs and white bum, fluting cries of pleasure as I splashed about while the animals challenged me from their dignity and repose.

Running water on a hot day plays on the senses. I dried off, laced up my boots and followed the river up past Black Tor. The temperature was in the high eighties and the air was windless. Pony mares and foals lay panting in the reeds and cotton grass, and the trickle of the river made me thirsty enough to drink from it which wasn't intelligent.

Below Hart Tor a dead sheep lay on its side in the bog. A crow that had been feeding on the animal's face flapped off. Hart Tor was protected from the sightseer invasion by the mire which was still green despite the drought. I've never tired of this 'cottage loaf' of granite with its horseshoe of turf within walls of blocks. Whortleberries were growing in cracks between the granite. Ahead on an horizon that rippled, South Hessary Tor was a pimple on the skyline.

I walked beside the Meavy to Devil's Bridge which must have some sort of satanic affinities although it looked innocent enough in the sunlight. Then I loped over the turf beside the road to Princetown and the lager. Cars and coaches swished by and sheep lined the wayside totally oblivious to the traffic.

I glanced at my watch and noted with relief that the pubs were still open. Normally Princetown is grey and inhospitable, but that afternoon it could have been somewhere in Spain. Tourists in shorts and sunhats thronged the pavements and the cafés, and ponies paraded through the main street. I brought my thirst to The Three Plumes.

WALES

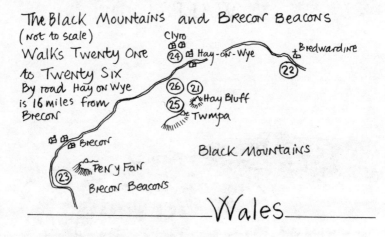

The Black Mountains and Brecon Beacons
(not to scale)
Walks Twenty One
to Twenty Six
By road Hay on Wye
is 16 miles from
Brecon

Clyro
(24) Hay-on-Wye
(22) Bredwardine

(26) (21)
(25) Hay Bluff
Twmpa

Brecon

Black Mountains

(23) Pen y Fan
Brecon Beacons

_____ Wales _____

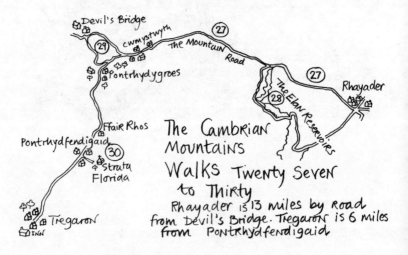

Devil's Bridge
(29) cwmystwyth
(27) The Mountain Road

Pontrhydygroes

(27)
(28) The Elan Reservoirs
Rhayader

Ffair Rhos
Pontrhydfendigaid
(30)
Strata
Florida

The Cambrian
Mountains
Walks Twenty Seven
to Thirty
Rhayader is 13 miles by road
from Devil's Bridge. Tregaron is 6 miles
from Pontrhydfendigaid

Tregaron
INN

4

Mid-Wales and the Borders

The Welsh Marches to the south have always been for me the frontier beyond which the Celtic dream flourishes. Look across the plain of Herefordshire and the dark reef of the Black Mountains in waiting. The landscape of the Marcher country is rich in black and white, half-timbered cottages but over the Black Mountains the magpie style gives way to something more austere. The English shires run into a wall of Welshness and walking the Black Mountains is like walking a ridge above time's high-water mark. All unspoilt hill country can lift you out of your moment in time but few British hills possess the mystery of these mountains.

WALK TWENTY-ONE
The Black Mountains – Pen y Beacon (Hay Bluff).

Length: 3 miles
Grade Ⓐ

A fine experience in the summer for a grandparent and grandchild.

At least the almost continuous autumn rain meant I had that part of the Black Mountains to myself. Apparently Pen y Beacon which previous generations have known as Hay

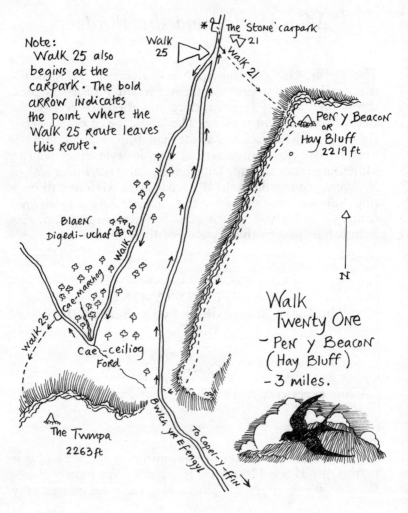

Note:
Walk 25 also begins at the carpark. The bold arrow indicates the point where the Walk 25 route leaves this route.

Walk 25

The 'Stone' carpark

Walk 21

Pen y Beacon OR Hay Bluff 2219 ft

Blaen Digedi-uchaf

Walk 25

Cae-marchog

Walk 25

Cae-ceiliog Ford

N

Walk Twenty One
- Pen y Beacon (Hay Bluff)
- 3 miles.

The Twmpa 2263 ft

Bwlch yr Efengyl

To Capel-y-ffin

Bluff is popular with hang gliders but thankfully the only things sailing over it as I parked the car in the carpark near the Stone were rain clouds.

After checking to make sure all the doors were locked I walked away from the car a few yards along the Capel-y-ffin single track road, and there was the well-defined path to the Bluff running over the common. Between the gorse bushes sheep were quietly grazing. I walked the waterlogged turf among them and thought of Kilvert. Much of his work is a Wordsworthian expression of delight in the living world. Dafydd ap Gwilym demonstrates a similar love of nature and both poets were also fond of pretty girls, so another Celtic connection had surfaced from the more obvious links of the Welsh place names. But it was good to be surrounded by pen, bwlch, bryn, cwm, bach and fawr. It was apparent, too, the way the Celtic language lost ground the further east I looked on the map.

A map isn't necessary on Hay Bluff or the approaches to this striking 2,219 foot summit. If you can't find your way onto it I suggest you give up hillwalking.

Cloud swirled over the Bluff and it vanished. Down to the south west the high mass of Twmpa was also being rubbed out by rain. On such a day you shouldn't take young children onto even the safest mountains unless you really know what you're doing. Hay Bluff isn't dangerous as Tryfan is dangerous but rain, low cloud, fog and snow can dramatically change things.

Walkers' boots had scarred the hillside revealing long 'clawmarks' on the old red sandstone which runs throughout the entire range. In shadow this rock can look black from a distance – hence the name of the mountains. But I have seen them radiant in spring sunlight when the whole of the Brecon Beacons have worn a pink flush wherever the grassy slopes have given way to crags.

I looked up as the slope steepened. Cloud pressed down with sheep darker grey lumps in the prevailing greyness. Although the Bluff is over 2,200 feet high the 'climb' from the Capel-y-ffin road to the top takes in a mere six hundred feet. And yet the feeling of height once you are on the whaleback is extraordinary. The cloud thinned when I negotiated the tiny summit crags onto the whortleberry plateau. White wisps of cloud lifted off the hills below – Kilvert's Radnorshire hills.

Great steeps rose from the farmland to create that In-the-Sky sensation central to all hill walking of quality. Crows craarked to each other from below and even when new clouds gathered the gloom seemed to generate its own light, like a sea mist.

I walked to the Trig Point before returning to the edge of the ridge to stride along roughly north east to south west, gradually losing height. The summit was puddled with peat wallows and the occasional brook threaded white down the hillside. The sound of flood water running off peat coursed through the hush.

Twmpa had returned, silhouetted black against the paler profiles of the other huge heads which were the ramparts of the enormous wall of crags and steeps marching down to Pen y Manllwyn and y Crib.

The path was ankle deep in peat gruel but as the ridge dropped with rather more urgency towards Bwlch yr Efengyl the going was less messy.

The single track road back to the carpark shouldn't be written off as an anti-climax. It afforded the brief but keen pleasures of a close-up of Twmpa and the narrow valley at the foot of the Bluff. Although the day lacked clarity, the golden brown, almost orange colour of the beech leaves stood between the half wild country of bracken and turf and the cultivated land that spread over an immense distance. The low cloud base brought its own element of drama to the scene. Rain was falling in the Wye Valley and white vapour rose from the low hills.

Striding through my thoughts it wasn't hard to imagine how a primary school child would react to an ascent of Hay Bluff, a traverse of the short ridge and the walk back under the dark steeps. The lack of height and challenge (in physical terms) doesn't detract from the Bluff's merit. I have been up a lot of higher, more rugged mountains to the disappointment of the views from their summits. The Bluff has to be savoured throughout the year. A sun-bright snowscape with the whole of Powys visible to the extreme horizons can make

114

you very reluctant 'to come back to earth'. And a summer dusk on the Bluff blurring slowly to twilight can send you to bed elated as if you have just sat through the definitive performance of Mahler's 5th symphony given by an orchestra and choir of angels.

WALK TWENTY-TWO
Red Lion at Bredwardine to Arthur's Stone, Moccas Park and back.

Length: 5 miles
Grade Ⓐ

In May this is a 'must' for lane lovers.

In 1877 the Rev. Francis Kilvert became vicar of Bredwardine and Rector of Brobury, and in June 1987 David Abrahams, David Baker and I parked the car outside the Red Lion in Bredwardine filled with the desire to walk some of the local lanes. Kilvert was the spur but I've no intention of getting bogged down in cult obsessions, although the Vicar of Bredwardine was a colourful, kindly figure capable of some evocative prose. I've always felt the need to weigh a countryside for its own worth, but I must confess it was the quest for Wordsworth that first brought me to the English lakes.

The day was breezy and showery, more like April than June. In the pub we had a bar snack first and the landlord gave us permission to leave the car outside his place while we spent the afternoon exploring. The Red Lion stands at the crossroads with the B4352 running directly in front of it. We took the narrow country road opposite the pub and walked to St Andrews Church – Kilvert's church. The sky was grey but we weren't depressed. We were Devonians and enjoyed each other's company and for a couple of days shared that freedom that was pivotal to my childhood. Dave Abrahams' ears were as red as my nose and Dave Baker had raindrops on the tips of his moustache.

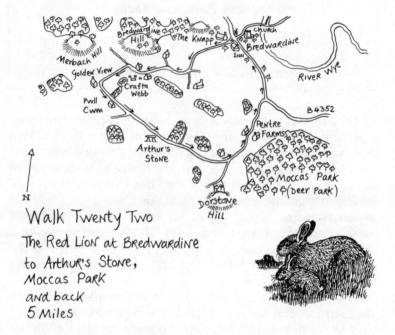

Walk Twenty Two

The Red Lion at Bredwardine
to Arthur's Stone,
Moccas Park
and back
5 Miles

Thick stands of angelica stood between the nettlebeds in the hedge. Then we were walking an avenue of young beeches to the churchyard where Dave Baker took photographs of us, the church, the yew tree and Kilvert's grave. The other Dave and I were content to stand about looking thoughtful. The sun came out and the giant sycamore roared in the wind which sent the raindrops flying. Kilvert's grave was marked by a white cross inscribed with a fitting epitaph for a diarist: 'He being dead yet speaketh'.

We didn't feel like going inside the church. It was exhilarating between showers so we came back up the sun-dappled road which Kilvert must have walked so often before peritonitis killed him. Rain fell when we reached the Red Lion and set off up the hill beside the pub. The big ostentatious Victorian house to the right beyond the stream was The Cottage before it was re-christened Bredwardine Hall. Kilvert often visited the place, probably because he was fond of a relative called Julia Newton who lived there.

We strode on, eager to stretch our legs. The wind rushed through the trees overhead and we were forced to shelter under the hoods of our cagoules like overgrown, disgruntled pixies. But on both sides was the lovely compensation of green banks holding the glitter of raindrops. A cock crowed and there were chickens scratching around in an orchard and a huddle of houses with the hill steepening.

The high leafy hedges had angelica and bracken at their feet then up on the right the plough behind the tractor was opening a field of red soil. This, for me, was the keenest reminder of my home county. A Celtic connection? Well, only perhaps if I cheat. The hill was called The Knapp.

Down below, the landscape crossed by the Wye was darkening under rain. I regretted that I did not know this countryside well, for it possessed a remarkable and individual beauty. We climbed higher keeping an eye out for the lost village of Crafta Webb of which only a few slabs remain scattered about an open field. The village had belonged to Kilvert's world. But perhaps we had been misinformed. Perhaps the map was misleading. We never found it, possibly because we didn't search too hard. The superb half-wild hawthorn hedges captured our imagination. They divided the small fields and adorned the hillsides. I can't remember seeing hawthorn hedges to compare with these. Rain beat down, blotting out the upland. Behind it was blue sky and soon we were swinging left, upwards into the sun.

At the wayside was herb robert, yellow deadnettle, purple vetch, wild strawberries, red campion and a great mass of Queen Anne's lace. Over the hedges were fields and woods running to the sky. But as so often happens in such a pastoral scene the human touch can lend the landscape something we relate to as human beings. It may all hinge on mood but on that occasion the sight of cat bowls and dishes in the porch of a white cottage at the roadside balled the emotion in my throat. I was reminded instantly of my home and my family and our cats.

A little further on two donkeys stood in a field staring at us through the bars of a gate. They talked through their noses as Dave Abrahams fed them with considerable expertise. (He was once an elephant keeper at Paignton Zoo.) They laid back their ears wearing expressions of absolute repose.

Up ahead the windswept slopes of Merbach Hill ended in trees and the sky. Then the rain fell heavily and we came with heads bowed onto the ridge to find the sun once more. Pushing back our hoods we could look down towards Bredwardine and the great vista of Herefordshire. A spotted flycatcher was singing and the hawthorns were catching the wind and shedding blossom. At either hand were grassy verges full of clover and buttercups. Beyond the hedges, which were waist high, larks sang despite the squalls.

The house on the ridge was Golden View. We could look over a field of flowers across the valley to hillsides covered with tiny fields, bounded by those gone-wild hawthorn hedges. Sheep bleated and the wind sang in the telegraph wires. It was like walking back into the childhood countryside, the hedges being what they were and us being in the sky.

The next house was called Pwll Cwm and beyond it the weather was coming in off the Black Mountains. But we didn't care. Those marvellous hawthorn hedges marched downhill and we were walking between the Queen Anne's lace into the interchange of light and shadow on that dizzy afternoon.

'It's bloody incredible,' Dave Abrahams said, lifting his voice above the noise of the wind. 'Where have I been all my life while this has been here waiting?'

The other Dave lifted his camera and froze Abrahams' serious, red face for posterity.

The rain returned, our hoods went up and we retreated into our own worlds. With the shower crumbling to a rainbow we reached Arthur's Stone, a Celtic connection which has its echoes in Spinster's Rock on Dartmoor. Both are the remains of chambered tombs of the late neolithic period, erected between 2,000 and 3,000 BC. Originally the stones would have been under an earth mound.

In that place, at that moment I think we all felt the far-off past in our blood. Arthur's Stone was the burial place of a community, the end of the cul-de-sac where the seasons ceased to renew themselves and darkness prevailed. Yet was this so? Sunlight was streaming over the hills, pursued by rain. The world was alive and we were part of its life. Standing before the Stone I wondered if the enigma would ever click into focus.

Leaving the tomb we passed a fenced-off wood, more Queen Anne's lace and more high hedges. Where the plantation ended there was a drive on the left and a mysterious signpost bearing the name: Miss O. Osborn. Further on, we found a delightful little farm, Caeperthy, and hedges laid in the traditional style which advertised the craftsman's skill. In the field behind one of them a grey pony snuffled her cry above the roaring of the wind in the wayside trees. Now the lace was rocking wildly to match our enthusiasm for the place. The great vale below was catching the rain we had missed. It was suddenly dark down there while we strode on through brightness. For all the gloom we recognised the beauty of the Wye and the way it affected the landscape.

I knew it was an experience I would resurrect often in old age; but we were coming down off the ridge now, with Kington Hill Cott on the left and a glimpse of the great Welsh river below. We were walking into a rainbow, under the walled and wooded Moccas Park, past Pentre Farms and an unpleasant collie that ran at us, barking. The hedges were hung with dogroses and the rain washed off a faint fragrance.

Looking left over the hedge we saw the tower of Bredwardine Church. A stream bubbled and gurgled behind the other hedge on the right but we had lost the noise before we reached the B4352 again and made the left turn which would bring us back to The Red Lion with some of the rapture still intact.

WALK TWENTY-THREE
The Brecon Beacons – Pen y Fan.

Length: 5½ miles
Grade Ⓑ

A good introduction to mountain walking but in the winter go with an experienced companion.

Brecon with its cathedral and narrow streets, which led to the mediaeval market place, had been washed by the wind and rain that were always around in mountain districts. It stood on the north bank of the River Usk, a clean, compact community of small stone houses, shops and pubs. My son, Chris, and I left it and drove along the A470 to the Storey Arms. The heatwave had ended and it was cool for May even when the sun came out between showers.

The car was left in the carpark across the road from the Storey Arms which is an outdoor education centre and mountain rescue post and not, alas, a pub! With just an afternoon to spare, the short ascent from here to the summit of Pen y Fan was acceptable although I would have preferred a longer route and an entire day on the Beacons.

The Storey Arms was a dull looking building standing at nearly 1,500 feet in the pass. Chris, who was twenty-three, wasn't impressed. But at 2,907 feet Pen y Fan is the Beacons' highest mountain and he was young enough to be fascinated by that sort of thing. The mountain towers above its companions in a National Park of outstanding beauty which

The Brecon Beacons

Walk Twenty Three
Pen y Fan
5½ Miles

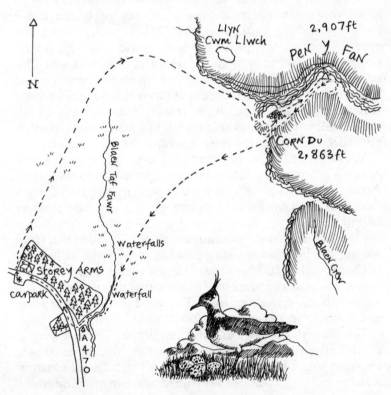

N

Llyn Cwm Llwch

2,907ft

Pen y Fan

Blaen Taf Fawr

Corn Du
2,863ft

Blaen Crew

Waterfalls

Storey Arms

carpark

Waterfall

A470

attracts only a fraction of the visitors that invade Dartmoor in the summer.

Thankfully the Beacons haven't 'gone commercial'. As far as I know there aren't any pixie shops or the Welsh equivalent of Widecombe and Princetown, and no heights as accessible as Hay Tor. You have to work to get to the summits. Nature in the Brecon Beacons demands that it be met on its terms – and this is very good news for those who care about the environment.

The Beacons lack Snowdonia's melancholy grandeur. The hills are open to the light and the sensation of being far above the rest of the world is keener than it is on Dartmoor. It may sound like sacrilege to Devonians but I often wish Dartmoor had half a dozen peaks like Tryfan – teeming with wildlife, of course!

Chris and I followed the trail up the hillside, trying to avoid the occasional peat gruel. The sky darkened and a shower fell. We looked at each other and knotted the drawstrings of our cagoule hoods under our chins and slogged on. Ahead was the concave profile of Corn Du, masked in rain; but the sun was shining by the time we had reached the red-brown scree to peer over the ridge. The view was startling. We were on the crest of a great wave of hill above miles of farmland that spread in all directions to other hills. Brecon's rooftops were catching the sun, far off.

We sauntered on to the summit. Down in the cwm to the north-west was Llyn Cwmllwch – a perfect mountain tarn. Across the saddle to the east were the craggy heights of Pen y Fan with its Trig Point standing on the top like a white knight.

Coming up Pen y Fan's summit slopes I decided this rated among the best hill walking I had ever enjoyed. Wherever fell boots hadn't laid bare the rock, the turf was springy, and those mountains of grass really captivated me. Pen y Fan was a good place, an aesthetic treat. The wind whistled in my hair and turned the sweat on my body to ice water.

We came to the cairn and the Trig Point. The last shower of the afternoon fell and the sky was blue over Wales. Looking south I could see the gleam of the Bristol Channel and the hills of Exmoor. Westward were more mountains, eastwards swelled the hills of Radnorshire and Here-fordshire. To the north was a suggestion, perhaps, of Cadair Idris.

Is it so strange to love a tree or a hill as much as you love your own kin? Maybe it's the Celtic weakness – the inability to separate the human condition from Nature. Or maybe it's the great strength.

The northern crags of Pen y Fan were spectacular surges of grassy rock culminating in the protruding lip of rock at the crest of the ridge. I crossed the summit and looked south over the cwm and Blaen Taf Fechan to the tree-fringed Upper Neuadd Reservoir. Ravens sailed down the wind into sunlight which the clouds always kept on the move.

Often in my life mountain country has provided me with visions of an extraordinary beauty. On Pen y Fan I discovered it again above a pastoral perfection which seemed divorced from this age of vandalism with the environment as victim. And I enjoyed in my son's company that sense of well-being which grows out of the beauty of a landscape. We retraced our steps without haste.

It had been one of the easiest ascents of my life. But Pen y Fan possessed a purity which most mountains in England and Wales have lost. I reflected on this as I soaked in a hot bath at the pub where we were staying in Brecon; and I continued to think about it as I came down to the bar for ale. Some old soldiers were mulling over Good Times at the corner table and I recalled that the South Wales Borderers had their barracks in Brecon. Soldiers from the regiment had per-formed heroically at Rorke's Drift against the Zulus when Victoria was Queen-Empress.

Twilight was deepening outside and the air was cool when Chris and I ventured into it. There was a pub next door, a pub two doors down the street and one over the road but we were heading for the 19th-century Shire Hall which had the sort of neo-Greek portico Victorian businessmen loved.

A handful of teenagers were eating Chinese takeaways on the steps and sparrows lurked hopefully for largesse. I grinned. Between the rooftops were the black silhouettes of mountains against a sky that would soon be full of stars.

We came on to 'Sarah Siddons' in the High Street. The

pub was once called The Leg of Mutton but was renamed after the famous actress who was born there in 1755.

The mediaeval streets and the occasional Georgian house were pleasant surprises but the fish and chip shops provided two dinners for two quid. Chris and I liked the town. It was the heart of a great rural district walled in by mountains and Welshness which my mother would have appreciated.

We strolled to The George and sat chatting over pints. History was coming alive in a way that saddened me. I thought of all the families, gone and forgotten, who had once walked the streets of Brecon and sat in pubs and watched the stars come out through windows before the curtains were drawn.

WALK TWENTY-FOUR
Hay-on-Wye to Clyro and back.

Length: 2½ miles
Grade Ⓐ

A stroll for romantics and nostalgia addicts.

Hay-on-Wye is one of those warm unspoilt corners of Kilvert Country that I love to re-visit. The Rev. Francis Kilvert (1840–1879) walked the Welsh borders and documented the life of its people, against a landscape he passionately loved, in his famous diary. But despite admiring Kilvert's prose and the way he brought an area of Victorian rural life so poignantly alive it was not our intention to make the usual literary pilgrimage. Hay's architectural eccentricities were sheer delight after the building society plate glass and supermarket functional of the South Devon seaside resort we had left twenty-four hours earlier. Feral pigeons chortled their border Welsh and there was a peculiar odour of second-hand books baking in the afternoon heat of high summer. The Hay Cinema Bookshop in Church Street was extraordinary. Outside, like slices of toast, faded volumes were

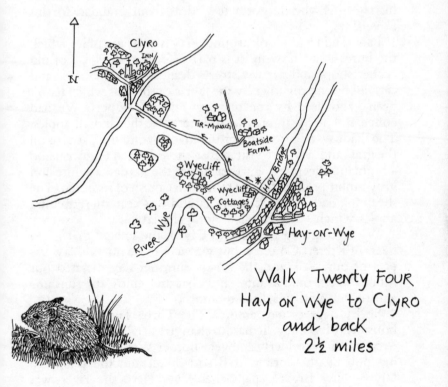

Walk Twenty Four
Hay or Wye to Clyro
and back
2½ miles

cooking and buckling on their racks at 15p each, ten for a quid!

Young jackdaws sat on the guttering while my wife and I walked the scolloped pavements, aware of attending the marriage of two cultures, English and Welsh on the banks of the River Wye. The Wye was my maternal grandfather's river. He was a salmon ghillie, Richard Morgan, who caught giant fish and felt naked without his gaff and rod. He took the rich and titled out in his boat and cursed them or praised them according to their skill at the fishing. John Buchan was one of his rods. Maybe he got a few ideas from grandad for his novels!

Patsy and I had a look around. Hay is in Breconshire which the bureaucrats now insist is part of Powys. It is full of old corner shops and narrow streets designed for the horse and cart, all bound together by the fabric of the past which hasn't been vandalised by the planners and developers. We had coffee at The Swan on a lawn littered with windfall apples. The shadows of garden furniture made geometric patterns on the grass and we were visited by a three-legged tabby cat and a highland sheepdog. Further down the garden a white and grey rabbit pressed its nose to the wire mesh of its hutch. The sheepdog had a long, serious face and was keen on retrieving apples which Patsy bowled along the lawn.

We were going to walk to Clyro, the village that is the heart of Kilvert Country, but we were in no hurry. Hay was part of our walk and the lovely summer day dictated our mood. We would saunter and chat and enjoy the sunshine and to hell with Hazlitt's dictum!

So by degrees we came to The Three Tuns, a little ale house run by Lucy. It hasn't changed at all for five or six decades. Lucy is elderly and very border Welsh. Not far from her pub on the corner of Broad Street and the B4351 to Clyro, Hay Bridge spans the Wye. Here the river was picking up light from the sky. It ran silvery-brown, holding reflections of trees and clouds, over shallows and through the deeper fish swims. Under the arches children were bathing and the day was full of the swifts' shrilling and the hum of insects. Along the banks flies danced over cowpats which the sun had turned to poppadums.

The road to Clyro was busy. Passing vehicles set the cow parsley dancing in their draught. The waysides were full of flowers and the hedges were plump and butterfly-haunted. It was easy to imagine Kilvert making this walk when the road was quiet and the only sound teasing the hush would have been the cries of the swifts. Below Wycliffe Cottages the Wye looped into its broad field-patched valley. To our left was a drive leading to Wye Cliff and a little beyond on the right the lane to Boatside Farm and Tir Mynach.

The countryside leftwards was expansive and enchanting. The flowers on the verges, rocking with the grasses whenever a car passed, shook out their winged insects although the petrol fumes were a reminder of how far we really were from Kilvert's world.

There were so many trees in the great valley and the wooded hills of Radnorshire waited ahead. The scene was sylvan and the grazing farm animals lent their calmness to its tranquility.

The walking was easy and the views down towards the Wye became more generous as we approached the junction with the A4153. The boggy little field corner and its willows on our left were quivering in the heat that danced in the lap of the magnificent valley. Then we passed a most handsome hawthorn hedge and came along by some houses to the A4153. Across it to the right was the road leading into Clyro which was once part of Radnorshire although that shire of great character is now lost in Powys.

But Clyro is still itself despite pockets of modern development. The rooks and the swifts loosed their cries into the summer day unaware that humanity had made such a mess of the world elsewhere.

Left of us was the warm smoky honey of a stone dwelling and on the other side a row of red brick cottages. Before us now was the churchyard with lots of headstones standing in the grass under the grey church and its blunt tower complete with steeple cock. The old close-by churchyard had solid hill country character. The surrounding hills were steep and the skyline tree-hackled.

We came into the churchyard and wandered among the grasses and plantain before going into the church to see the commemorative plate erected in Kilvert's memory. The interior was quiet and austere and we were happy to leave it for the fresh air again and walk beneath the yews to the lych gate. A blackbird sang out against all the evidence of mortality. In front of us were two white cottages under ancient tiles which were covered with moss. Over the road to the right was Clyro Post Office Stores and left of this neat white building was Ashbrook House. According to its wall plaque the 'Rev. Francis Kilvert, Diarist, 1865–1872, lived here'. It was an elegant house of warm grey stone which seemed common in the area.

We walked past it to The Baskerville Arms which used to be The Swan in Kilvert's day. But the name Baskerville provided the Devon link. The family that had once lived at Baskerville Court were 'transported' to a fictional home on Dartmoor by Conan Doyle in his *The Hound of the Baskervilles*. Above the fine white portico of the pub a stone hound gazed symbolically into space. Then as we sat on the steps outside sipping our refreshments a big black three-legged dog joined us, which Patsy thought odd after the three-legged cat at The Swan in Hay! Alas, the interior of The Arms has moved into this age with its pool table and we weren't tempted to linger.

So we strolled back to Hay, towards those hills above the little town that must have moved Kilvert – heights named Pen-y-beacon ('Hay Bluff' to Herefordshire folk), Cusop and other hills where the Offa's Dyke path ran along the bottom of the sky.

We ate a good meal in Hay at dusk and went on a modest pub crawl before returning to our room at The Swan. The hotel was a great rambling Pickwickian coaching inn with a lofty dining room and massive sashed windows. From our bedroom was a moon-hazed vision of Kilvert's hills which we carried into sleep.

Note: The Swan at Hay on Wye has since changed hands and I don't know if it is still an inn. But good accommodation can be found almost anywhere in the town. Try The Seven Stars in Broad Street or The Black Lion.

WALK TWENTY-FIVE
The Black Mountains – Twmpa to Y Das and back.

Length: 9 miles
Grade ©

A walk along the edge of an impressive escarpment.
Wonderful in the autumn.

F.S. Smythe called it 'The Spirit of the hills'. 'Mountaineering,' he claimed, 'is a search for beauty . . .' He went on: 'The hills are beautiful. They are beautiful in line and form and colour; they are beautiful in their purity, in their simplicity and in their freedom; they bring repose, contentment and good health.'

Certainly I felt that Spirit as I left the car at the Stone car park on the Capel-y-ffin road under Hay Bluff and walked right to take the right-hand turning down towards Cae Ceiliog. The day was wild. Cloud and sun competed under the influence of the wind to make those swift changes of light and shade which turn panorama to spectacle. And I was an 'extra' in the drama, walking towards the great escarpments of the Black Mountains that began with Twmpa and ran north to south in a series of blunt crests to Y Das.

Twmpa is probably a corruption of twmpath meaning 'hillock' – and there's a nice touch of Celtic irony! This 'hillock' makes the highest point on Dartmoor look like a pimple; but I didn't have to remind myself that in the hills everything is relative and should be weighed for its own worth.

I strode down through the trees which the October gale was thrashing into a dance. Leaves fell and were sent flying again. A couple of ponies watched me from the verges of the narrow road. Then I came round a bend littered with storm debris and had to jump the twin water splashes of Cae Ceiliog. Below them the stream ran away in cascades under the trees.

I walked on until I reached the grassy lot where cars may

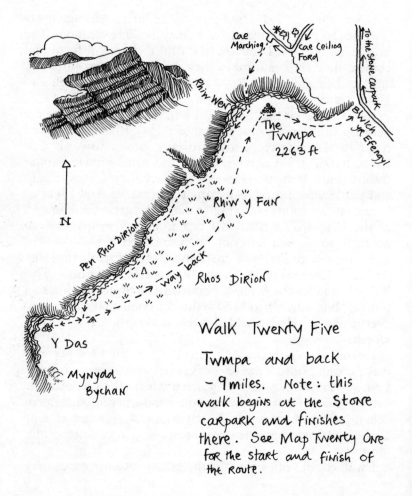

Cae
Marchiog

Cae Ceiliog
Ford

To the Stone Carpark

Rhiw Wen

The
Twmpa
2,263 ft

Bwlch yr Efengyl

Rhiw y Fan

Pen Rhos Dirion

way back

Rhos Dirion

Y Das

Mynydd
Bychan

Walk Twenty Five

Twmpa and back
— 9 miles. Note: this
walk begins at the Stone
carpark and finishes
there. See Map Twenty One
for the start and finish of
the route.

park above the place called Cae Marchiog. To my left was the broad turf path leading to Twmpa across downland. Ponies and their foals were grazing with the sheep among the bracken. Three ewes sauntered ahead of me on what appeared to be another of those pop trails that receives a pounding during holiday season weekends. Outside the tourist season it is a path into solitude and the quiet excitement hills can provoke.

Soon the bracken-smothered lower slopes became steeps of thin, tussocky grass with sphagnum showing on the turf. Then the 'lip' of Twmpa was above me, clad in whortleberry bushes. A tiny crag lent the summit dignity. And for all the irony of its name Twmpa at 2,265 feet was a mountain. To seal the moment a merlin launched itself from the rocks to my left and flickered over my head to depart, twisting and turning along the cliffs. The little falcon provided an unexpected moment of delight to bring with me onto the top. Lured by the bird and the craggy profile of the next crest on the right I followed the edge of the steeps of Rhiw Wen. But straying briefly back onto the broad summit after spotting what I thought was another merlin I found a small, reed-fringed tarn about the size of a pool table.

Walking the edge of the windy, amazing tableland of bog and rock, in and out of light, under a sky that was forever moving, above a landscape where cloud shadows raced was satisfactory. Immediately below, the half-wild downs met pasture bounded by tree-fringed hedges. There seemed no end to it. The view from the summits on this walk ranks with any of the Great British Mountain panoramas.

The wind hissed and whined in the reeds on bluffs which carried the eye to the crags beyond Rhiw Wen. In the flare-up and fadeaway of light the big stuff towards the end of the ridge left an ache inside me.

Below the large reed beds of Rhiw y Fan – which literally means the Crest of the Hill – were some distinctive little outcrops poking from the steeps. Several paths plunged to the vale from this part of the ridge and the views, streaming with light, were ready to mesmerise. The crags were of that beautiful, dark Old Red Sandstone and always, not so far away as it looked, other huge profiles waited against the sky.

And the movement in the sky created the illusion of the moving mountain.

Just down on the steeps under the edge ponies were feeding. I walked above them, above the rest of the world, along a clearly defined path towards the next distinctive crest, and from the top I had another merlin's eye view of the bracken below. It was criss-crossed with grassy rides. A squall of rain struck the mountains and I sheltered among the rocks under the edge. Here I found the litter some moral bankrupt had stuffed into a crevice. It mocked the autumn beauty of the scene stretching between me and the horizon.

Back on the table top I kept putting up pipits that fluttered low for a few yards before diving back into the reeds. Between gusts of wind their lisping hinted at a frailty that existed solely in my imagination. Really they were tough little creatures like everything else that survived in that place at that altitude.

The narrow sheep walk traced the very brink of the plateau. Above me to the left were great hanks of wind-flattened coarse grass and wind-bent reeds. Light swelled, dimmed almost to darkness and blazed again. I had come under the shoulder of Rhos Dirion and was tackling the moorlike bogs, reeds and grass tussocks on the approach to Y Das. Then it was heartwarming to be met by the vision of lofty steeps and the path from the vale cutting diagonally across them. Moments later I was off the sog walking a track of large loose stones past two cairns onto the broadspur. The small cairn of rocks daubed with red and yellow paint didn't suit the surroundings or do justice to the summit. It was another casual expression of species selfishness. Mountain wilderness character is of primary importance but accepting that this is a minority notion I'm grateful to meet Nature on wilderness terms whenever I get the chance.

Fit walkers can stride on to Pen y Manllwyn and take in another half a dozen or so summits to complete the escarpment at Table Mountain above Crickhowell. A magnificent route would be Hay Bluff, Twmpa, Y Das, Mynydd Bychan, Pen y Manllwyn, Waun Fach, Pen Trumau, Mynydd Lysiau, Pentwynglas, Pen Allt-Mawr, Pen Cerrig-calch and Table Mountain.

Meanwhile, lesser mortals or those with a limited amount of time to spare must consider how they will make the return from Y Das to Hay Bluff carpark. Even on detailed maps the labyrinthine system of paths winding back to Cae Marchiog and the road looks daunting. From the great spur on the escarpment the conundrum seems insoluble. Alas, when it boils down to this sort of thing I'm hardly Mensa material. Then again, the mental block may spring from a desire to prolong the mountain top pleasures.

I chose to retrace my steps to Twmpa. Second helpings of what you really like need no justification.

For those who have tired of crag-top crawling above the magnificent plain of Herefordshire there is an easier return. From the cairn with its yellow and red daubings walk back the way you came but instead of cutting off to the left onto the edge of the plateau go up the rough stone track past the cairn and take the broad path of peat and turf across the plateau towards Twmpa. It is well defined and hard to lose even in mist.

The views to the right across bleak upland are a direct contrast to the panorama of hills and farmland to the left.

At the Twmpa cairn continue directly on, letting the path lead you down the pleasant descent to Bwlch yr Efengyl (Gospel Pass). Turn left here and the single track road will bring you under Pen y Beacon to the Stone carpark again.

WALK TWENTY-SIX
The Marches – Hay-on-Wye, Hay Bluff and Llanigon.

Length: 8 miles
Grade Ⓐ

A lane lover's walk into the mountains and back.

As I've said, Hay is a confluence where the Welsh and English cultures meet in happy confusion, but the town is definitely Celtic rather than Saxon. Drink at any of its pubs and you'll

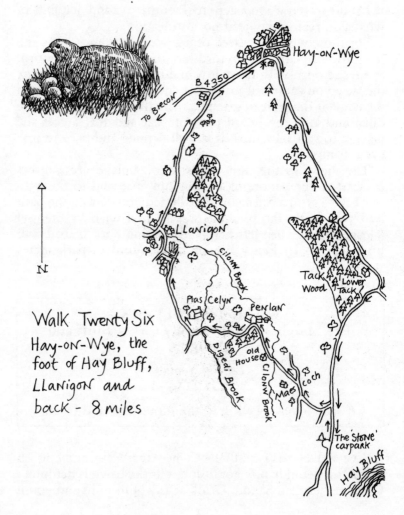

Hay-on-Wye

B 4350

To Brecon

N

Llanigon

Cilonw Brook

Plas Celyn

Penlan

Digedi Brook

old House

Cilonw Brook

Tack Wood

Lower Tack

Maes

Coch

The 'Stone' carpark

Hay Bluff

Walk Twenty Six
Hay-on-Wye, the
foot of Hay Bluff,
Llanigon and
back — 8 miles

understand what I mean. An evening at The Blue Boar or The Black Lion can be long and enjoyable.

That autumn I was tucked up in The Seven Stars, a snug little guest house near the Town Clock in Broad Street. After a hard day on the hills I could enjoy a swim in the heated pool or sweat the aches and pains out of my body in the sauna. One morning I had had enough of rain-soaked high ground and decided to take a long stroll to Hay Bluff. This fine summit is also marked Pen y Beacon on some maps, hinting again at a mild identity problem, perhaps, or the way the Welsh language has suffered until quite recently.

The drizzle had stopped when I took the B4350 Brecon Road out of Hay and turned left a little beyond the petrol station. The way proved to be high-hedged with all the character of a lane and little traffic to trouble the walker. A bend carried me past mature conifers up the incline, with the long hump of Cusop Hill big across the fields to the left. The hedges were full of trees and that bold half-wild ridge was always in view. I ignored any right-hand turnings.

Creeping ever uphill the road passed below forested steeps until it levelled out at the old conifer plantation. I came around another bend to find a farmhouse of weathered grey stone and a magnificent yew tree at the wayside. The wind had risen and leaves danced along the metalled surface before me. Cusop Hill was directly opposite across the valley with the firs of Tack Wood on my right.

It was three miles from my starting place to the signpost and fork where I swung right for Capel-y-ffin. Now the countryside was taking on a wilder aspect and I experienced a lurch of the heart as I went over the cattle grid below ferny banks and above the stream running beside Lower Tack. Where the water cascaded and cut under the single track road I came up left onto a windwashed common.

The landscape was most attractive. The bracken made rust-brown patterns on broad sweeps of turf and there before me was the cloud-smoky head of Hay Bluff. In the distance, where the road wound on and vanished, were more hills with a remarkable view across the Radnorshire farmland on the right – a view that brought Elgar's cello concerto alive in my head.

Also on that side was the carpark and standing stone which thousands of visitors to the Bluff have admired before departing for the summit. For people who dislike scrambling around in the hills this walk will enable you to experience the wonderful exhilaration which mountains impart without any of the discomforts ascending them can produce. I find the business OK in small doses but even then after several days of upland walking I still felt the urge to get amongst the summits. Yet, one-track roads and lanes winding over such a pleasant part of Britain can be idyllic, and if you are unfamiliar with them you walk in quiet expectancy, keen to discover what lies beyond the next bend.

In this frame of mind I made my way back along the road and swung off it to the left where a side-turning dipped and curved away from the common. At the obvious right-hand bend I passed a rough track that led to Blaen Digedi Fawr. Keeping right I went over the cattle grid and down a narrow lane with beeches to the left.

Where the road divided I took the left-hand fork between banks crowned with neat hedges. Soon I was in a dip passing a most incongruous but obviously necessary metal crash barrier on the right above a little tree-choked coombe. An unhill section brought me past an old byre. Through the screen of trees to the right I could look down onto a valley of small fields which were strong with the character of the region. Then the gradual descent over mud and leaf-mush coaxed me into a magnificent view of the Vale of the Wye.

I walked beneath a vault of branches, pausing to admire the barn with its roof of mossy tiles. The rain-drenched landscape smelt of farmyards and decaying leaves. The colour of the native trees glowed from the morning's greyness. The streams were brim full.

At Penlan Pony Trekking Centre I swung left down a steep hill under the trees and was beseiged by three crazy farmdogs. My tactics were to growl back and walk on as boldly as possible. But the conifer gloom was spooky and everywhere the havoc caused by the recent gales and deluge was in evidence — fallen trees, torn branches lying at the wayside, water pouring down banks into the road. To my left were tight ranks of conifers and on the opposite side, views of the vale over woods and pasture. Plump, shaggy sheep returned my gaze from a hillock in front of the slow fall-away of cultivated land with the A4350 in the distance. Again, I was reminded of Elgar and how he turned landscape into music.

The hamlet of Llanigon lay under its chimney smoke in the coombe below. Beyond the main road and the river the countryside lifted to the half-wild hills of the Begwns.

The red soil banks at either hand were comforting with their echoes of South Devon. The farm on the left and the lovely old barn with its chunky tiles, beautiful stonework and weathered doors was familiar only because I've encountered similar buildings throughout England and Wales.

A sudden sharp descent pursued the bend on the right and I came around with it to the Digedi Brook. Where the road crossed the stream there was also a wooden footbridge. The water was high and fast-flowing but I put it behind me and walked uphill to the junction where I turned right for the chance to peer once more into the Vale of the Wye.

A long descent brought me to the house called Troed-y-Rhiw. I came on past other neat dwellings into the outskirts of Llanigon where I stopped to talk to a Jack Russell that was mooching about in a wayside field. The red brick houses of St Eigon's Villas led me to a signpost that informed me it was two miles to Hay providing I went to the left and kept the church on the right.

On the church-side of the hamlet The Old School turned out to be a private house. It faced some white cottages. Beyond it, on my route, were more cottages, a telephone box and a bus shelter. The next signpost insisted Hay-on-Wye was still two miles away. Trusting it, I swung right onto the two-track road which was most pleasant and a little later crossed over the Cilonw Brook and passed a white and black house and Old Forge Garage with its mass of parked vehicles.

Sparse, mixed ribbon development and fussily trimmed hedges were blessed with the occasional rural statement of an orchard and a giant oak or an unblemished field.

A mile later I reached the A4350 and made the abrupt right turn to stride on past the fire station and almshouses to my starting point and Hay itself.

After a sauna at the Seven Stars I went next door for a pint. Sitting in the bar I learnt of Jacqueline du Pré's death that day. Beyond the chat and the laughter and the drinking was the memory of Hay Bluff, the autumn countryside and all the melancholy of Elgar's cello concerto.

5

Powys and Dyfed

For me this is one of those really Welsh corners of Wales
where the Old Tongue is the first language and the hill farms
and villages are heartbeats of a culture that hasn't been
swamped by the rising tide of mid-Atlanticism so apparent in
much of England. The countryside with its coombes and
river valleys, rounded hills and open moorland is very similar
to Devon. This was the homeland of some of the greatest
Welsh poets, including my favourite – Dafydd ap Gwilym.

The hinterland of Aberystwyth is typical of the countryside of central Wales. Here you will find those rare fork-
tailed hawks, the red kites, and a human warmth that sits
well on hill country that is remote and beautiful.

WALK TWENTY-SEVEN
The Cambrian Mountains – The Mountain Road:
Rhayader to Devil's Bridge.

Length: 13 miles
Grade ©

Really a long lane over moor and hill.

Rhaeadr is Welsh for 'waterfall' and this reveals much about
the character of the little town of Rhayader in the upper
valley of the Wye. 'Rhaeadr Gwy' to give the place its old

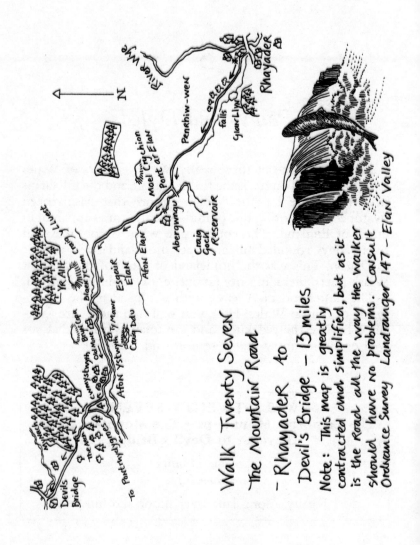

Walk Twenty Seven

The Mountain Road

– Rhayader to
Devil's Bridge – 13 miles

Note: This map is greatly
contracted and simplified, but as it
is the Road all the way the walker
should have no problems. Consult
Ordnance Survey Landranger 147 – Elan Valley

name – the falls of the Wye – is the centre of a hill farming area of Powys. Nearby the Wye and the River Marteg meet and the whole of the surrounding countryside is beautiful even by Mid–Wales' standards.

In 1975 I spent a whole autumn living in the Dyfed village of Cwmystwyth. I was writing a novel and walking the hills and playing soccer for a small community close to Tregaron, about ten miles away. After I had exhausted the routes over the hills it occurred to me that a walk from Rhayader to Devil's Bridge might be rewarding for a number of reasons. I would be able to trudge along close to two rivers and fix my mind on what I wanted to get down on paper.

Rhayader is Welsh Wales grey. It has a market square and a clock tower; and once upon a time the falls, 'The cataract of the Wye', thundered with the life of the river. Then the bridge was built and the falls vanished in the process. But the town is one of those outposts of the past that has an undeniable charm. It carries history well but my opinion may owe much to ancestral affinities.

Four roads meet at the Clock Tower in the centre of Rhayader but I was interested only in the Mountain Road. The name was evocative and provocative. 'THE' Mountain Road – I chewed over the definite article as I wolfed my lunch and washed the crumbs from my teeth in that quaint little pub The Cwmdeuddwr Arms.

It was mid–afternoon when I left the inn and turned right to head down the hill to the Mountain Road. My companion thought I was crazy. He drove past me with a wave of the hand and a shake of the head, reminding me that I had burnt my bridges. But there is a wonderful sense of freedom in the act. It's like kissing goodbye to convention. You are going where the road takes you and although it is a direction society has to discourage it can be fun once in a while – more so if you are greying at the temples.

The Mountain Road was clearly signposted and I swung along it to leave the houses behind me in the sunlight that had no strength. I crossed the bridge and came under the leaf-fall beeches and oaks to see the waterfall up ahead over the low hedges and a hillside covered in the autumn splendour of our native trees. On my right was a wood and below, in the coombe, a pool was catching the light and playing with it. According to my old friend John Jones of Tyn Fron, this is Glan Llyn. John is headmaster of the primary school Swyddffynnon at Ystrad Meurig.

In those days we played soccer for the Aberystwyth and District League side, Pontrhydfendigaid.

Walking through the leaf patter in the oakwood I glimpsed the nameless waterfall pouring off the hill. The road carried me up to the right of it but I made a quick detour and walked alongside the series of cascades, taking the spray on my face. I wonder why most adults are bogged down in adulthood with its boring conventions.

It doesn't require much to tear off the tie and ruffle up the hair before heading for the hills or the pub or any of the Dream Places you've denied yourself all your life.

Soon I was striding over fine open moorland with the stream and the series of cataracts and falls spurring me on. The afternoon was fading as I returned to the road. Dartmoor came to mind. There was a sluice gate to the left and reedy streambeds under a round shoulder of moor. To the right sheep-dotted wilderness swept to the vagueness that precedes evening on fine autumn days. The views from the right-hand side of the road were a blend of rolling downland with the inevitable hills beyond hills which I can't resist. It was Dartmoor without the tors.

I walked the bend watched by sheep that stood in the reedy margins. Behind them was that attractive wind-rounded upland. But I was coming downhill under Penrhiw-wen and Afon Elan was flowing under Pont ar Elan to the left showing white water at its cascades as it felt its way into the Elan Valley to keep the reservoirs topped up. Although the river meandering through the broad valley was delightful I can rarely work up enthusiasm for reservoirs but the Elan lakes are the exception. For all their beauty though, they remain symbols of how the Welsh have been trampled on so often by English bureaucracy. Birmingham's water supply can still make a Welsh Nationalist hot under the collar.

The countryside all around me offered consolation. With the sun low now the bleakness was taking on a warm flush, and so was I. On the little bridge spanning a brook I paused to say hello to some lean sheep. The river was a grey glitter in the last of the afternoon. Above me to the right was the hill, Moel Crychion. At the confluence of the Elan and Nant Hirin across the valley was Aber Glanhirin with its bridge and conspicuous white house flanked by firs, with a small square conifer plantation above it.

The river was brimful of flood water. Beside the road sheep were settling into their hollows for the night and the early evening was still and cool. Then from the next bridge I saw far up in the hills the thread of a waterfall. There across the valley, where the Elan and Nant Gwngu met at Abergwngu, was an old white house among a few broad-leafed trees.

The stream in front of it and the hills behind it cut the dwelling off from a world that has no love of silence and solitude. As if to emphasise my point a motorist leaned hard on his horn to tell me I was too far out on the road; Attila the Hun and Mrs Hun were taking a joy ride with Mr and Mrs Nero. I moved aside and let them pass but I couldn't resist lifting two rigid fingers of scorn.

The Mountain Road wound on, light grey and narrow in the brown and sere landscape. The ruins of a house belonged to the desolation and the deepening tones of evening. I crossed a broader stream and suddenly the Elan was gone. In its place was an erratic brook looping this way and that.

At the wayside was a brake of conifers and sheep feeding tight against it. Over the left where the sky was brightest the thin wisps of waterfalls were clearly visible with the hills darkening to monotone. My side of the valley was boggy and gulls were plunking down in the pools of the flooded levels. The road went up and down before it swung me gently round a bend from Powys into Dyfed which I considered my home territory. On my right was the bonny Ystwyth – a hill river of immense character bounding along under Craig y Lluest and Yr Allt with Esgair Elan leaping up on the left.

Both sides of the defile could boast those steep rounded heights that remind you that you are in the Cambrian Mountains. The crags over the Ystwyth ended in boulder strewn slopes and I was walking into the sunset, accompanied for a while by a tattered old sheep with a limp and the sort of cry that fills you with helpless pity.

Dusk deepened but the streams running down off the hillsides lost little of their brilliance. The river became broader and noisier and the road ran along the steep craggy hillside above it. Some cars passed, headlights glaring. Bright red jewels blazed in the sheep masks at the wayside. I walked through the blueing air down into the lovely wooded hollow of Blaenycwm. Lights were on in the windows of the hill dwellings and above them the streams fell from the high places that belonged to the hawks and the foxes.

Mistlethrushes clattered out of the hawthorns in the field where Man had claimed a corner of the wilderness with his homestead and drystone walls. The dark flanks of the hills climbed up into twilight. I walked over the bridge and put the Ystwyth on my left. The road crept skyward leaving the river to its gorge. I knew this part of Dyfed well and could have walked it with my eyes shut. Over my right shoulder were Tyllwyd and the hill, Bryn Copa; down by the Ystwyth were the lights of the dwelling, Ty Mawr.

The river made its descent dramatically. The sound of the torrents and falls was amplified by the hills and the hill silence. The stars of autumn burnt coldly above the black silhouettes: Polaris, Cassiopeia, Cepheus, Andromeda, Ursa Minor – the poetry of astronomy matched the living poetry of the cosmos. By starlight I looked across the small fields that ran beyond the Ystwyth to the blank blackness of Craig Ddu – the aptly named Black Cliff.

Then I had reached Mrs Sidebottom's house where the derelict lead mine began. The living room light was on and the lady and her husband were reading by the fire. I loped along past the screes and crags, shafts and workhouses until the cattle grid warned me I was entering the outskirts of Cwmystwyth. Bwlch y Gwynt cottage was on the left, one light showing through the curtains of a downstairs room.

I marched on through the village where I was staying, past the Post Office Stores and Pentrev Farm, the chapel and the old schoolhouse, and the house I had been loaned by kind friends. It was called Dan y Rhos then, although I believe it is now Gate House. The temptation to nip in for a swift glass of cider was strong but I walked up the hill and on into the conifer gloom beyond Bryn. Any left turn would have sent me off to Pontrhydygroes.

At night conifer plantations are the nearest thing you can get to a corner of hell but I reached The Arch and headed downhill nursing a glorious beer thirst. Before long the dense firs on the right had given way to bare muscular hills which showed their ribs in places. It was hawk country of feminine curves and hard weather.

The hateful conifers crowded in on the left but I had seen the lights of Bodcoll Farm, one of the most beautiful farms I know. The buildings form a neat square on the hillside overlooking the valley of the River Mynach.

The Mountain Road's final bend presented me with the welcome sight of the Hafod Arms Hotel and Devil's Bridge. The Welsh name Pontarfynach has a gravelly satanic ring to it but David was waiting at the bar and the Guinness was smooth and creamy and I could have eaten a whole elephant – curried, of course, with pilau rice and a hundredweight of chappatis.

Note: Transport at the end of this walk is politic unless you really want to trudge back.

WALK TWENTY-EIGHT
The Cambrian Mountains – Rhayader, the Elan Valley Reservoirs and back.

Length: 19 miles
*Grade © *

A good route, especially when low cloud makes walking the hilltops a penance.

The autumn rain had stopped an hour or so before I left Rhayader clock tower to walk the road marked Elan Valley, B4518. Soon the shops and houses were behind me and a watery sun did its best to brighten the morning. I had a cold

Walk Twenty Eight
Rhayader, the Elan Valley
Reservoirs and back
19 miles

N

Pont ar Elan

Craig Goch Resr.

The Mountain Road

falls

Llyn Glan

River Wye

Rhayader

Esgair
Pen y garreg

Penygarreg Resr.

Y Glog Fawr

Afon Elan

Y Foel

Carreg ddu Resr.

Elan Village

Caban Coch Resr.

and a slight hangover but neither had gone to my legs. A grassy track at the roadside made the going reasonable although I was in no mood to be drenched by the spray tossed off the wheels of passing cars.

Floodwater was trickling into the road from the fields but the sky was clearing. Maybe it would stay fine, I thought, passing the Elan Valley Hotel and noting the signboard which told me there was 'Trout Fishing for Residents'. Wooded hills studded with crags stood in a sky of misty blue. A sheep rose on her hindlegs to browse the wayside hedge like a goat. Up ahead were more crags and a wooded gorge. The road ran high above the Afon Elan, walled in by massive cliffs and steeps.

The first dam was a blunt reminder of what the Victorians had done to the valley. The Elan is a bonny little river and you only have to read Shelley to appreciate the wild grandeur of yesterday's coombes. Today we have a handsome man-made Welsh Lakeland but I'm sure I would have enjoyed the original place before 1892 when work on the reservoirs began. And yet the whole complex has a compelling beauty that owes much to the nature of the surrounding countryside.

The walking was undemanding. Caban-coch lake on the left is very Swiss, unlike Dartmoor's Burrator Reservoir. Here the conifers climb high hillsides beside the water as they do around many a Swiss lake.

The right angle brought me to a more ostentatious dam and a folly-like tower sheltering under a green dome. Then I was out of the 'Christmas trees' loping along beside the placid waters of Carreg-ddu Reservoir and its fringe of silver birches. The wood of broad-leafed trees opposite had laid its old golds and browns on the surface of the lake.

The walking was now up and down below massive hills carved open here and there by gulleys. Eventually the road descended to the water and crossed a bridge before doing its mild switch-back again until it ran through some mature conifers. Before I entered the trees I looked up at the sky. The blue had spread and there was a great lagoon of it between two long reefs of cloud.

A hump-back bridge spanned the Elan at the end of the

reservoir. The river was in spate and the air smelt of spent
rain. On the other side an S bend saw me past The Flickering
Lamp Hotel and Restaurant. I blew my nose, took out the
flask of Nescafé and gulped down a couple of Paracetamols.
The Flickering Lamp, I mused, getting under way again.
Maybe Florence Nightingale had spent a weekend there. It
looked a nice place but I wasn't hungry or in need of a bed.

Presently I came upon a startling sight. Before me on the
right was an enormous man-made waterfall gushing in a
curtain of whiteness over the dam containing Pen-y-Garreg
Reservoir. It was 'Homeric' as my old man would say
whenever he was confronted by anything extraordinary; and
Homeric is a word that travels well even in this age of tabloid
hyperbole.

The shining lake beyond the wall of water was a contrast
but far ahead was another 'fall'. Sunlight shafted down.
Colour was coaxed out of drabness. Oak leaves glowed. And
there I was struggling to snare ephemera with the desperation
of a drunken Welsh poacher trying to grab a salmon with his
bare hands.

A modest little bridge saw me over a mountain brook that
roared. Wet sheep returned my gaze, unembarrassed. The
landscape was a mixture of small crags and large slopes of
bracken that was yellow-brown. The reservoir was a field
away but the road brought me down closer to it as I walked;
and all at once the dam and the green-domed tower eclipsed
everything. Froth had curdled on the water just below the
monumental and artificial falls.

I crossed another bridge over another mountain stream
and walked above Craig Goch Reservoir. Birds were
flinging their calls across the silence. The flats of reeds and
coarse grass and the treeless slopes gave the lake the character
and atmosphere of a Scottish lochan. I walked up and on into
desolate moorland which the National Trust-type picnic
table and benches at the roadside, a little beyond the next
bridge and torrent, did nothing to enhance. Grey squirrels
scattered from the mast and leaves beneath a row of beeches
as I passed. Boggy land lay to the left with the reservoir on the
other side. Soon I was high above it, accompanied occasionally by watchful sheep. Locked within the eternal Now of

their existence the sheep stopped to graze the verges.

I was seeing with a stranger's eye the beauty and idiosyncrasies of the landscape at a glance. Novelty enables you to distance yourself from a place and yet regard it with a kind of gleeful passion which in the native has matured to something more profound.

After all the crags, trees, water and dams, the Welsh hill farm was a welcome change. It was there at the roadside with its cow houses and barns and belving cattle – a pulse borrowed from the solitudes of Welsh history. Something older than stones and slates was in residence, something changeless amidst all the changes, something unmolested.

The ponies continued to crop the grass although the road had eased me closer to the lake now. The great valley and the water stretched northward between low-rounded moorland hills. And the sadness of the countryside and the season was beginning to get to me. I started to stride out undismayed by a glimpse of the Mountain Road ahead on the side of Moel Geufron. A starling flock passed low with a concerted whisper of wings and I came over the brow of the hill to look down on the Elan meandering through its valley to replenish the 'lakes'. Then I crossed Pont ar Elan and the loud river to bear right at the Mountain Road and the signpost that read: Rhayader 5 miles.

The afternoon was mellow and the autumn hills 'Nearer Heaven than Earth below'.

WALK TWENTY-NINE
The Cambrian Mountains – The 'Vampire' Trail: Devil's Bridge, Pwllpeiran, Pont-rhyd-y-groes and back.

Length: 11 miles
Grade Ⓑ

A fine autumn stroll for a couple content to be with each other.

Loneliness can drum up encounters with the unexpected but in the not too distant past little I did was censored by logic. Living at Cwmystwyth on the Mountain Road, without transport, meant long walks not only over the hills searching for wildlife but to either Devil's Bridge or Pont-rhyd-y-groes for the occasional ale. Return trips in the dark were often eventful, especially when the weather confined most folk to their firesides.

Autumn's bright mists and colours illuminated the landscape. The world had a stained-glass window glow and as I buckled my rucksack at Devil's Bridge I was thinking of Dafydd ap Gwilym's small mediaeval world. Dafydd was the greatest Welsh poet and one that steps easily into world literature. He was born at Bro Gynin near Aberystwyth around 1330 and died about forty years later. He was buried in the Cistercian Abbey of Strata Florida, Ystrad Fflur – Valley of the Flowers, in Dyfed.

I was in Dyfed, in red kite country, and Devil's Bridge with the holiday season dead and buried was quiet. The bridge is actually three bridges, one above the other, and the lowest and the oldest is Devil's. The Welsh name is Pont-ar-fynach, the Bridge over the Mynach. It is part of a grandeur of wooded gorges and waterfalls ghosting down ravines. Where the Rheidol and Mynach meet the steps leading down are called Jacob's Ladder. Then there are the Falls of the Rheidol and the Mynach's headlong plunge over Devil's Bridge Falls.

Afternoon was drawing in when I left Pont-ar-fynach and

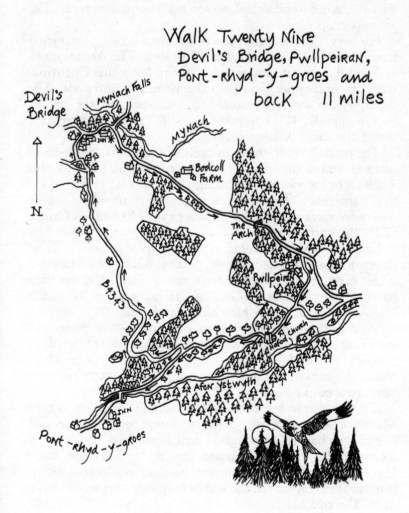

Walk Twenty Nine
Devil's Bridge, Pwllpeiran,
Pont-rhyd-y-groes and
back 11 miles

Devil's Bridge

Mynach Falls

MYNACH

INN

Bodcoll Farm

N

The Arch

B4343

Pwllpeiran

Hafod Church

Afon Ystwyth

INN

Pont-rhyd-y-groes

took the B4574 for Cwmystwyth intending to reach Pont-rhyd-y-groes at opening time. A swift half at The Miners Arms would set me up for the return along the B4343. Light slanted across the trees, touching the hills above Bodcoll Farm. A whiff of bleak upland reached me on the breeze. The air was crisp.

Forestry Commission plantations are a little less inspiring than yesterday's cold porridge. The one at The Arch with its walks and picnic areas was true to form. Now that Christmas trees are grantable, God help the British countryside. The Arch, by the way, was erected to commemorate the Jubilee of George III. Why, I asked myself, considering what a stirrer the third George was.

The road through the trees came downhill to a right-hand turning and a sign which read 'Experimental Husbandry Farm'. On the right was a picnic area but I was looking for my 'vampires'. There were none on the roofs of the houses and there were none lurking close to the Husbandry Centre of Pwllpeiran.

I walked briskly downhill in the fading light. The views on the right towards the Ystwyth Valley and the hills beyond were mysterious. I stopped to enjoy them and recalled passages from Dafydd ap Gwilym's fabulous poem *Morfudd's Pilgrimage* in the Nigel Heseltine translation.

'And now deep Dovey with your wine-dark flood and shivering waters, let nine waves carry her to sweet St David's country. Rheidol for your honour's sake give passage to her: Ystwyth grant this to me – a crossing of fair waters between your two banks . . .'

But the hills losing their colour weren't the place to find Morfudd – 'the chaste jewel' with her golden hair and beguiling charms. I thought I had unearthed her once in Conway but the lady turned out to be a visitor from Liverpool capable of telling the barman to do something impossible to himself in the sort of language that would have made Dafydd blush.

Before long my little side road through reverie met the B4574 and I followed it, right, for Pont-rhyd-y-groes. At the waysides were stone walls and a chapel-like building almost lost under the trees. It was Coniferland broken by beeches, but at the cottage at the head of a farm track part of my past assumed a curious and vivid reality again.

It was here one autumn evening in the mid-seventies that I saw my 'vampires'. I was on my way from Cwmystwyth to The Miner's Arms and the dark shapes leaving the trees before me took me by surprise. Five lovely red kites, the fork-tailed hawks of Dyfed, had left their roosts and were flying off like vampire bats. So, the road from Cwmystwyth to Pont-rhyd-y-groes became the Vampire Trail; and whenever I returned from the pub I expected the night to be full of the hawks. Benign Welsh vampires!

The tower of Hafod Church rose from the trees. I walked up the hill past the little churchyard. It was a silent place carved out of the pagan past. The Goddesses of an older religion, Epona and Morrigan, would find no comfort here; and the Celtic horned god, Cernunnos, who loved and comforted sick animals would have shunned the place. The early Christian missionaries said he was the Devil, him and his antlers. It was a slander.

The way was rough. It climbed between tumble-down walls and presented glimpses of the coniferous slopes of the Ystwyth valley and the coniferous slopes of the high ground beyond. Fortunately pleasant, rocky moor bulged skywards to the right. Rooted in it, like a tooth, was an old farmhouse with a barn of rusty, corrugated iron. Could this be Caermeirch? The Ordnance Survey Landranger 147 map seemed to think so. The bare hillsides around the farm were beautiful.

At another time I might have left the road and taken to that fine unbroken country. Yet the narrow way, snaking upwards, was a nostalgia arterial, carrying me back rather than forward. The solitary tree on the skyline and the sheep in the nearby pasture held the dream-structure together as a drystone wall is held together by gravity.

Then I was walking beneath oaks and beeches and it was downhill. Soon I had swung left onto the B4343 with deciduous trees on the Ystwyth side and the bridge over the river waiting. Pont-rhyd-y-groes means The Bridge of the Ford of the Cross and beyond the bend was The Miners Arms. I entered the bar and asked the landlord in Welsh if he spoke English! It was an exercise in courtesy. In France you don't assume everyone speaks English so you try out your 'O' level Français. In Dyfed and Gwynedd intelligent foreigners realise Welsh is the first language.

Ten minutes later I was closing the door behind me and swinging through the dusk, back over the bridge to the Cwmystwyth turning which I passed to take the notorious bend uphill into the trees. Open country stretched before me as I came over the brow of the hill. Cars passed holding me briefly in their lights. I looked across the pastures to high hills and walked on. Muscular, half-wild countryside reared on the right with a wood of young oaks and farmland opposite that hadn't been fully tamed. But the farmhouse and outbuildings at the roadside were one of those outposts of human warmth you find everywhere in rural Wales.

Although the road was busy compared to the Vampire Trail it ran over a wind-washed upland of grass and reeds. It was quite dark now and the lights of the scattered dwellings were on. Above me the star dance had begun in the vast, clear October sky. The hills were low and the countryside was open to the weather and the seasons. After Coniferland its spaciousness and simplicity were remarkably attractive.

Walking towards an inn through the autumn dusk always makes me cheerful. I was really striding along by the time I had passed the school and the stores and was following the bend around to The Hafod Arms Hotel. The Three Bridges Inn the notice informed me and I smiled at that magic word: 'Carvery'.

WALK THIRTY
Ffair-Rhos to Strata Florida.

Length: 3 miles
Grade Ⓐ

The perfect chance to explore the Welshness of Mid-Wales.

I was going in search of Dafydd ap Gwilym and a bit more of my past, and May was the perfect time of the year to visit the backwaters of Dyfed. From the Pont-rhyd-y-groes to Ffair-Rhos road I had looked down on a Chaucerian world of sheep, cattle, foxes, hawks and hens. Under the bloom of sunlight Tregaron Bog – Cors Caron – was a vague expanse of reeds dotted with scrub willow. I drew a couple of deep breaths and David Abrahams nodded his approval. We had seen red kites on the wing and had walked a beautiful stretch of mountain country which I prefer to keep to myself. Now we were outside The Cross Inn at Ffair Rhos above the Teifi Valley. Afon Teifi, Afon Towy – Wales, and the River Tavy in Devon. There was another of those almost diffident Celtic connections.

A thrush sang from a wayside tree as we began our short journey from the black and white inn. Catching the sun away across the sheep pasture to our left was the great shoulder of Pen y Bannau. A pleasant descent guided us past the white school house with cultivated land to the right and the hills looming larger as we neared Pontrhydfendigaid –which means The Bridge of the Blessed Ford. For me it was an emotional moment. The little farm with ducks and chickens in the roadside field brought the past into sharp focus.

During a stay in these hills when I was in my mid-thirties I played soccer for Pontrhydfendigaid – or Bont FC as it is known in the Aberystwyth and District League. After a week of loneliness stuck out in the wilds with Brother Fox, Brother Hawk and Brother Salmon, the kindness of the Welsh-speaking lads of Bont every Saturday kept me from despair. Glowing from the battle and the bath we came to The Red

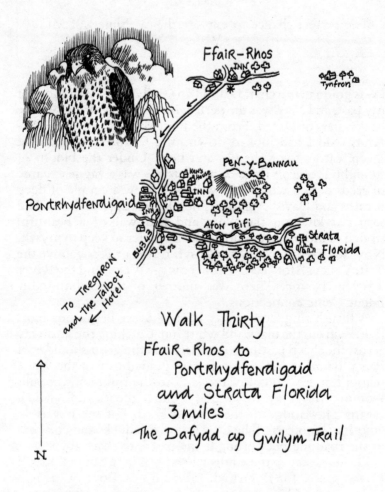

Ffair-Rhos
INN
Tynfron

Pen-y-Bannau

Ken's
House
INN
INN
Pontrhydfendigaid
INN

Afon Teifi

Strata
Florida

To Tregaron
and The Talbot
Hotel

N

Walk Thirty
Ffair-Rhos to
      Pontrhydfendigaid
  and Strata Florida
      3 miles
The Dafydd ap Gwilym Trail

Lion or The Black Lion to eat and drink and celebrate or hold post-mortems. There were my friends Ken Jones and John Tyn-fron, and my team mates and drinking companions, Drws, Lodger, Dicky Mint, Ieuan, and Lloyd. And there was the language, mellifluent Welsh, and the magnificent melancholy of autumn dusks as I drove back to the Mountain Road and my cottage.

Strolling with David across the soccer pitch I considered the obvious Celtic connection. Wales and Devon and Cornwall share a geographical affinity. The land is formed of pre-carboniferous rocks and the soil has provided the sort of nourishment Celts seem to require. I don't think the Welsh Celt is spiritually deeper than the rest of us but he enjoys celebrating the spiritual-animistic side of his nature. He also enjoys his independence, with the mountains as a fortress protecting him from the tidal surges of European culture. Perhaps a barren upland forces people to turn in upon themselves and become dreamers and idealists.

We left the football field and walked through the village past the row of neat little cottages and Evan Jones' Butcher shop. The grey stone Presbyterian chapel stood amongst its firs on the right, opposite the general stores. The Christian religion was alive and well in Bont. The village was as Welsh as ir hen iaith itself.

Up a side-turning on the left was The Black Lion, a white pub with a splendid porch and black paintwork. Here you could get Allsopps and a good game of darts. Further down the main street were more small houses in a row, another old chapel and The Red Lion by the bridge that spanned Afon Teifi. We crossed the river and saw the signpost the other side of the petrol pumps: Strata Florida Abbey.

'It's more of a pilgrimage than a walk, isn't it?' David said.

A couple of ponies were rolling in the grass and dandelions in the meadow on the right, watched by a handful of chickens and a black cat. The river was on the other side, running through tree-fringed rough pasture. Pen y Bannau towered above it.

We walked under the birdsong and the young leaves of beech and oak. The way was sun-dappled and the sunlight held the smell of the river. Then we went over a little bridge

157

and a tributary stream of the Teifi. At the bend was a mossy stone wall. Over it we could see some fine hills.

The sheep were small, healthy and contented, walking around in the nearby pastures like adverts for careful husbandry. The way to the abbey was bounded by leafy hedges. A buzzard mewled. Birdsong, streamsong, treesong – the living world took its life from the seasons just as Dafydd ap Gwilym took his poetry from the poetry of Earth and his emotions: '. . . I must pass through the coppins of this year's May, and along the wooded hillsides bright like my love's hair before I can drink of the lake on the high hill and see our couch under the birch tree'. From *25 Poems by Dafydd ap Gwilym*, translated by Nigel Heseltine, and published by The Piers Press. Lovely stuff!

The remains of the Cistercian abbey stand in a meadow on the south-east bank of Afon Teifi. Strata Florida is the Latinised form of the Welsh Ystrad Fflur – 'the valley of the flowers'. The once magnificent building and centre of Welsh culture was brought to ruin by Henry VIII and I daresay the puritan iconoclasts had a hand in the final vandalism.

We went through the shop and found the outline of the church, chapter house, cloisters etc., beyond a splendid stone archway. Lines of low stone walls patterned a lawn of green turf. We strolled down what was once the nave, the sun warm on our heads. Crows alarmed, a jay screeched and from somewhere close at hand came the song of a white-throat. The hill rising from the pasture behind the south transept chapels was dotted with flowering hawthorn and clumps of oak. The hush emanated from the time-worn carcass of the abbey. The decorated tiles of the chapels hinted at the beauty of the former building. Looking at them I felt angry and sad. The destruction of Strata Florida Abbey was an indictment of bigotry and intolerance and all fundamentalism that is life-denying within the limitations of its own blinkered vision.

On a wall to the left at the end of the ruins is a memorial plaque to Dafydd ap Gwilym. David, son of William, the great Welsh bard. The words cut into the slate are in Welsh and Latin. The sound of running water and the cries of birds and farm animals might have been plundered from his verse.

They were the voices of defiance. The abbey had been razed to the ground but the place was alive in its Welshness. Here was the slow heartbeat of a nation clinging to its traditions and culture. If the North Wales mountain, Carnedd Dafydd, was a fortress of resistance to the invader, then Strata Florida is a stronghold of the Celtic spirit.

A cuckoo began to call across the hush. I waved an imaginary wand over David's head as he walked in front of me under the arch; but he did not turn into Morfudd.

In the road outside an ash tree grew on the bank of a brook. It was the sort of living monument Dafydd would have appreciated. But his work deserves greater recognition because he is one of those poets necessary to the Celtic spirit. I said this in the back bar of that beautiful old inn, The Talbot Hotel, in Tregaron that evening. It was frosty and Sally Williams, who runs the inn with her family, had built up the great log fire in the dining room. This fire burns magnificently in a high, long, deep fireplace.

After we had bathed and eaten some of Sally's delicious chilli con carne in the bar with its pine wood furniture, we sat and talked with the hill farmers who had come to Tregaron for the market. The Talbot is one of my five favourite hill country inns; the others are Pen y Gwyrd, Snowdonia; The Kinloch Hotel, the Isle of Mull; The Black Lion, Hay-on-Wye, Powys; and The Rock Inn, Haytor Vale, Dartmoor.

The Talbot has supplied many memorable occasions. I recall a long spring evening by the fire listening to the great Welsh male voice choirs on tape while we drank and chatted. Then there was the autumn night with Graham Williams pulling the pints and cracking the jokes until we were joined by the members of the local rotary clubs. The singing went on for hours – Myfanwy, Hyfrydol, Nant y Mynydd, Llef, Mae D'Eisiau di bob Awr . . .

Going to some inns is like going home, and The Talbot has its own highly individual and compelling atmosphere. The food is excellent, the beds comfortable, the fire almost as warm as the landlady and, when Tregaron male voice choir opens up on a Saturday night, you'll find the ghost of Dafydd ap Gwilym pressing his nose to the window of the back bar. At The Talbot the Celtic spirit, which can be so elusive elsewhere, is a definite presence. It is an inn with blood in its stones.

Note: You return by the same route from Strata Florida to Ffair Rhos.

6

Snowdonia

Snowdonia is that wild and rugged part of North Wales surrounding the celebrated mountain, Yr Wyddfa, which the English know as Snowdon. At 3,560 feet this peak dominates an area which is mostly a National Park and offers not only tough mountain walks but also climbing of quality. Apart from the Snowdon group of peaks the other two most notable mountain groups are the Glyders and the Carneddau – and the latter, especially, is a real wilderness challenge of high ridges and deep valleys. At the villages of Beddgelert, Bethesda, Capel Curig, Llanberis and Nant Peris climbers and walkers are always welcome.

The fourteen Welsh mountains of 3,000 feet or more are all in Snowdonia. My favourite peaks are Tryfan and Crib Goch.

WALK THIRTY-ONE
The Snowdon Horseshoe Ridge.

Length: 8 miles
Grades © and ⓓ

Not for the inexperienced mountain walker.

When I first hitch-hiked to Snowdon I was as lean as a racing snake. My Welsh relatives were amazed that a fifteen-year-

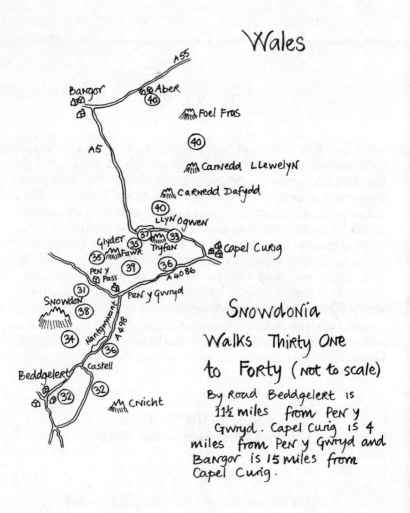

Wales

Snowdonia

Walks Thirty One
to Forty (not to scale)

By Road Beddgelert is
11½ miles from Pen y
Gwryd. Capel Curig is 4
miles from Pen y Gwryd and
Bangor is 15 miles from
Capel Curig.

old with so little flesh on his body should even be considering the ascent of the highest mountain south of Scotland. In the early 'Fifties the mountains of North Wales were the horizon of my dreams and the reality of confronting them for the first time on the approach to Capel Curig left me warm with excitement. I scanned their silhouette, aching to be there, against the sky, alone.

During that autumn pilgrimage I wandered among them sleeping in cowhouses and barns, glad to hear my mother's tongue but unwilling to seek human company. The hills were everything. For some people The Dream never has a chance but for me the first glimpse of the peaks descending from Yr Wyddfa was the hardening of the childhood vision that had been fed by my mother's stories.

After a long apprenticeship on the South Devon sea cliffs the Snowdon Horseshoe surprised me. The rock was generous compared to some of the climbs I had done on Berry Head. At first I followed an experienced party up Crib Goch and as far as the Pinnacles, then the path led me on easily to the top of Yr Wyddfa. The rest was straightforward despite a little confusion on the south-east face of Yr Wyddfa.

I remember how the combination of autumn mist, sunlight and silence and the high rock undulating on forever filled me with awe. Certain details return whenever the Horseshoe comes to mind as I 'go down' with a dose of mountain fever: the Hunter's Moon of October shining on the hill farm above Nant Gwynant, a vixen screaming across shining fields as I stood at the beudy door staring at the stars; mist like a cobweb on my face; hailstones bouncing off my head; rain departing noiselessly to leave the morning sparkling.

Easing the car into the carpark at Pen y Pass I recalled the first visit right down to the smell of the animals in the cowhouse and the rats running through the straw as I tried to go to sleep. The autumn morning was sunny and the mist was clearing. There were less than half a dozen cars in a car park that is always crowded at weekends and is full in the summer. Even the youth hostel that was once the famous Gorphwysfa Hotel seemed empty. The Gorphwysfa was one of the cradles of British mountaineering in the Edwardian era

163

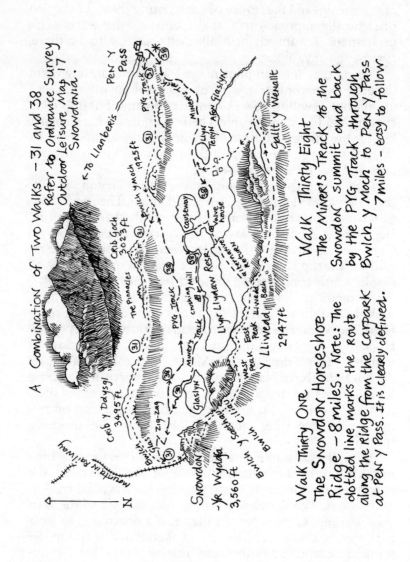

A Combination of Two Walks — 31 and 38

Refer to Ordnance Survey Outdoor Leisure Map 17 Snowdonia.

← To Llanberis

Pen Y Pass

Crib y Ddysgl 3495 ft

Crib Goch 3023 ft

Bwlch y moch 1925 ft

The Pinnacles

PYG Track

Miner's Track

Causeway

Valve House

Crushing Mill

Llyn Llydaw Res'r

Llyn Teyrn

Afon Glaslyn

Gallt y Wenallt

Glaslyn

Bwlch y Saethau

West Peak

East Peak

Y Lliwedd Bach

Y Lliwedd 2947 ft

Zig-zag

Bwlch Glas

Snowdon
~ Yr Wyddfa
3,560 ft

Mountain Railway

↑ N

Walk Thirty One

The Snowdon Horseshoe Ridge — 8 miles. Note: The dotted line marks the route along the ridge from the carpark at Pen Y Pass. It is clearly defined.

Walk Thirty Eight

The Miner's Track to the Snowdon summit and back by the PYG Track through Bwlch y Moch to Pen Y Pass. 7 miles – easy to follow although it has never captured my imagination in the same way as The Pen y Gwryd Hotel just down the road.

I had booked in at The Gwyrd, eaten a good breakfast and driven up to Pen y Pass to begin the Horseshoe. Things had changed a lot since my first visit; but as I came up the Pyg Track towards the dark red peak of Crib Goch the old excitement returned. The Pyg Track is a well-marked right-hand turning a little before the more obvious Miners' Track. It was easy and rather irritating walking over compressed stone chippings with all the additional 'assists' which I suppose have become necessary on well-trodden National Park routes. But beyond Bwlch y Moch, where I had left the Pyg Track and taken to the lower slopes of Crib Goch, the path became less assertive the higher I went. Before long I was putting hand to rock to enjoy some steep scrambling.

Nowhere was the ascent difficult and the holds were safe and numerous but there isn't a better way of getting to the top of a mountain.

The path was always visible and cairned and I hadn't broken into a sweat by the time I reached the top. From the windswept summit, 3,023 feet above sea level, I could look across the Llanberis Pass to the Glyders and glimpses of the Carneddau or south east to Moel Siabod. The views were ravishing. Ahead of me the way followed the knife edge of the ridge to Crib y Ddysgl (Garnedd Ugain, 3,493 feet) and I walked it with respect for the precipices on my right, negotiated the Pinnacles and came down to Bwlch Coch. (The Pinnacles can be skirted by dropping a little below them to the left.)

The wind and the nip in the air had brought a glow to my face. A raven cronked, clouds sailed by, the sun shone. Even on the easy approaches to Crib y Ddysgl I was aware of the drops on my right-hand side. I was also aware of the mountain solitude although in front of me I saw a couple of bright cagoules moving up Crib y Ddysgl. Down to the left was Glaslyn, steely grey despite the sun.

Several paths ascended Crib y Ddysgl but unless you are a competent rock climber the one furthest on the right should be avoided. It leads onto the sort of crag that could spoil your enjoyment of the Horseshoe and bring you in contact with a

Mountain Rescue team. The other paths present no difficulty providing you don't go too low, but care is essential on all mountains and this great classic ridge walk isn't recommended in heavy mist, rain or snow; and ice would render it suicidal. Obviously this advice isn't aimed at experienced hill walkers and climbers.

I chose a pleasant scramble over friendly rock onto the ridge, overtook the couple in the orange cagoules and let the path bring me the Trig Point and the top of Crib y Ddysgl which is a mile from Crib Goch – a sky mile! From here the descent to the Snowdon Mountain Railway and Bwlch Glas was kind to the legs and knees ruined by years of soccer.

At the Bwlch I followed the railway towards the summit of Yr Wyddfa. Under the crags to the left of me were the ugly Zig-Zags – disfigurement caused originally by the erosion brought about by hundreds of thousands of feet. The new look Zig-Zags were born of necessity but do not enhance the mountains. Neither does the bunker-like café and railway station stuck on the top of the loftiest mountain in England and Wales. That morning it was closed and shuttered but for all my purist cant I confess to enjoying many a glass of ale there on hot days. I also realise I contribute to Snowdon's erosion problems although I rarely tread the popular trails. Maybe I can be forgiven for side-stepping an issue whose solution will probably result in No-Go areas.

At 3,560 feet the coffee from my flask tasted heavenly and the peanut butter rolls were a feast. From the summit I could gaze down upon Glaslyn and Llyn Llydaw and take in the immense panorama of the mountains and hills that swam away into far-off misty places the imagination could visit.

When I departed I passed through the little walled enclosure at the far end of the Summit Station, came down the path and turned left at the rock monolith to descend the great shattered south-east face of Yr Wyddfa to Bwlch y Saethau – the Pass of Arrows where King Arthur is supposed to have died in battle and a most obvious Celtic connection if one is necessary in a place that is pivotal to the entire Welsh Celtic consciousness.

Ignoring the Watkin Path that swung down to the right I crossed Bwlch Ciliau and climbed the long steeps of Y

Lliwedd, taking the west and east Peaks at a good pace. But I allowed myself time to look down the thousand foot precipice that falls to the slopes above Llydaw. Ravens were on the wing below me, catching the sun in a coal glint of feather.

On Lliwedd Bach I sat and swigged more coffee.

Leaving the peak I avoided the usual descent to Llyn Llydaw and pushed on along the greening ridge to complete the Horseshoe on the delightful Gallt y Wenallt. The wind licked over my face as I came down to Afon Glaslyn and forded it somewhere below the old sheepfolds to pick up the Miners' Track the Snowdon side of Llyn Teryn.

I met several Snowdon enthusiasts as I walked back along the Track to Pen y Pass, and I was at peace with myself when I arrived at Pen y Gwyrd. That most celebrated of British Mountain inns has always stood at my personal crossroads where adventure begins. For over a hundred and fifty years Pen y Gwryd has been a special place to generations of climbers, mountaineers and hill walkers. I go there because I need to share the mountain past with kindred spirits.

Towards the end of the 1940s Christopher Briggs and his wife bought the inn and gradually restored it to its former glory. Illness has forced Chris to take a back seat now and the PYG is run by his daughter Jane and her husband Brian Pullen; but the atmosphere created by that honest, straight-talking Yorkshireman endures.

When I was old enough to drink I sank a couple of pints in the Everest Room. Collecting my pot from the bar I had a tantalising glimpse of Pen y Gwryd's inner sanctum – the Smoke Room, where the hotel guests sat laughing and talking. The exclusiveness of that gathering was seductive to the extreme. By then I was drunk on the romance of mountains and Snowdon dominated my nostalgia for the Golden Age. Oxbridge capers, tweed, cakes and ale, hemp ropes, stiff upper lips and a 'Jolly Good Show' yodelled in a breezy public school accent across the heights, were the ingredients of that romance. Sepia photographs brought Pen y Gwyrd's past alive. Fuel for nostalgia came from Smythe's mountain books and W.H. Murray's splendid prose. Behind the climbs and walks and booze-ups were decent values.

In these days of the Philistine triumphant Pen y Gwyrd remains an inn where mid-Atlantic vulgarity finds no lodgings. The baths are deep, the cuisine excellent, the company good. Among the guests that evening were a curate, a Lord and Lady, a university professor, a postman, a shopkeeper and a senior Nato Officer. Love of mountains was the bond.

I dined well and supped ale in the oak-panelled Smoke Room where the Everest team had relaxed during the training for their successful assault on the world's highest peak. The Gwyrd was the party's H.Q. and they returned in 1953 for a celebration dinner. Chris Briggs invited them to write their signatures on the ceiling of the Everest Room and to those historic scrawls have been added other names including Bertrand Russell, H.V. Morton, Chris Brasher and Roger Bannister.

I never fail to enjoy the absence of television at the 'funny old inn'. Peace and quiet and some intelligent conversation make a welcome change from what a lot of hotels offer. And I remember on my first visit how intrigued I was by the name on my bedroom door: Tryfan. By a fortunate coincidence Pen y Gwyrd has fourteen bedrooms and Snowdonia has fourteen mountains over 3,000 feet.

Settling in a corner of the Smoke Room by the fire I drank my beer while the conversation lapped at the edge of my thoughts. Outside the darkness had deepened and the stars shone above the mountains.

Note: The normal conclusion to the ridge walk is to descend from Y Lliwedd to the cairn on the grass and follow the path left down the steeps to the Miners' Track at Llyn Llydaw. Here you turn right for Pen-y-Pass.

WALK THIRTY-TWO
Beddgelert to Castell, Nant Gwynant and back.

Length: 12 miles
Grade Ⓑ

A superb road and lake walk through the mountains.

The story of the Welsh prince, his wolfhound Gelert and the grave where the dog is buried has a universal appeal. Llewlyn the Great had a favourite wolfhound called Gelert and according to legend left the loyal old animal guarding his son. Returning from a hunting trip one day the prince was horrified to see the dog and the cot where the baby had been left sleeping, covered in blood. In a fit of grief and anger he put the hound to the sword only to discover the body of a dead wolf behind the cot. The baby was safe because Gelert had killed the wolf.

Full of remorse Llewlyn buried his dog and now tourists flock to the spot in their thousands. Whether the tale is true or not doesn't matter. It sits comfortably in the Celtic imagination and goes well with the surrounding mountain grandeur.

Bedd-gelert – the Grave of Gelert – is one of those mountain villages which occupy more than a corner of a valley in Snowdonia. If you love mountains this quiet little community with its slate roofs and smoking chimneys will constantly call you back to it. The houses stand each side of Afon Glaslyn not far from Llyn Dinas among the foothills of Eryri. I make sure I walk there out of season to become part of the Welshness of the place.

Anyone who visits a Welsh-speaking village should make a real attempt to pronounce the words correctly. Learn a few basics and treat the language with the respect it deserves. I get irritated when TV newscasters get the Welsh place names wrong yet are so particular over the pronunciation of, say, Russian or words like 'guerrilla'. Beddgelert is pronounced Bethgelert – the 'dd' is like 'th' in 'thee'.

I love the sound of the Old Tongue – ir hen iaith – in the

Walk Thirty Two
Beddgelert to
Nantgwynant
and back – 12 miles

N

Nantgwynant

Bethania

Afon Glaslyn

Return Route

Llyn Dinas

Castell

Bryn Bedd

Blaen Nanmor

A498

Gelert's Grave

Beddgelert

Footpath (alternative)

YR ARDDU

Dolfriog Woods

Coed Caeddafydd

Pont Aber Glaslyn

Bwlch Llechog

Dolfriog

Cae Dafydd

Bwlchgwernog

bars and shops, but for me Beddgelert will always be the village of the jackdaws. Whenever I stay at the Tanronan Hotel near the bridge I watch the daws from my bedroom window before breakfast. One particular spring morning a couple of years ago they were chacking to each other as they came and went at the chimney-pot nesting sites. The comical, sociable beautiful daws sent their cries across the rooftops. It is a sound I can rarely separate from mountains and grey stone cottages and the Welsh language.

The birds were nesting in the chimneys immediately above my room. Standing on the bridge over the Glaslyn I would watch them slide headfirst into the chimney pot to rearrange the nesting material and emerge like sailors leaving the conning tower of a submarine.

The rain had stopped and the sky was clearing. I left the Tanronan carrying a good breakfast inside me. The sun was out and the roofs gleaming under the crisp 'chak-chak' of the daws as I turned left and took the A498 Tremadog Road. Three or four days of sweating hard on the heights had dampened my enthusiasm for mountain tops. Soon I was out of the village following the road above Gelert's Grave with the cliffs of Craig y Llan away to the left. The bend brought me over Pont Aber Glaslyn for the chance of a close up of the craggy hillside. The river was behaving according to the laws of romantic fiction; it was 'brawling over rocks'. The old disused railway was visible on the left where it ran along the base of the cliffs among conifers. Afon Glaslyn was now on my right but before long I said goodbye to it and took the left hand turning sign-posted Nantwm and walked uphill, delighted to have shown my back to the main road.

On the brow of the hill was a row of striking grey stone cottages displaying plain porches. Beyond them was the chapel, a tall, austere building typical of Welsh religious architecture; further on I could look over the drystone wall on my left across craggy ground to the mountain tops. Spring greenness was showing but it was all so late and had nothing like the intensity of a South Devon spring. But after a long wet winter there was birdsong and the season's wayside flowers and grass standing to attention in the sunlight.

I continued up the next rise in the lane under broad-leafed trees. Fields and little groves and copses of birch lent a softness to the landscape which the nearby mountains couldn't eclipse. The lane was narrow, rough underfoot, and the drystone walls beside it seemed to have grown out of the earth. The countryside in the heartland of Snowdonia was a repository for so many of the deathless elements of the Celtic spirit and the Celtic way of life.

There was the smallness of the pastures, the birds and farm animals, sunlight, trees and grasses with the mountains beyond. It was the world of my ancestors and the world of poets like the 7th century bard who wrote the lullaby *Dinogad's smock* and spoke of weasels and hunting dogs, fish, deer, wild pigs, grouse and foxes. This was also the world of the mythology that was mead to the Celtic imagination, enhancing and distorting, and supplying meanings to a life fraught with bewilderment and drenched in wonder as the spring morning was drenched in sunlight.

A fine grey house called Bwlch-Llechog stood on the frontiers of this magic place. There were silver birches to the right and the song of a thrush and wood pigeons crooning. The panorama of hills and farmland was rendered even more pleasing by the birdcalls.

The lane went up and down, following the edge of a wood. The drystone walls at the wayside were mossy and the beeches in their prime. I passed the entrance to Dolfriog Hall which is a youth holiday centre. Why can't the generations mix as they did in my youth when you got sixteen- and sixty-year-olds at the same dance? The notion made me smile. The soldier out of step was berating the rest of the platoon!

So, between musing and simply looking about me I came on to Bwlchgwernog and walked left up the hill under the trees with the stream, Nanmor, down below on the left. After Cae Dafydd rare breed farm I found young broad-leafed trees on the slopes to my right screening Forestry Commission conifers, and thick birch woods in the valley opposite. Clouds sailed overhead. The hills were dark then light and I thought of the child Dinogad in her small world of birdsong, sun, rain and the seasons watching the shadows cancel out detail on the mountains.

Above the dark firs of Coed Caeddafydd were the crags of Yr Arddu. A gate across the path barred my way to stop the livestock straying. I opened it and made sure it was closed behind me. Far too many walkers treat farmers with contempt and as I swung on into mountain country I heard the sound of running water and thought of my friend John Jones who keeps sheep in Dyfed and has to contend with some irresponsible ramblers. The craggy slopes reaching high to the left had many handsome woods. Nanmor was far below in the ravine on the left. Beyond it was wild pastureland and the disused quarries of Blaen Nanmor. I went through another gateway with drystone walls at either hand, crossed the bridge and saw the stream tumbling over a waterfall.

The way upwards was never strenuous. Then, as a reward, I was greeted by the vision of Snowdon itself, Yr Wyddfa and the peaks of the Snowdon Horseshoe over the next brow. The summit of Yr Wyddfa was lost in cloud but once I was past the white and blue house, Blaenant, hill country grew around me with a remarkable telescoping of horizons. The long ridge of Cnicht stood in the north east, its distinctive high waterfall like white sealing wax on black rock.

The next bend brought me before the spectacle of the Watkin Path on the far side of Nantgwynant. I stood for a while and gazed at the great waterfalls. Yr Aran and Lliwedd seemed enormous. Between them Yr Wyddfa was still brewing its own cloud.

I walked on past Bryn Bedd and looked down on the outbuildings of Castell Farm as the past rose between me and the moment. Another gate was left behind, then another, as I paced downhill. Then there was the white farmhouse and green paintwork of Castell. Well, the last time I slept in the byre not far from the farmhouse was in the early seventies. Coming down through the rhododendrons I recalled dusks laden with the smell of cattle and the heavier tang of corned beef curry cooking on a paraffin stove.

So I walked the last of the lane, crossed over the bridge and the river to the A498 and turned left to stride back towards Beddgelert. And soon I was enjoying the glassy calm of Llyn Dinas on my left and the wooded slopes above the far shore which rose to the countryside I had passed through during the walk. With so much mountain work under my belt I cruised along beside the lake, looking across to the waterfall of Pwll Pair Sygun. Cars and coaches swept by to the right but that was a part of my world it was easy to dismiss. Llyn Dinas ended but Afon Glaslyn wound on down the valley into Beddgelert under high hillsides with their woods and crags.

Before returning to the Tanronan I had a Guinness in the Prince Llewlyn, listening to the Welsh of the regulars at the bar lapping over the English of the visitors at their tables, and feeling a bit lost between the two languages.

WALK THIRTY-THREE
Tryfan – Heather Terrace (The East Face).

Length 2½ miles
Grade Ⓑ

A very easy ascent of a beautiful mountain.

Once Tryfan gets in your blood you are hooked for life and will keep returning to the mountain year after year. Often I lift my head from some task, close my eyes and let the vision of the East Face grow with the hiraeth. 'Hiraeth' is one of those peculiarly Welsh words which defy accurate translation into English. It is a word layered with meanings built around a longing for homeland that is at once melancholic yet desirable.

The New Year was still in its first week when I drove into the North Wales village of Beddgelert and got myself bed and breakfast at the Tanronan Hotel. Angharad was serving tea to a couple of guests before the coal fire in the lounge. I had a bath and came down to read before the evening meal. Snow had fallen heavily on the mountains and more was expected; but I had the winter gear and wanted to experience winter conditions on Tryfan. The sound of spoken Welsh

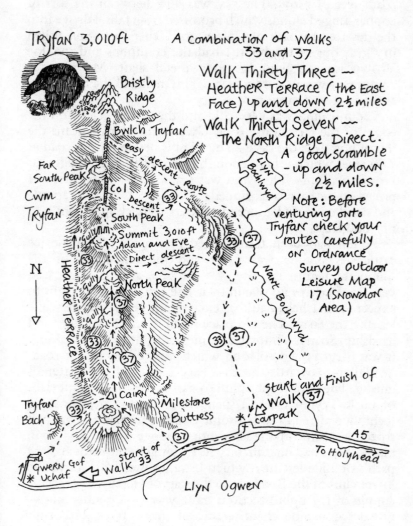

Tryfan 3,010ft

A combination of Walks 33 and 37

Walk Thirty Three — Heather Terrace (the East Face) up and down 2½ miles

Walk Thirty Seven — The North Ridge Direct. A good scramble - up and down 2½ miles.

Note: Before venturing onto Tryfan check your routes carefully on Ordnance Survey Outdoor Leisure Map 17 (Snowdon Area)

Bristly Ridge

Bwlch Tryfan

easy descent

Llyn Bochlwyd

Far South Peak

Cwm Tryfan

Col Descent

Route

33

South Peak

Summit 3,010ft Adam and Eve

Direct descent

N

33

Gully

Gully

Gully

North Peak

37

Nant Bochlwyd

33

37

33

37

Heather Terrace

37

33

37

Cairn

Milestone Buttress

Start and Finish of Walk 37 carpark

Tryfan Bach

33

Start of Walk 33

37

A5 To Holyhead

Gwern Gof Uchaf

Llyn Ogwen

filtered through from the bar. I was relaxed and slept well that night.

After breakfast the next day I found white mountains and roads free of snow. The sky was blue between the sort of copper-tinged clouds which promised fresh falls. I drove into the deserted carpark of Gwern gof Uchaf Farm and fished my gear out of the boot. I had the crampons and the Joe Brown ice axe with the long metal shaft. My survival equipment was in the rucksack. This included the bivvy bag and fifty feet of nylon rope.

The morning was very cold and there were icicles on the edges of the farmhouse roof. Gwern gof Uchaf means the 'High bog near the cave'. The farm is beside the A5 road at 1,000 feet which is high enough to woo the arctic spells that visit Snowdonia. The wind was razor sharp on my face as I pulled on the balaclava, zipped the Goretex Ultimate cagoule and checked to make sure my gaiters were clipped firmly to my bootlaces.

Tryfan had been transformed into a kid's fairytale ice castle. Its skyline was silver and the remainder of the silhouette against the sky was the blue-grey of shadowed versglas. Perhaps no one in their late forties had the right to expect such a heavy jolt of excitement as I received while leaving the farm. The old place smelt of sheep, weather and hardship. So many human lifetimes had gone into its making. It was part of the desolation which existed beyond the road.

Walking towards the East Face I felt a slight flutter of unease. The path crept uphill to pass below the elegant slabs of Little Tryfan where I spent hours honing my climbing technique. Then I crossed some boggy ground that was half frozen and came up the scree into a groove which was iced in places. But I had no difficulty scrambling to the cairn and the path's oblique left turn which brought me airily above the lower cliffs of the East Face to the start of Heather Terrace. A couple of icy uphill sections gave way to a gentler snow-powdered incline characteristic of the Terrace with runs diagonally south to north along the face. Above me towered the cathedral façade of Tryfan with its glinting buttresses and icicles hanging from every overhang. The ice in the gulleys was polished white. The solitude was overwhelming.

I trod the wide path carrying the ice axe in my right hand like a walking stick. The route was, perhaps, too well-defined but this is common to all the popular mountains in Britain and it would be petty to carp about it. The scree and heather on my left were coated in ice and snow. The higher I went the thicker was the ice. At the bottom of many of the slabs and crags ice lay in great whorls and breast plates, snow-encrusted; but it was possible to pick my way around it.

Out of the sun the cold was intense. Sprigs of heather had been turned into Christmas Tree decorations. I looked across the dull gleam into the valley of Nant Gwern y Gof. Maybe the stream was running under ice. It was difficult to tell in the white, hushed landscape with everything except the buzzards and myself frozen to apparent lifelessness. The traffic on the A5 didn't count. Nothing mattered except me and the mountain and the path rising to meet the demands of the mountain.

Above me a lot of naked rock showed between the lumps that were ice-plastered. Maybe the feral goats of the Glyders were up there peering down at me. I grinned and nearly cracked my face. My fingertips ached and my toes had become dead. I stopped and ran on the spot for ten minutes.

From North Gulley the Terrace brought me to the bottom of Central Buttress. I buckled the ice axe to my rucksack and took the upper path which wasn't hazardous. But at the foot of the slab below the col where I could pick up the South Ridge I was tempted to strap on the crampons. Surprisingly a more careful examination of the rock revealed accommodating ice-free patches and soon I was sitting under the drystone wall in the col drinking coffee and eating chocolate. The sun shone on me to celebrate the occasion.

Five minutes later I climbed up the South Peak and on to Tryfan's summit and the Adam and Eve Stones. In the magic of that winter noon, alone among the mountains which I loved as much as the Devon tors, I experienced something close to rapture. The sun had the snow glittering on the high ground all around me. It was remarkable but not unusual for the mountains of winter Snowdonia.

A little to the right of the Adam and Eve Stones is the steepish, well-worn rock and rubble descent of the West Face.

Normally it can be done without alarm or fuss, but that day the conditions had transformed it and I took a long time to reach the bottom. Then it was a relief to come down over the frost-hardened turf to the road by Llyn Ogwen and swing back to the farm and the car.

WALK THIRTY-FOUR
The Watkin Path to Yr Wyddfa and back.

Length: 7 miles
Grade ©

A spectacular walk with nearly 3,500 feet of ascent.

Late May of birdsong and hawthorn blossom. Two days of hot sunshine had come on the heels of a week of prolonged rain. Nigel East, Mike Taylor and I were staying in a cottage above the Vale of Gwynant. We could look from the alp across the valley and see the waterfalls pouring off the hillside in Cwm Llan beside the Watkin Path. The lure proved irresistible and shortly after breakfast we came down to the Lower Gwynant Valley, three miles from Beddgelert; and after buying chocolate and drinks at the Post Office checked our gear at Pont Bethania and came along the lane over the cattle grid. The Public Footpath to Snowdon was clearly marked where the rough road departs from the tarmac. The sign read: Llwybr Watkin Path.

Mike could not stay serious for long and by the time we had passed through the gate onto the old mine road Nigel and I were close to tears. Between us we had created this bizarre character, the Reverend Theobald Yahoo, a coloured clergyman with a long head, pebble glasses and plus-fours who spent his spare time on cycling tours. His adventures are a little too bawdy for these pages but they kept us amused whenever the landscape released us from its magic.

The wood on the left gave way to open turf at either hand. The path looped with Afon Cwm Llan on the right and the wooded slopes of Coed yr Allt above it. Then it crossed the

178

YR Wyddfa 3,560 ft

Bwlch y saethau

Walk Thirty Four
The Watkin Path to
YR Wyddfa and back
7 miles

N

Bwlch Ciliau

Cwm Tregalan

Y Lliwedd
2,947 ft

Disused QUARRY

Craig Ddu

Afon Cwm Llan

Gladstone Rock

Cwm Llan

falls

coed-yr-allt

waterfalls

Afon Merch

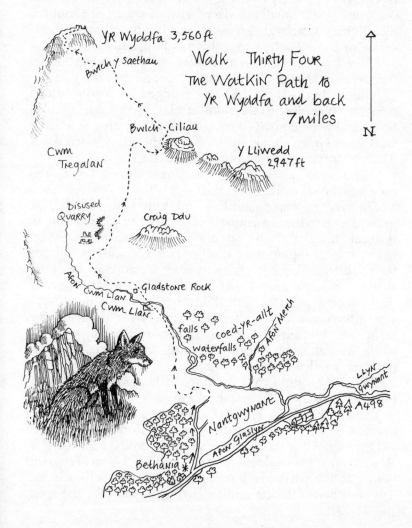

Nantgwynant

LLYN Gwynant

A498

Afon Glaslyn

Bethania

dismantled tramway to bring us within reach of the waterfalls. Mike and I were fresh-water fanatics, addicted to torrents and pools; but we knew there was an even more seductive splash-pot further upstream. A cuckoo called and Mike answered it. We were hot and needed a good laving.

Beyond the waterfalls which were really a series of spectacular cascades in two parts, the incline steepened. The path crept along the bottom of some rugged steeps with the river flowing swiftly below it on the right. Then we reached our pool. It was small and deep below a waterfall about ten feet high. We struggled to untie our boots and pull off our socks, impatient to get into that natural jacuzzi.

The water was the colour of chartreuse. Below the bubbly fizz we could see the white glint of pebbles on the bottom.

A long thrash-about later we trudged on to the bridge over the river close to the ruins of Plas Cwm-Llan. The old house had been destroyed by commandos during simulated warfare in Hitler's War. Even on a bright sunny day it was a doleful spectacle.

'The sort of place where one might encounter Yahoo moping about', Mike observed.

The walking was delightful. The stony path wound over grassy levels to the Gladstone Rock with Yr Aran standing in the heat quiver on the far side of Cwm Llan, and the river also to the left, dropping over another fall. We walked right of the Gladstone Rock, pausing to have a glance at the tablet that reminds passers-by that W.E. Gladstone M.P. opened the path on September 13th 1892 when he was eighty-four. I was more interested in the Gladstone Slabs along on the right. There I found a lot of high easy rock on the tilt and made three attempts to get from ground to top in under two minutes. I failed – but only just.

'Theobald would have done it,' Mike said, after making his own way up at an ursine amble.

The sun beat down but after a few swigs from the flasks we decided to save our thirsts for the Snowdon summit café.

Once again the path looped and bore to the right and Yr Wyddfa loomed colossal at the head of Cwm Tregalan before us. The shale track brought us past the shells of what had once been the slate miners' barracks and on by the spoil heap to the quarries with their depressing air of dereliction. We had left Cwm Llan in our wake and the Watkin Path was assuming real wilderness character. The west flanks of Y Lliwedd swept down from the right while the South Ridge of Snowdon towered on the other side of the valley. The ascent was continuous but made no demands on stamina.

I think the phrase 'melancholy splendour' could be applied to this corner of Snowdonia. The absence of wildlife, save for the daws and ravens, emphasised the bleakness. But we pushed upward undismayed and our cheerfulness intact. Certainly Theobald Yahoo helped and the desolation was to my taste.

As the ascent steepened cairns appeared and the odd sign that was baffling because we didn't see how it was possible to lose such a well-defined path. Only in thick mist could a walker be conned into taking the right-hand path above Cwm Tregalan onto Y Lliwedd. Yet approaching Bwlch Ciliau the way made a very abrupt right-hand turn and misty conditions might have persuaded careless walkers to continue in that direction at the next swing left. A definite path goes from here to Y Lliwedd's three summits.

But we came with more urgency along the correct path close to the edge of the precipices above Llyn Llydaw. Nigel had pointed out that the bar on the summit of Yr Wyddfa might close at two, and a desperate consultation of watches had prompted us to accelerate. We quick-marched from Bwlch Ciliau to Bwlch y Saethau, exulting in the views but operating now on the high octane fuel of a beer thirst. The thought of a tall glass of cool Tartan bitter spurred us to greater efforts.

After glancing for the tenth time at his watch Mike saw me champing at the bit.

'Fancy going on, Bri, and getting them in?' he said, and I was away up the drunken diagonal path and the great shattered South East face of Snowdon to the summit Station. I reached the bar with three minutes to spare to be told that it was open till two-thirty! Before long my friends joined me and when we had slaked our thirsts we sat outside by the cairn and drank in the panorama which was beer to the spirit. A train hooted as it climbed the track to our left, puffing smoke and bringing up another load of tourists.

'It's one hell of a pub,' Mike said, yawning from a grin.

Note: The quickest and best way back to Pont Bethania is the way you came.

WALK THIRTY-FIVE
Ogwen Cottage, Tryfan, Bristly Ridge and the Glyders to Pen y Pass and on to Pen y Gwryd.

Length: 5 miles
Grade Ⓑ

Mountain work without a lot of effort.

Most walkers were coming off the high ground as I trudged up the path from Ogwen Cottage one June evening. A long dry spell had left the mountains in excellent condition. Llyn Ogwen was ruffled by the gentlest and warmest of breezes and I could hear the shouts of children down by its waters. The evening smelt of dew and sheep. A moth ricochetted off my head with a soft thud. I crossed the stream, Nant Boch lwyd and followed it up to Llyn Bochlwyd. Keeping this gloomy little tarn on my right I walked the gentlest incline until the path brought me under the crags of Tryfan's South Peak to Bwlch Tryfan. The top of the mountain up on my left was flushed with sunlight as I came over the ladder stile and drystone wall and took to the Miner's Track. After a little while I could bear right where the ascent of the screes beside Bristly Ridge had been scarred by thousands of boots. Usually I scramble up the Ridge on a route which is almost as clearly marked as the scree path, but that evening I felt lazy.

Two climbers greeted me halfway up and told me it would be dark soon. Maybe I looked old or incompetent. They were young and anxious rather than haughty. I knew I had plenty of daylight left and if I was overtaken by darkness I would bivouac under the rocks somewhere as I had often

182

Ogwen Cottage

LLYN OGWEN

A5

LLYN Idwal

LLYN Bochlwyd

Tryfan

N

Bristly Ridge

Bwlch Tryfan

Glyder Fach

Glyder FAWR

Castell y Gwynt

Walk Thirty Five
Ogwen Cottage, Bristly Ridge and the Glyders to Pen y Pass and Pen y Gwryd – 5 miles

LLYN Cwmffynnon

Pen y Gwryd Hotel

A4086 To Capel Curig →

Pen y Pass Hostel

LLYN Pen y Gwryd

Cafe

A4086

A498

To Beddgelert

done in the hills. I was in my late forties and full of self-confidence.

The Glyders are the forty-square-mile central range of the three main groups of mountains in Snowdonia. The summits of my intended traverse from Ogwen to the Llanberis Pass were situated on the chain from Tryfan in the north to Glyder Fawr in the south. Compared to the Snowdon Horseshoe Ridge it was a stroll – providing you had read the map and could avoid the odd dangerous spot in bad weather.

The path was idiot-proof. Above Bristly Ridge it swung right and ran across a broad 'cat-walk' with Glyder Fach and Fawr impossible to miss on such a clear sunlit evening. All around me mountains were blueing in that shadowy way that hints at impending dusk. The sun was picking out their peaks.

I stuffed my hands in my pockets and walked to the first heap of giant slabs and found the Cantilever – the big, horizontal rock beam that was balanced on two blocks with one end jutting out like a Neolithic diving board. I walked to the end of the beam and checked my route although this was unnecessary.

The boot-erosion trail and its cairns skirted Glyder Fach's enormous jumble of rocks and slabs which were too strange to ignore. It looked as if an outcrop bigger than Dartmoor's Hay Tor had been wrecked by an internal explosion. But beyond it in the theatrical light was a far weirder vision. Castell y Gwynt, the Castle of the Wind, was an amazing loose structure of rock spires, rock fingers and upright slabs on the edge of a steep crag. I chose the left-hand path away from the drop on the right and came along an easy stretch to Glyder Fawr which is seventeen feet higher than Glyder Fach – hence the Fawr! (In Welsh, Fach and Bach mean 'small'; and Fawr and Mawr mean 'large' or 'great'.)

The sun had left the mountain tops and against the haze Snowdon's peaks were firming to silhouette. Glyder Fawr was even more shattered than Glyder Fach. I picked a way through the rock litter before returning to the cairned path on the left to begin the descent towards Pen y Pass. The way over the rocky shoulder was splashed with red circles of paint. Before long I was walking down the end of the ridge with Llyn Cwmffynnon in the shadows below to the left and the Llanberis Road on the right.

Twilight brought out the faint stars of summer. I came beyond the steeps and walked a boggy stretch to the bluff above Pen y Pass. A short descent, made conspicuous by the red circles, and I was over the stile and on the road north-west of the youth hostel. Lights were on in the building that had once been the Gorphwysfa Hotel. A group of teenagers crossed the A4086 as I walked left in the fading light. Their laughter reminded me of summer evenings and friendships which had come to nothing and others that had grown stronger over the years.

I swung along down the hill, whistling, as I had done in the early 1950s when I had walked the Snowdon Horseshoe for the first time. So I came in the summer darkness that is never opaque to Pen y Gwryd. Dimly through the trees gleamed the lights of the old inn and all around it were the mountains I had come to love as if I had been born to them. The night intensified a longing for what I had been enjoying an hour or so earlier on the Glyders.

Now those mountains were lost to me and I wanted the warmth of the Everest Room and company I could relate to.

The sweat had cooled on my back and I was shivering slightly by the time I reached the bar. Nothing had changed. There was the usual Pen y Gwryd mix of youngsters, middle-aged walkers and tough old timers sitting on the wooden benches, deep in conversation. Bringing my pint to a table I recalled my first drink in the Everest Room and how I had sat at the fireside trying to imagine how I would feel in middle-age doing the same thing. Well, inside I was still the boy who had come to Snowdonia full of passion for the mountains. That devotion to the hills hadn't diminished.

Emily Brontë distilled it into one verse:

What have these lonely mountains worth revealing?
More glory and more grief than I can tell;
The Earth that wakes one human heart to feeling
Can centre both the worlds of Heaven and Hell.

But mostly Heaven, Emily.

Note: It is no penance for a companion driving a car to wait for you at Pen y Gwryd. Purists can always stride back to Ogwen along the road via Pen y Gwryd and Capel Curig. See map.

WALK THIRTY-SIX
Capel Curig to Beddgelert.

Length: 11½ miles
Grade Ⓑ

A road walk of quality

I hitched a lift from Beddgelert to the general stores in Capel Curig, needing a rest day after walking and climbing in the Glyders and on the Snowdon Horseshoe. I wanted to saunter and relax and give my muscles a chance to shrug off the faint ache and stiffness. I bought chewing gum and followed the bend to the right as I left the stores and walked out of Capel Curig on the Nant Gwynant road. There wasn't much traffic and once I had crossed the bridge over Afon Llugwy and left Plas y Brenin Mountain Centre behind me I could enter into the mood of the occasion.

Often a landscape reminds me of a piece of music – Dyfed and the Welsh Male Voice Choirs, Dartmoor and strangely enough Elgar's Cello Concerto, Snowdonia and Mahler's 4th, the Hebrides and Bruch's Violin Concerto. That morning belonged to the slow movement from Mahler's 4th. I was perfectly at ease and walked into the beauty of the day, and the music I carried in my head brought me closer to the spirit of the place. My wife calls this, 'the romantic switching on the automatic'.

The sun on the hills and mountains played on the rock faces. Mist streamed up the North face of Y Lliwedd and vanished. The sky was the sort of blue that would cloud over later but its repose was reflected on Llynnau Mymbyr which were so calm they really did look like glass – nothing but that cliché would do them justice. Despite the clarity and the way

186

A combination of
Walks 36 and 39
contracted and
simplified

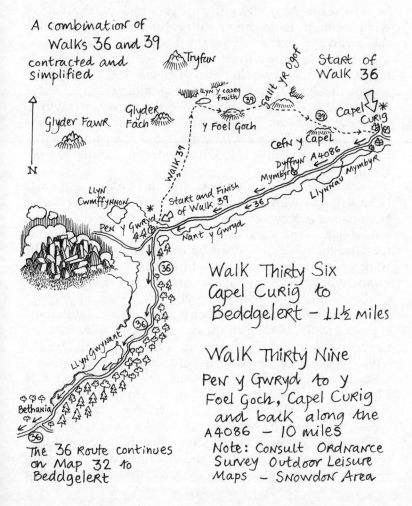

Tryfan

Gallt yr Ogof

Start of
Walk 36

Llyn y caseg fraith 39

Glyder Fawr

Glyder Fach

Y Foel Goch

39 Capel Curig

Cefn y Capel

Walk 39

Dyffryn
Mymbyr A4086

Llynnau Mymbyr

N

Llyn Cwmffynnon

Pen y Gwryd

Start and Finish
of Walk 39

Nant y Gwryd

36

36

36

Llyn Gwynant

Bethania

36

Walk Thirty Six
Capel Curig to
Beddgelert – 11½ miles

Walk Thirty Nine
Pen y Gwryd to y
Foel Goch, Capel Curig
and back along the
A4086 – 10 miles

Note: Consult Ordnance
Survey Outdoor Leisure
Maps – Snowdon Area

The 36 Route continues
on Map 32 to
Beddgelert

the peaks of Y Lliwedd up ahead of me were revealed in marvellous detail, the Snowdon Horseshoe managed to convey the illusion that it was insubstantial like the mist it was loosing into the sky.

On both sides of the valley were craggy hills. Ascending the lower steeps of Moel Siabod beyond the two lakes of Mymbyr the conifers managed to look less like the farm crop they were. The slopes of Cefn y Capel to my right were dissected by drystone walls and patched with bracken. I had come to the end of the lake where there was a garth and the broad stream. Nant Gwyrd flowed across marshy flats to wind through the Mymbyr valley. Streams were tumbling thin and white off the steeps at the foot of Moel Siabod. Low, thick reeds, loved by foxes seeking a kennel for the night, lay to my left with a waterfall and farmhouses on the right.

In such a broad, open valley farm buildings tend to catch the eye. At the right-hand side of the road was Dyffryn Mymbyr, the farm that featured in Thomas Firbank's best seller *I Bought a Mountain*. The mountain was part of Glyder Fach. Esme Firbank still lives under it in the famous farmhouse.

Those huge hillsides embossed with boulders and crags were streaked with the torrents which are characteristic of Mountain country for three seasons of the year. Often I would halt to marvel at one of the roadside falls or cascades catching the sun as it foamed off the ridge to the right. The traffic passing by could not diminish the beauty of the moment or perhaps mountains have the power to lift us out of the moment into something close to 'a state of grace'.

Nan y Gwryd clattered over its stony bed and I wandered along above it listening to the deep cronking of ravens and the bleat of sheep. Every so often the slopes of Dyffryn Mymbyr supplied their surprises of falls and rustling streams. Then I reached the bend that brought me the full view of Lliwedd's peaks which had assumed a Himalayan majesty. Before long I was striding past Llyn Pen y Gwyrd and crossing the road to pop inside the hotel for morning coffee.

The transformation of hill ascetic into bar room sybarite requires no defence. The joys and discomforts of mountains are replaced by the pleasures of the inn at the end of a day that has become part of your being. But I hadn't reached my destination and the coffee was sufficient although the quiet bustle of Pen y Gwryd coming to life made me itch for Smoke Room evenings after a long soak in a hot tub.

Outside again a coach passed and the kids in the back window gave me the V sign and I waved a hand in acknowledgement. They were short of targets for ridicule and, if I obliged, it in no way impaired my feelings for the rest of humanity. Away on the right Afon Glaslyn tumbled down the steeps between Gallt y Wenallt and Craig Penlan into the vale of Gwynant. The peaks of Snowdon soared above it and the road carried me downhill to Llyn Gwynant. The canoes on the lake were paddled by eager youngsters. More teenagers had congregated on the near shore. I strolled on and posted some cards at Nantgwynant Post Office which must be everyone's idea of the corner shop in a mountain district.

Then I lengthened my stride and found another gear. Soon I was at the fireside in the residents' lounge at The Tanronan and Angharad was serving the cakes and tea before a cheerful blaze of Welsh coals.

Note: You can catch the bus back to Capel Curig but ideally a less active companion with the car can bring this walk to a delightful conclusion.

WALK THIRTY-SEVEN
Tryfan – The North Ridge.

Length: about 2½ miles
Grade Ⓓ Map on p. 175

A long, beautiful scramble – not for the fainthearted.

Tryfan catches the eye as you motor down the A5 from Capel Curig towards Llyn Ogwen. There are the three peaks in dark profile, beside the road on your left. There are the crags, gullies, grooves, ribs and buttresses of rock favoured by generations of climbers that have preferred this friendly old mountain to others with more demanding pitches and scrambles.

The North Ridge is that skyline you admired from the A5 before parking in the allotted space at the head of Llyn Ogwen. My daughter Becka had frowned when she had seen Tryfan's profile. It was a blustery autumn morning and she was eleven but could climb like a squirrel.

'It looks big and steep, Dad,' she said, watching me shoulder the rope and do up her rucksack. 'Are there lots of steep bits?'

'Some,' I said. 'Nothing you can't handle. It's only 3,010 feet high.'

We walked back along the wayside towards Capel Curig. Three big lorries swished by followed by a line of cars. A hundred yards or so beyond Milestone Buttress and the busy rope parties we went through a gate and made the winding ascent over rough ground beside the drystone wall to the shoulder and its heather. The track had been worn to clear definition by the boots of those who had gone before us for nearly a hundred years and on the shoulder it met other paths at a cairn.

I looked at the sky. Cloud was massing in the west but I guessed it would disperse when it hit the mountains. Becka popped a boiled sweet in her mouth and sat on a rock to tighten a bootlace.

'Which way?' she said eventually.

'Straight up the middle one,' I said. 'Maybe we'll see the goats.'

'Goats – up here?'

'Gone-wild goats,' I said and the wind lifted her shoulder-length fair hair like a wing as she grinned.

The goats which wander across the Glyder Range of Snowdonia's mountains and are sometimes found walking the horizontal terraces of Tryfan by surprised climbers, are small, shaggy animals. They are nimble and shy yet elsewhere they have been persecuted often to the point of local extinction – especially where there are trees because they eat almost anything. But I like the creatures and enjoy meeting them in some high wild solitude with just the weather and the rock for company. We can always find an excuse for killing an animal when it ceases to be useful in our terms – the workhorse, the goat, the mink. The ethics behind the original exploitation are rarely questioned.

Well, a mountain like Tryfan can cleanse a person of any silly notions of 'godhood' or 'superiority over lowly life forms'. Tryfan has to be faced on its terms or the arrogant will come badly unstuck. But Becka had a long way to go before she became burdened with cynicism. She babbled on about goats, Billy Goat Gruff and nannies and kids and kept looking about her in case we were under observation from goat eyes.

Like other popular routes in Snowdonia the way was conspicuous, thanks to the passage of so many boots but it required handwork as well as footwork. Whenever I thought a pitch might give Becka problems we roped up and I let her feel the 'line' at her own pace, admiring her suppleness and rhythm. The 'jug-handle' holds enabled her to dismiss the odd problem with an ease that didn't surprise me. She had climbed with me before on many occasions.

So we came around the bulges of rock and the corners, rising all the time and absorbed in the scrambling, until we passed the big leaning slab called the Cannon and reached the second shoulder. From here there was a spectacular view of Llyn Ogwen far below and the surrounding mountains split by the head of Nant Ffancon.

The cloud was boiling now over the Carneddau and thunder carried over the hills. I glanced at Becka but she seemed intimidated neither by the height nor the approaching storm.

'Where are the goats?' she said.

'They could be anywhere up here,' I smiled. 'Keep your eyes open.'

A shadow crept across the valley and engulfed Tryfan. We put on our cagoules and gaiters and moved off. The path had run up against a rock wall but I climbed it comfortably and Becka followed suit without hesitation to join me on the North Peak. The grumble of thunder deepened to a broken growl and after a moment's silence the sudden clap was an explosion that made me jump.

'It's frightened away the goats,' Becka said, gazing about her in the hope of seeing the elusive creatures. I coiled the rope and nodded.

The teacher and his party of a dozen or so teenagers from an English secondary school couldn't hide their amazement at the sight of my daughter's tiny figure coming along the peak towards the Adam and Eve Stones. Nor could the teacher resist asking me if we had 'done' the North Ridge. My 'yes' had the hefty adolescents in his party giving Becka some searching looks.

'Bit tricky for a little girl,' said the teacher, disapprovingly I thought.

'She's done the Snowdon Horseshoe and several difficult rock climbs in South Devon,' I said, eager to be away.

The storm broke and Becka and I sheltered under Adam, or was it Eve?

'Funny names,' Becka said. The rain fell like a curtain to hide the hills and reduce the visibility to a hundred yards.

'The freedom of Tryfan is granted to whoever jumps from one to the other,' I said. 'But if you slip you're likely to fall down the East face.'

'What's the freedom of Tryfan?' she asked.

'I dunno,' I said. I only knew that the Adam and Eve Stones standing on Tryfan's summit like a couple of dinky Dartmoor menhirs were natural geological oddities entirely in keeping with Tryfan's character.

When the rain eased we departed in the opposite direction to the way we had come. At the col between the summit and the South Peak was a path to the right snaking down over the rock jumble and boulder-littered steeps. Again it was conspicuous and well-cairned but the wet surface was treacherous and we descended carefully, avoiding wherever possible the tilted slabs.

Eventually we reached the grassy slopes and the easier path down to the A5 once more. Becka continued to look for goats and couldn't hide her disappointment at their non-appearance.

'You didn't make them up, did you, dad?' she said. The rain was spent and she had dropped the hood of her cagoule to loose her hair to the wind.

'They're up in the hills somewhere,' I said. 'Cross my heart.'

'Still – we got to the top of the mountain,' she said. 'Which way did those big kids go up?'

'The way we came down.'

'Boring,' she said, splashing down the boggy slope and thinking how she would tell it all to her mum and brother that evening by the fire in the cottage in Deiniolen.

WALK THIRTY-EIGHT
Miners' Track to Snowdon, Pyg Track back.

Length: 7 miles
Grade Ⓑ Map on p.164

The great pedestrian Way to Snowdon and back.

The great truncated pyramid of Snowdon towers above the grandeur of the surrounding mountains. Five long ridges fall from its summit. There is no doubt that the highest peak south of Scotland is also the most beautiful, attracting climbers, hill walkers and day trippers who have never considered themselves mountain aficionados. The pilgrim ways converge at the summit where the café is also the terminal for the rack and pinion railway that operates throughout the summer from Llanberis.

The Welsh name for Snowdon – Yr Wyddfa Fawr – the Great Tumulus, has the majesty of the actual mountain in its poetry but is difficult for English tongues to get around. Try 'Er oithva vawr'. On Snowdon Celtic influences are a powerful presence. The summit is the vortex where folk instinct whirlpools but I've often stood by the cairn looking north, with something just as strong tugging at my innards. At first I put it down to the 'hills beyond hills', a craving for the unknown. Then I discovered that Snowdon was halfway to Iona, a place where all the Celtic paths converge.

Shortly after the New Year I had a morning to myself before going off to climb on Tryfan so I decided to walk the

Miners' Track to Yr Wyddfa and return by the Pyg Track (now written as the Pigs track on the Ordnance Survey Outdoor Leisure Map No. 17). Snow had fallen and the clouds massing around Yr Wyddfa, Crib Y Ddysgl and Crib Goch promised further falls. I left the carpark at Pen y Pass noting the absence of cars. It was Monday and no one was about.

The Miners' Track is the Holiday Season pedestrian's highway to Snowdon, but it is always a good return route if you've had a hard day on the crags of Y Lliwedd.

The snow on the broad stony path warned me that conditions on the actual mountain would demand the use of ice axe and probably crampons although the route is very easy in the summer.

I was walking the track that led to the old Copper Mines. To the left it provided a magnificent portrait of Moel Siabod, snow-covered and catching fresh falls as clouds drifted over it. The vale of Gwynant was greyish white, soft on the eye among the hard geometric shapes of the mountains.

The Track rose gently, swinging left then right again to present the daunting spectacle of Y Lliwedd, dark and snow-plastered directly ahead. The wind scattering the powder snow brought a tingle to my face and made my eyes water but I had hit a rhythm which generated body warmth by the time I was passing above Llyn Teryn. This little tarn was iced at the edges.

Shortly after leaving it the path looped to the right with the Valve House on the left and dazzling views beyond Llyn Llydaw to the North-East Face of Snowdon. The vision of that splendid peak, white and glistening, prompted me to sample a chunk of Stilton while the ravens of Y Lliwedd performed their aerobatics and sent their cries ringing across the vast amphitheatre. Then I walked over the causeway that spanned the north-east end of Llyn Llydaw and came on briskly along the Track which was about twelve feet wide and hugged the edge of the lake.

Just after the remains of the Crushing Mill the path departed from Llyn Llydaw and ascended to the right of Afon Glaslyn which was flowing down from Glaslyn. Before me Yr Wyddfa occupied half the sky. White columns of snow silently veiled the summit. Gazing up at it as I walked I slipped on some ice and thudded down on my behind. My language probably amused the ravens doing their sky dance above the Cribin Ridge on the far side of Glaslyn. I've often scrambled up this little-used approach to Bwlch y Saethau and continued to Snowdon's summit on the final section of the Watkin Path.

Glaslyn is nearly 2,000 feet above sea level and was sheeted in ice. I trod warily beside it because the ice looked thin and the ice on the Track was making me feel vulnerable. The night-before's celebrations in the bars of Beddgelert were revenging themselves on me; but I left the ruins of the mine buildings behind and followed the path where it mounted steep ice-glazed screes. Here the work of the National Park authorities to minimise erosion is apparent and necessary.

Above the junction with the Pyg Track the path becomes the notorious Zig-Zags. Yet en route to Bwlch Glas there was the bonus of Glaslyn wedged like a discarded monocle under the enormous face of Yr Wyddfa. And between the lake and the mountain and the mountain top the ravens were still up to their tricks.

At the Bwlch Glas monolith I met the full force of a wind cold enough and rough enough to sandpaper an eighth of an inch off my features. But it was a relief to escape the Zig-Zags which I've never liked. Cloud closed around me. Snow fell. When the squall passed I had a look at the railway track which would lead me to the mountain top. It was sheathed in ice several inches thick. Snow had drifted deep on top of it in places. Here a slip would have been fatal for the drop on the west side was nasty.

I glanced about me as the cloud lifted. I was alone and the next snow flurry accentuated the isolation. But I walked the incline to the railway station without incident and perched myself on a snow-crusted rock under the summit cairn. Between clouds was the familiar spectacle of the lakes below and the ridges running through snow smoke into more cloud.

I feasted on Stilton so ripe it would have floored a hungry mouse. Then I drank coffee and made a cautious return to

Bwlch Glas and descended the Zig-Zags to pick up the Pyg Track. Its point of departure to the left of the Miners' Track is obvious and occurs at about the height of the Cribin Ridge directly opposite over Glaslyn.

The Pyg Track was a much more exciting prospect than the Miners'. It was a twenty-four carat mountain path contouring five hundred feet above Llyn Llydaw, very rough and ready after the way below. It carried me under Crib y Ddysgl to undulate along the flanks of Crib Goch to Bwlch y Moch and the view down the Llanberis Pass.

The walk to the carpark brought me into contact with my first human beings since I had left the road at Pen y Pass. A young couple and their friendly border collie stepped aside as I came slithering down a short flight of steps with all the aplomb of a pig on stilts.

WALK THIRTY-NINE
Pen y Gwryd to y Foel Goch, Capel Curig and back.

Length: 10 miles
Grade Ⓑ Map on p. 187

Mountains out, road home and Pen y Gwryd at the end of it all.

Occasionally it was enough to walk out of the inn at the crossroads where the road from Llanberis met the road to Capel Curig and follow the Miners' Track into the mountains. But the Miners' Track snaking into the wilderness behind Pen y Gwryd mustn't be confused with its more celebrated namesake beside Llyn Llydaw and Glaslyn.

We lunched on ham, pickled onions and coffee at the inn. Patrick and Simon had been chasing around Conway the night before looking for young ladies with a desperation that was almost alarming. Ron and I called it the Headless Chicken Rally. But burning the candles at both ends had taken its toll and Simon slept in the car while we walked the fifty yards from Pen y Gwyrd along the road towards Capel Curig and made a ladder stile ascent of the drystone wall to the left beyond the last building. The path was peat gruel running with water after the rains of early October. It led us towards the crags above Cwmffynnon and the Llyn of that name to another ladder stile to the right of some falls on the nameless river that flows down into Llyn Pen y Gwryd. The approach to the stile over the river was made on a beam covered with wire mesh.

The other side of the wall was a sog. We splashed through it and jumped the stream. The sky was clearing. The wind blew and clouds raced over the mountains. Everything was strong with the life of the place. We felt it as we walked diagonally up across the long mountainside pausing to look back over left shoulders at Crib Goch and Yr Wyddfa rising dark in the sky.

A drystone wall was also climbing the slopes to our left bringing that human touch to the landscape that is often absent from more remote wilderness areas. The jagged summit rocks of Glyder Fach were above us and on the top of the next ladder stile I turned to take in the full sweep of the Snowdon Horseshoe. Llyn Cwmffynnon was a patch of light before the solid darkness of Crib Goch.

We came directly up a rocky slope on a rocky path whose waysides were decorated with small cairns until we were beside the waterfall below Glyder Fach. Then Ron and Patrick took photographs and expressed their delight in language slightly too colourful for this book. But I could understand their reaction. We could look down the Vale of Gwynant to the sea and those horizontal bands of light that trick you into believing earth, sky and water are one.

The waterfall crossing was easy and the path on the other side led us onto a boggy plateau where we strode along over grassy flats puddled with peat wallows. That lovely mountain, Tryfan, was poking its head above the horizon. As we approached it on the 'trampoline' of bog and grass it grew larger and darker in hard silhouette against the sky and distant Carneddau. Eventually we could sit among the rocks and eat some cheese and swig fruit juice from our bottles.

Ron stroked his beard and asked about the routes on

Tryfan and I told him about Heather Terrace and the harder path above it and my daughter Becka's ascent of the North Ridge while she was still at primary school. Ron sucked at his fag and nodded. The ravens pitched and rolled in the sunlight above Bristly Ridge up to our left and as we prepared to depart a group of four young walkers overtook us. Until that moment we hadn't settled for any particular route but the path to our right in the direction of the tarn called Llyn y Caseg fraith looked good.

Again it was one of those days of cloud shadow which had light streaming away before us pursued by darker moments. We walked over tussocky grass to the right of the Llyn and the collection of small tarns beyond it. A ewe gazed at me and elegantly lifted a hind foot to scratch under her ear. The air was crisp with a hint of snow in it.

The young climbers had left y Foel Goch, a charming little mountain. Foel is Welsh for bald and this summit is just that. It reminded me of the larger Dartmoor tors, outcrops like Down Tor and Hayne Down Tors; but the impression of height created by the deep valleys and ridges before me ended any further comparison. To the right below were Llynnau Mymbyr and Capel Curig, and when I lifted my eyes the whole of North Wales was spread out under the sky before me.

We were lightly clad and fit as mountain goats after a week of intensive mountain walking. Eager to push on we came to the rocky summit of Gallt yr Ogof to stand on the edge of the high steep crags and gaze down into the valley and over it to the Carneddau. Then we began to run across the plashy ground to the end of the ridge called Cefn y Capel where we overtook the four youngsters who were lolling around eating and laughing on the hillside. Our descent was rapid and we were whooping as we took the final steeps to the next rounded summit and hurtled on past a couple of little tarns to the path beside the drystone wall. It brought us less hurriedly to a ladder stile at the bottom and the trudge along the lane to the gate and the open ground by Joe Brown's climbing shop.

We swigged Lucozade and marched and ran along the A4086 towards Pen y Gwryd. History buffs may be interested in the site of the Roman marching camp by Llyn

Pen y Gwyrd. The legions, presumably of Agricola in his war against the Ordovices, would have rested here as they pushed north to conquer Gwynedd. Once inside the hotel we peeled off our wet shirts and pullovers, and put on dry sweat tops before ordering tea and cakes. It was half an hour to opening time and we spent it pleasantly before the fire as the Everest Room filled with thirsty walkers and climbers, and Dolores prepared to meet the rush from her side of the bar.

WALK FORTY
The Carneddau Ridge.

Length: 13 miles
Grade ©

Wilderness mountain walking best done with an experienced companion.

I spent the night bivouacked in the trees below Rhaeadr Fawr. Here Afon Goch plunged over crags for two hundred feet in a spectacular and elegant waterfall. It wasn't as spectacular as it could be because no rain had fallen for days and the weather of early June was doing its best to live up to its reputation.

At daybreak I strapped the lightweight sleeping bag to the top of my rucksack and walked back down to the wooded gorge. The evening before I had arrived in the little village of Aber on the A55 Bangor–Conway coast road prepared for the traverse of the toughest of the three main mountain groups of Snowdonia – the Carneddau. Unlike the Glyders or the Horseshoe Ridge group, the Carneddau represented something approaching real wilderness. Those high, rugged and featureless ninety square miles of deep valleys and great hump-backed summits linked by ridges, were easy to get lost in – especially in poor conditions. To venture onto that upland with its sudden surprises of crags without mountain-walking experience would be very unwise.

Beginning at Aber you come up the road following the

199

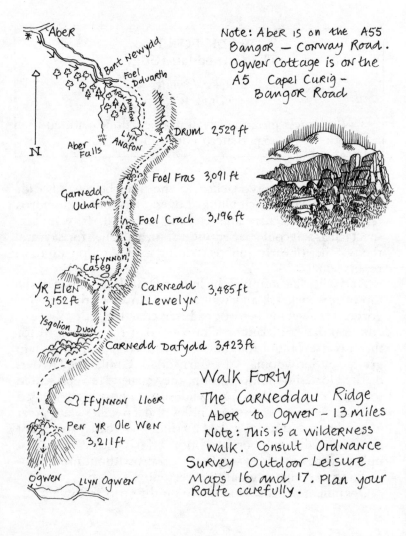

Aber

Bont Newydd

Foel Dduarth

Afon Anafon

Llyn Anafon

Aber Falls

DRUM 2,529 ft

N

Foel Fras 3,091 ft

Garnedd Uchaf

Foel Crach 3,196 ft

Ffynnon Caseg

Yr Elen 3,152 ft

Carnedd Llewelyn 3,485 ft

Ysgolion Duon

Carnedd Dafydd 3,423 ft

Ffynnon Lloer

Pen yr Ole Wen 3,211 ft

Ogwen   Llyn Ogwen

Note: Aber is on the A55 Bangor — Conway Road. Ogwen Cottage is on the A5 Capel Curig — Bangor Road

Walk Forty
The Carneddau Ridge
Aber to Ogwen – 13 miles
Note: This is a wilderness Walk. Consult Ordnance Survey Outdoor Leisure Maps 16 and 17. Plan your Route carefully.

signs to Aber Falls and turn left over the bridge, Bont Newydd. Despite the temptations of Rhaeadr Fawr this becomes a far better route onto the great six-mile ridge that will take you over half a dozen 3,000 feet summits to the descent to Llyn Ogwen. Careful route planning and the ability to read map and compass are essential when the weather is bad.

There was enough light at a quarter to five that morning for me to stride out without difficulty despite the valley mist. I went through the gate and up the rough road, across a track, and on up the hillside to another high, simple farm road. This brought me under Foel Dduarth with Afon Anafon on my right, almost to Llyn Anafon.

The mist was thin and patchy. Above it was the cloudless blue sky I had prayed for. Sheep scattered as I abandoned the road and came hard up the steeps on the left to the crest of the ridge at Drum, choosing my own line of ascent where there was no actual marked path. Once on Drum, though, catching the end of a dazzling sunrise, the way was clear enough and the ridge broad enough for me to jog. The startling beauty of the situation, the undulating heights sailing above mist that rose and vanished in the sunlight, fed my sense of complete well-being.

The Carneddau seemed to charge me with energy and the animal thing was gripping me as it often did when I was a boy.

The fence and drystone wall running along the top had surrendered their human associations to the seasons and hard weather long ago. A lark sprang from the thin grasses ahead of me and began to sing. Then the nature of the Carneddau asserted itself. The mountains were a remarkable flexing of rock muscle that never developed into peaks but the desolation lacked the arctic emptiness I had encountered in Scotland's Northern Highlands. The bleating of sheep and the larksong gave it a life of its own. Maybe desolation was the wrong description. High solitude was better.

The grassy, rock-littered slopes were part of the assembly of great, green, hump-backed ridges and enormous summits with their crags, boulder sculptures and cairns. Wraiths of mist crept around Foel Fras and disappeared. Foel Fras was

the first of my 3,000 footers. It was a disappointing collection
of low boulders on a plateau that was dissected by a drystone
wall.

Foel Crach was next and it turned out to be a funny little
summit. The upright stones each side of the path had
presumably been placed there to guide weary or distressed
travellers to the refuge hut to the north-east. The top of Foel
Crach would be easy to miss in cloud but cwt Jacob (Jacob's
Hut) might prove a lifesaver in bad weather. And at least
from the summit I had my first view of Carnedd Llewelyn,
the second highest mountain south of Scotland.

Most of the mist had gone and the morning was calm and
sunny and very warm. I came up the ridge and the loose
stones of Carnedd Llewelyn to find myself on a table top,
open to everything hard weather could muster, and lumpy
with stones pushing out of the turf. Around the large cairn
were huddles of mis-shapen boulders. Carnedd Llewelyn,
the Cairn of Llewelyn, last of the born and bred Welsh
Princes, was the fulcrum of several ridges, one of which led to
Yr Elen. This was bow-shaped, falling and rising in a narrow,
high saddle to the top of Yr Elen. The dangers here in bad
weather are obvious. Sheer summit crags fall to Ffynnon
Caseg, a dark tarn in a bowl of cliffs. Ffynnon Caseg is Welsh
for Mare's Fountain and is a reference to the half-wild
mountain ponies which drink at the tarn or used to in the
past.

I returned by the same ridge to Llewelyn and stood a little
to the south of the summit looking towards Tryfan printed
on the haze of Snowdon's peaks. The buttresses of Carnedd
Dafydd's crags, Ysgolion Duon, the Black Ladders, were
gleaming across a great gulf of sunlight. Then I changed my
T-shirt, rubbed some suntan lotion onto my nose and noted
the faint flush on my already suntanned arms.

Larksong chased me along the easy crest to Dafydd where
three massive heaps of rock, far too impressive to be labelled
mere cairns unless the word is awarded its prehistoric
connotations, stood like the shattered remains of old Celtic
towers. Showell Styles in his *The Mountains of North Wales*
suggests these giant cairns are 'the ruins of fortifications or
watchtowers dating from prehistoric times'.

To the left of the cairns was the edge of the craggy steeps that dropped to Ffynnon Lloer – the Fountain of the Moon. It was now an undemanding march to the enormous summit of Pen yr Ole Wen and the inevitable big 'carn'. But a little beyond it a smaller heap of rocks provided the vision across Llyn Ogwen immediately below to the Glyders and Yr Wyddfa – a sight that had me reaching for the water bottle and glancing at my watch. I had managed nearly thirteen miles in six hours without extending myself. I'm not patting myself on the back. Everything is relative and before anyone starts crowing about how they did the Carneddau in three hours or less consider the record of Joss Naylor. This Lakeland fell runner extraordinary did the fourteen Welsh 3,000-foot summits from Yr Wyddfa to Foel Fras in four hours, forty-six minutes! A distance of twenty-three miles.

Sitting on Pen yr Ole Wen I gobbled a quarter of a pound of Stilton, a peanut butter roll and an orange. I was not an obsessive summiteer but I knew I'd have a go at the Welsh fourteen in one day again, as I did many years ago, before I was too old. I still had personal demons to exorcise and challenges to meet which would have made less restless mountain walkers shake their heads in disbelief and contempt. Most of the time the beauty of the hills gives me all I require. Then the animal thing, the need to run or walk swiftly across high ground, has me sweeping along with it to the euphoria of journey's end.

I came left off the summit as you face Tryfan, down the loose, stony path, skirting everything vertical except the lowest of crags which presented no difficulties, until I had reached the valley at the Bethesda end of Llyn Ogwen. Here I had a cold bath in just my underpants while the traffic swished and roared by and the climbers on Tryfan's Milestone Buttress worked out their rock problems.

Note: A lift waiting by Llyn Ogwen is usually very welcome. The bus service is handy but a kindred spirit at the wheel of a car and a warm smile may seal your achievement.

THE INNER HEBRIDES

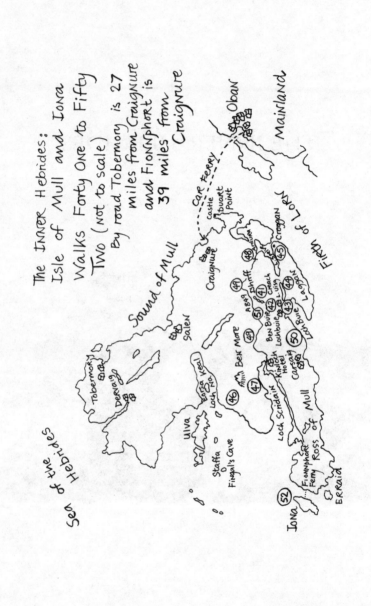

The INNER Hebrides:
Isle of Mull and Iona
Walks Forty One to Fifty
Two (not to scale)

By road Tobermory is 27
miles from Craignure
and Fionnphort is
39 miles from
Craignure

Sea of the
Hebrides

Tobermory

Dervaig

Salen

Sound of Mull

Craignure

Car ferry

Castle
Duart
Point

Oban

MAINLAND

Firth of LORN

Croggan

Lochbuie

Loch Uisg

Lochbuie

Carsaig

Kinloch
Hotel

Loch Scridain

Ulva

Staffa

Fingal's Cave

Fionnphort
Ferry

Ross of Mull

ERRAID

Iona

Ben More

Loch Na Keal

Ishriff

Creach

A849

Ben Buie

52 46 47 50 43 44 45 48 41 42 51 49

7

The Isle of Mull

Mull is the second largest island of the Inner Hebrides. It is a 'microcosm of all that is typical of the highlands'. Twenty-five miles long and twenty-six miles from east to west, it has three hundred miles of wild, rugged coastline and sits like a 'hound couchant' near the bottom of the archipelago.

About 2,000 people live on Mull but there are more red deer than humans and they bring the hills to life. Wild animal activity on the island is always intense and the place is a natural sanctuary for scores of different species, from wild goats to golden eagles, snow hares and corncrakes. For me it is the perfect wilderness retreat, Tir Nan Og – Sunset Land – a place that constantly calls me back.

WARNING: Deer Stalking and Walkers

At the height of the stalking season when rifles are out on the hills in the South of Mull killing deer, it is both dangerous and impolite to venture onto the open moors which are known as deer forests. Anyone thinking of walking the hills – especially Laggan, the Ben Buie and Ben More areas – in July, August, September and October should seek the advice of the local landowner.

Walking certain areas during the busy months will cause unnecessary friction.

The Close Season for red deer stags (when they aren't stalked) is 21st October to 30th June.

For hinds it is 16th February to 20th October although the main culling month is November.

Late autumn, winter and spring are obviously good times to visit the wild country in the South of Mull – although in the spring there is the lambing which is common to all the British hills.

Daft or uncaring walkers risk more than the wrath of those who own the sporting rights, but in all the years I've tramped across the South of Mull I've had no trouble. I keep off the deer forests during the really busy months wishing to be neither nuisance nor corpse! If in doubt, *keep away* or find out if that mountain top is safe.

The walks that should be avoided from 1st July to 20th October inclusive are marked with a stag's head.

WALK FORTY-ONE
The Ascent of Creach Beinn.

Length: 5 miles
Grade Ⓒ

Up and down a remote Scottish mountain.

That spring I had a real hunger for a landscape devoid of humans. I had heard the cry of mated peregrines in South Devon and had become homesick for the Hebridean hills.

Even after so many years of boarding the Caledonian MacBrayne ferry, the journey from the Argyllshire port of Oban to Mull could still excite me. Then at the cottage in Lochbuie when the gear was unpacked from the car and the logs were crackling on the fire, I peered out of the window to watch the deer forest over the water firm to purple-grey silhouette in the evening sky. Nothing had changed, I reflected, as dusk became darkness and Venus gleamed in the sea loch.

The two Daves and I were reluctant to turn-in although we intended rising early the next day to see the sunrise from Creach Beinn. Eventually we decided to stay up all night with the tipple of our choice to guarantee a start in the small hours.

Loch
Airdeglais

N

Creach Beinn
2,289 ft

Ben Buie
2,354 ft

Gleann a'Chaiginn Mhoir

Abhainn a'Chaiginn Mhoir

Old Drove Road (rough track)

Creach Bheinn Bheag

phone box
gate
School
House

Bridge

Loch Uisg

Lochbuie

Walk Forty One
The ascent of Creach Beinn
and back – 5 hard miles

Loch
Buie

Consult Ordnance Survey Sheet NM 62/72 Firth of Lorn (North)

Sitting by the fire drinking Guinness between spells of laughter, cat-naps and conversation, had all the elements of trance. So we joked our way through the night. By four fifteen we blearily departed and the cuckoos calling through the hush seemed to be addressing me personally. All around us songbirds were in voice and a curlew fluted from Laggan Beach.

Lochbuie is a tiny straggling community. The single-track road has grass in the middle and it ends at the shores of the sea loch. The crofts and cottages were asleep when we walked past them and the meadows where corncrakes nested, towards Creach. Above Laggan deer forest the morning star gleamed but the light in the east was swelling and torches were unnecessary as we left the telephone box behind us and came up to the Scots pines about fifty yards beyond the little grey building that had once been Lochbuie School. Creach's bulk stood dark among the stars. Across the glen to the left of it was Ben Buie and the beginning of the Ross of Mull with Beinn nan Gobhar a distinctive summit above the coast.

Creach is a mountain in two parts: Creach Bheinn Bheag (the first and lower of the two summits) and Creach Beinn – 2,289 feet.

At the Scots pines we left the road and followed a rough path alongside the trees where the ground was boggy and bracken-covered. In the half-darkness we came up the slopes under a small crag onto the ridge to some wind-ravaged pines and a line of telegraph poles. Behind us to the left was the featureless deer forest of Laggan and the waters of Loch Buie. No lights showed in the croftship. On the right was the glint of Loch Uisg, the tree-fringed freshwater lake.

We climbed slowly, raising red deer hinds from the corries and hoping the sun wouldn't beat us to the top of Creach Beinn. The ascent was gradually steepening but there was much to keep us occupied – unusual things like the hollows left in the grass where deer had been lying. The clatter of departing animals broke the hush.

Among the steeps and crags of Creach Bheinn Bheag were terraces of grass. We had the choice of rock scrambles or easier work on the grass. Then, as Dave Baker unscrewed the flask, we could look down on Loch Buie where the night sky had dumped half its wealth. Dave Abrahams was deeply moved but needed no goading to push him on for our goal. The other Dave stayed behind to take photographs.

Creach Bheinn Bheag's deceptions were typical of nearly every British mountain I've set foot on except the straightforward escarps of the Black Mountains. You think you've reached the top only to be confronted by another corrie and another rocky summit soaring above you. Small Creach was a step on the gigantic rock 'staircase' leading to Creach Beinn. It was rock-and-boulder-strewn with numerous flooded peat wallows haunted by hooded crows. From the dark countryside below came the mournful cries of red-throated divers.

Some of the best moments of my life have been spent on this mountain. I have lain in the grass watching snow hares grooming themselves and ptarmigan feeding and golden eagles flying higher than the summit. I have stood on the top in deep snow looking north to the Merry Dancers and I have been there in an autumn dusk with stags roaring and greylags calling as they passed overhead.

Now I was moving comfortably over high ground again towards the light swelling in the sky. Through a gap in the rocks on the left was a glimpse of Loch Airdeglais in the glen under Ben Buie. Passing the rusty posts of yesterday's deer fence we crossed the saddle to the screes of Creach Beinn's shoulder. The col was patched with lochans. Then the screes and slabs provided scrambling up to the ptarmigan scrapes and levels of grass and the sun that had risen to mock us. Ahead was the Trig Point and the cairn. A snow hare lolloped off into the rock jumble and we were standing before the sun which was an enormous sphere of brilliance. Clouds and mountain tops picked up a pink flush.

'Look,' Dave whispered.

A pair of golden eagles slowly swung across the sky to quarter the slopes for ptarmigan and hares. Ghostly bens rose before us – Beinn Fhada, Glas Bheinn, Ben Buie and huge 3,169 feet Ben More. At our feet now was Loch Airdeglais.

Sunlight bathed the rocky summit of Creach and we suddenly realised we were being watched by half a dozen ptarmigan. These trusting little mountain grouse possess a charm that goes well with calm spring mornings and a wilderness landscape.

The stars had vanished when we left the summit cairn and the ptarmigan and walked down the slopes to Loch Airdeglais via a little lochan, making the descent close to a burn whose progress to the glen was more direct.

Then we marched back towards Lochbuie along the old Drove Road and ate a snack breakfast beside a waterfall under the scrutiny of a pair of hoodies.

Note: This Creach Beinn stands above Loch Uisg in the south east of the island. It should not be confused with the height of the same name on Ardmeanach.

WALK FORTY-TWO
The Lochbuie Drove Road.

Length: 4½ miles
Grade Ⓑ

Through a lonely Hebridean glen.

In the old days cattle were driven along grassy tracks between communities, many of which were abandoned and fell into ruin. One of these Drove Roads links Lochbuie to the A849 Craignure–Fionnphort Road above Loch Sguabain where this walk begins.

It was autumn and snow was lying on the tops. Sgulan Mor, which we called Armchair Mountain, had a sparkle and Ben Buie down the glen was as beautiful and mysterious as the great mosque in Samarkand. The afternoon was clean and fresh, the sky cloudless and the sun was disappearing behind the Ross.

From the road we headed for the deserted shepherd's cottage and walked beside Loch Sguabain to Loch an Eilein and Loch an Ellen across rain-soaked ground, secure in the knowledge that the stalking would be over for the day. Up on the ridge of Beinn Fhada the ptarmigan were calling and

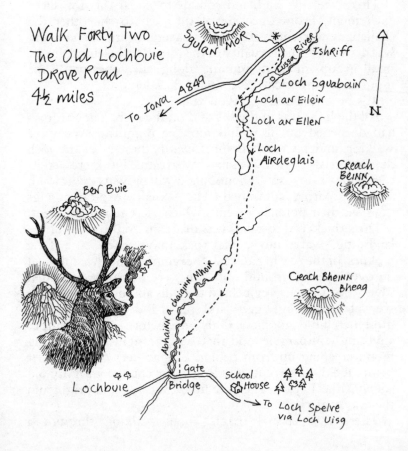

Walk Forty Two
The Old Lochbuie
Drove Road
4½ miles

Sgulan Mor

Lussa River

Ishriff

To Iona

A849

Loch Sguabain

Loch an Eilein

Loch an Ellen

Loch Airdeglais

N

Creach Beinn

Ben Buie

Abhainn a chaiginn Mhoir

Creach Bheinn Bheag

Lochbuie

Gate

Bridge

School House

To Loch Spelve
via Loch Uisg

water was running off the hills. Our breath condensed on the cold air.

I was with Patrick Blair, Simon Brooks and Ron Walter. Our base was the cottage at Lochbuie. My companions were awed by their surroundings. It was Ron and Simon's first visit and the assault on their senses had left them a little dazed.

The walking was easy if wet. We strode alongside the water until the way looped to cross the neck of land between Loch an Ellen and the largest loch of the group – Airdeglais. We were now well into the broad, deep glen with the steeps climbing to craggy ridges and summits. One ford led to another and as we advanced and the day died around us the stags began to roar.

There are few highland sounds to equal this for sheer excitement. From one side of the glen to the other the challenges were delivered and answered until the evening was dense with the sexuality of the Rut. The belching din set small groups of hinds running along the slopes while the mountains amplified the animals' thunder.

'It's bloody amazing,' Ron said.

All the light was in the sky and on the loch. The shadows had deepened but it would soon be moonrise. We were walking under Creach Beinn towards the end of the loch that was criss-crossed with narrow streams. Dusk brewed its own valley mists as a high mountain will brew its own cloud; and the roaring continued. The sexually explosive stags stamped their potency on hills which were normally silent.

Dusk thickened to a darkness that exhaled the smell of the landscape – water, moss, grass, rock, maybe even some of the rankness of the roaring animals. Leaving the loch we splashed on over marshy ground until we were halted by a sudden silvery glow in the sky behind the hills ahead. Slowly while we watched the light grew and spread and we witnessed the most incredible moonrise. Only once before can I remember anything comparable, and that was the sight of the spring moon creeping up from behind Laggan deer forest as I sat before the dining-room window in the cottage with my old friend Mike Taylor. Then the moon was full and bright and the way was clear.

There is a special magic about walking through a

Hebridean glen by moonlight. Every so often the stags roared and the mountain walls tossed back the echoes; and the mountains themselves, cut so cleanly against the stars, were 'visions of delight'. I imagined what it was like for the hinds up there, feeding on the draw moss and mirroring Aldebaran and Vega in large, alert eyes.

It was great to have wet feet and to tread recklessly, blind drunk on the beauty of the night.

We crossed the fierce little river, Abhainn a Chaiginn Mhoir, by the falls, which probably wasn't the orthodox crossing point. But the path was waiting on the other side and we were walking above the river, cupping our hands to our mouths to imitate the stags.

The river wound on, taking us with it, and we were so high on the magic that we sailed over the terrain like deer. And the descent on the narrow path below Ben Buie deposited us at last in the pasture by the bridge on the outskirts of Lochbuie. The metal gate creaked open, and while the others passed through it onto the road I looked up at the moonlit crags of Ben Buie. Night accentuated the mountain's fine shape. It seemed to have been designed to stand against the star fields.

'Come on, Carter,' Ron called. 'Get working on that Bolognese sauce or we'll let Brooks cook the meal.'

'And perish,' I observed in a mordant tone.

The moon shone on Laggan. An owl cried and bats were on the wing. Rabbits scattered off the road before us and we marched through the croftship down to the sea and the cottage.

Note: Unless you wish to retrace your steps transport waiting in Lochbuie is essential.

WALK FORTY-THREE
Laggan Sands (Traigh Bhan Lagain).

Length: 3 miles
Grade Ⓐ

A there-and-back saunter.

Loch Buie is a sea loch, a horseshoe bound on one side by the great lump of Laggan deer forest and on the other by the hills of the Ross of Mull. The heel of the horseshoe is a fertile plain with a wood of oaks and salix and boggy pasture advancing to the beach and the ruins of Moy Castle. There are about a dozen small dwellings scattered along the road and the shore. The mansion, Lochbuie House, set against the trees above the sands, dominates the Croftship.

Ben Buie gains its 2,000 feet and a bit more in one great heave from the edge of the loch to lord it over a dramatic landscape. One spring morning Mike Taylor and I looked up at it with affection as we walked the road to the post office which in those days was run by a couple of Gaelic-speaking old ladies from their cottage near the telephone box. Passing the reedy margins we heard the unmistakable 'crex-crex' of a corncrake. And we swung round to see it walk with a deliberate gait into the middle of the road, cast an eye over us, hunch its shoulders, turn, and retreat into the cover again.

An eagle was soaring between Ben Buie and Creach Beinn when we set off on our beach stroll from the triangular monument 'erected by Lochbuie and his highlanders to commemorate the coronation of Edward VIII and Queen Alexandra'. The sands were strewn with rocks and giant pebbles known as cobbles and we kept to the track along the shore. Beside it was the Episcopalian Church of St Kilda and the big empty Vicarage. Chickens stepped cautiously about between the buildings.

A little further on we came to the gate of Lochbuie House which stands in its own private grounds, so we took to the shore, forded the river by the bridge and came down to the tidal island, Eilean Mor. When the tide is low you can walk

216

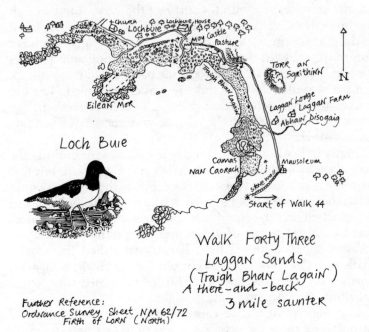

Loch Buie

Walk Forty Three
Laggan Sands
(Traigh Bhan Lagain)
A there-and-back
3 mile saunter

Further Reference:
Ordnance Survey Sheet NM 62/72
Firth of LORN (North)

over soft sand to it. For me and Mike it will always be Rabbit Island for obvious reasons. The place is pitted with burrows. On other visits to Mull we had come to the island after dark and grilled sausages over a driftwood fire.

A couple of divers fished the wavebreak and eider duck were also on the water. Curlew and oyster catchers sent their cries rippling through the sunlight. Rabbits fled before us and vanished underground. We wore shorts and trainers and carried a towel and our snacks in a small day pack.

The seal had hauled herself onto the mussel reefs. Around her the kelp swayed with the surge of the waves but through the binoculars we could see her drowsing, eyes closed, blind to the glare of the sea loch and deaf to the bird calls. She was a common seal with the profile of an earless dog and 'paddles for feet. Prettier than a grey seal she basked, tail up, head up, while the gulls swooped and the waves crumpled. The old stalker up by Loch Spelve called all seals 'selkies'. In the binocular window even the tufts of whiskers above her eyes were visible.

Many of her kind littered the sandspits and rocks along the Sound of Mull shore between Salen and Craignure but few common seals came to Loch Buie. From the turf we could watch her unobserved. Flopped on the rocks she looked like a big mottled, silver-brown fish. Between her world and ours was the snoring-purr of eiders and the piping of waders.

Then she was joined by a heron that fished the nearby shallows. The water was favoured by sea ducks and great northern divers. Across the hush we heard the selkie moaning her contentment.

Leaving the island we came round the spit of gorse and rushes to see the grey, ivy-clad tower of Moy Castle standing on the shore. Behind it was Lochbuie House. Moy was a Maclean stronghold with the sort of bloody history you expect from an island like Mull. Great black-backed gulls barked and were answered by a dog.

The Lochuisg River was difficult to ford where it flowed onto the beach near the castle. We went up onto the track over the bridge and back through the trees and gate onto the shore behind Moy. Sheep were on the beach but the rock litter made it uncomfortable walking so we returned to the track below the pastures and came under the bluff to Laggan Sands. The outgoing tide had ribbed and wrinkled the surface but higher up the beach the grey volcanic sand was pale as if it had been bleached by the sun. The fume of windblown particles drifted before us and the snoring of eiders rose from the shallows.

The outcrop above the pastures to our left was Torr an Sgrithinn. It reminded me of the torrs on the South Devon escarpment near Prawle Point. The Celtic connection was visible, but it went deeper than names of things and language and landscape affinities. Before us were the steeps and gulleys of Laggan deer forest.

We crossed Abhain Diosgaig below Laggan Lodge and Laggan Farm and were on the edge of a bay, Camas Nan Caorach.

The grass running into the sands of something resembling dune country was the closest terrain to machair I'd seen in the area. The chapel in its pocket handkerchief graveyard back from the shore under the vast flanks of Laggan is the Mausoleum of the Macleans of Lochbuie but human history couldn't compete with what the loch and its margins were supplying in abundance.

Off the dune-like spit were eiders, the black and white drakes and the brown ducks. The shores were part of the wild goats' territory. The animals came down from Laggan at dusk to feed on the seaweed with sheep, deer and brown hares.

We sat in the grass and ate cheese and nuts and drank fruit juice. Then we bathed in the water by the mussel beds and while we were drying off a porpoise swam along the length of the shallows as if nature hadn't done enough to fill the morning with beauty.

Then we followed our footprints back.

WALK FORTY-FOUR
Crossing Laggan Deer Forest:
from Loch Buie to Croggan.

Length: 8 miles
Grade ©

A classic wilderness crossing.

It was winter and I was alone in the cottage under the mountain. I burnt pine cones and pine logs on the fire, ate porridge for breakfast and kippers, stews or rice dishes for dinner. I carried no loose flesh and the glow of physical well-being was central to the whole experience.

The weather was hard. A north wind had whitened the hills and brought the deer down to raid the crops by the sea. Sometimes I would look out of the cottage window and see hinds and stags in the neighbouring field feeding on roots.

The history of the island deer and the people of Mull is curiously entangled. The creation of deer forests, which are great tracts of open, generally treeless moor, led to the clearances and the mass enforced exodus of the dispossessed native gaels. The whole business stank.

Laggan Deer Forest lay in the south-east corner of the island. It was a peninsula reaching to heights well over one thousand feet with the freshwater Loch Uisg and part of the sea loch, Spelve, to the north-west and the Firth of Lorn on the south-east shores. Two narrow isthmuses each side of Loch Uisg joined the peninsula to the southern part of Mull.

The forest was a wilderness of high ground, glens, bog and lochans. The hills in the south fell abruptly to the sea in precipices. Some of these rock walls were over eight hundred feet high. On the rough ground above them roamed the herds of wild goats—feral ancestors of the animals which had escaped or been left behind during the Clearances for sheep and deer. The shells of crofts still stood on Laggan as monuments to the islanders uprooted by landowners who were as grasping as they were uncaring. So the peninsula, which was eight miles long and rarely more than a couple of miles wide, had become

A combination of walks 44 and 45 – greatly contracted.
Walk Forty Four – Laggan Deer Forest from Loch Buie to Croggan – 8 miles
and back from the pier along
Walk Forty Five – Croggan, the deserted
villages and on to Lochbuie – 13 miles.

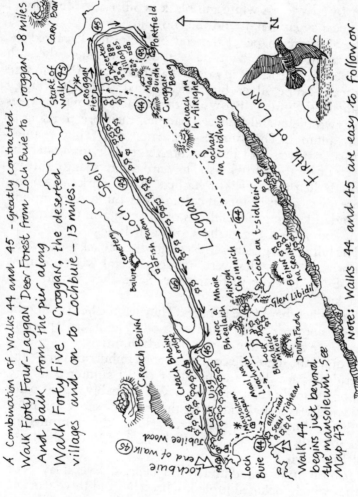

NOTE: Walks 44 and 45 are easy to follow, on
Ordnance Survey Sheet NM 62/72. 8 wilderness miles are 8 long miles!

Caol Ban

Start of Walk 45

Croggan Pier

Deserted Villages

Portfield

Maol Buidhe

Croggan Beag

Cruach na h-Airighe

Lochan na Cloidheig

Firth of Lorn

Loch an t-sidhein

Beinn na Sròine

Glen Libidil

Druim Fada

Loch Bhealaich Mhoir

Airigh Chrìonnich

Bhealaich

cnoc a' Mhoir

Fish Farm

Loch Spelve

Laggan

Balure cemetery

Maol na Luachraich

Creach Bheinn

Loch Uisg

Creach Bheinn Lodge

Jubilee Wood

Mausoleum

Allt-nan-Closan

Sgeir Tighean

Loch Buie

Lochbuie end of walk 45

Walk 44
begins just beyond
the mausoleum. See
Map 43.

N

an unofficial, unsignposted Nature Reserve. May the Lord preserve it.

One morning, after the blizzard, six hinds were in my front 'garden' and the chaffinches waited to be fed on the dining-room window sills. Across Loch Buie the hills of the deer forest were as white and bleak as Siberia. At first light I walked Laggan Sands and met no one.

Beyond the chapel at the end of the beach I walked the snow alongside the drystone wall to a gap where the path climbed the steeps. On my right was the brook, Allt-nan sean Tighean. Some silver birches sprouted from the craggy farside of the gulley. Browsing the terraces among the trees were two billies and fourteen nannies, their breath rising in white plumes. The animals fascinated me. They roamed comparatively free of human interference, living under the mercy of local landowners. They are small, shaggy throwbacks to their mediaeval forefathers. Black, dark brown and white, or variants of mixed colours they can be seen trailing in single file along the clifftops or browsing in the hanging glens above the Laggan shore of Loch Buie.

The billy I was glassing had a magnificent backward sweep of horns. The females were smaller: several were pregnant and obviously close to their time. Soon they would drop their kids.

The billies shared the females. They led the herd along the terraces and ledges in search of food. The goats' appetites were large and their menu seemingly limitless.

Around the ferals life continued at an unhurried pace – the Hebridean pace. Despite the bitter cold I sauntered up my side of the gully following what was probably a goat path. The wind was brutal and under the crags the snow was piled in drifts. Snowsmoke billowed along the summits of Laggan's hills and when a squall hit the deer forest big flakes whirled down.

I had on my thermal underwear beneath several layers of clothes which included moleskin breeches and three pairs of climbing stockings as well as a good tough cagoule. The air was so cold it hurt my lungs and set my teeth on edge.

The trail brought me up towards a hill outcrop. Deer were on the skyline and a stag and several hinds ran out of the gulley to my left. Where the snow had been blown thin by the wind the trails of goat, deer and sheep were visible. Any of these animal highways could be taken up the steeps.

I pushed on through snow and heather and the wind grew fiercer the higher I climbed. Kicking onto the magnificent tableland I kept Maol na Luachrach on my left and came through a breach. To the south-east (right) was the Firth of Lorn, a darker grey than the sky. All the mainland mountains over the water were white. The starkness of the scene was thrilling and just a little bit disturbing.

I should have left a route card (giving my starting place, direction and destination) with the people who looked after the cottage. In my eagerness to get onto Laggan I had broken a cardinal rule. Well, I'm no saint and that's for sure, and I'd be deceiving myself and the reader if I pretended to be a hill-walking perfectionist. But I had all the survival gear if things went wrong and I had winter weather experience to back up my solo effort. 'Escape routes' down to the lochs were always available.

A hind barked and led four companions swiftly towards Druim Fada. The map of Laggan is covered with Gaelic words that explain themselves once you have acquired the basics. It was a wild upland in the Celtic tradition, a little Kingdom of a place where you can expect to see golden eagles and smaller birds of prey and maybe even a horned god or two. Between the hilltops are many lochans; and the glens on the Uisg-Spelve side are tree-filled.

The deer forest isn't bleak and inhospitable as Dartmoor can be. I skirted several frozen, nameless tarns on my way to a pass in the crags, keeping Loch Bhealaich Mhoir on my right. Presumably the loch and the hill took their names from this pass. It is very conspicuous and the Gaelic word for pass or breach is 'bealach'. On the other side is a hanging wood of silver birches, Coill a' Bhealaich Mhoir, so even if you miss the pass but end up in the trees or near the trees you are doing OK. Steep crags are easy to avoid on your descent to the trees.

The valley below me was Glen Libidil. It was broad and deep. The Firth of Lorn stretched away on the right. I sat on my bivvy bag, back to a tree and drank soup from the flask.

The black grouse that live on Laggan had concealed themselves in sheltered hollows. Occasionally a covey leaving to forage would cry down the snow: 'Helluy, helluy, helluy' – like Sloane Rangers greeting each other. The eagles kill them and the blue and the brown hares and the ptarmigan, as well as feeding off deer carrion. Hard winters and springs left dead hinds lying on the hills. Whenever I saw the wind ruffling the coat of a deer stretched out lifeless on a lonely hillside I was saddened.

But I find it does me good to go alone into the winter hills. It stops me taking things for granted.

Across the glen I could see Loch an-t-sidhein and when I was ready I set off towards it, glad the frozen snow had buried the tussocky grass on the hillside. Once I was beyond the rusty remains of the deer fence and had crossed the bog and the stream it wasn't difficult to pick a diagonal route up the far steeps to the right of Airigh Choinnich.

I give you my route but this is one of those wilderness places where on a clear day the landscape unrolls before you and landmarks are abundant, although hills among hills can look very similar. Glen Libidil and the birch wood are the keys and Loch an-t-sidhein enables you to aim for the next hills in a north-easterly direction.

The heights under Beinn na Sroine, where the biggest lake on Laggan, Loch an-t-sidhein, was frozen solid, were playing host to the snow phantoms. Little white dust devils were gliding across the surface and a deep sonic whine rose and fell. I put up three more of the dark grouse and watched them hurtle away. Deer were on the skyline and others joined them. I got the feeling all the creatures of Laggan were watching me.

I was sinking knee-deep in snow that blanketed long grass, struggling to meet the challenge of the glens that cut across the peninsula. Crest after crest of high ground rose before me. Ravens croaked as they flew by. Then I was in a shallow glen, beside Lochan na Cloidheig. Before me loomed Cruach na h-Airighe and leaving its summit I raised five red grouse from a peat channer. The way was pitted with very small tarns and it was all downhill now to the mouth of Loch Spelve and Croggan Pier. The snow had helped disguise the odd lift of land but I wanted to walk Crogan Beag and stride on and descend between the two streams to Croggan.

Snow was falllng, and on the far side of the mouth of the sea loch a dozen wild goats were wandering up the white steeps of Carn Ban.

You can get back to Lochbuie on the road from Croggan as described in Walk 45 or you can arrange for a car to be waiting at Croggan Pier. I did the return road walk but anyone out of condition would find it a long, long way after crossing Laggan.

Note: On a fine spring day this walk presents no problems. It brings you across some of the loveliest wild country I know at a time of year when the red-throated and black-throated divers are wailing from the remote lochans. More than four people walking this together would constitute a crowd and a betrayal of the seclusion. There is no room on Laggan for the picnic table, signposts, twee wooden bridges and steps up and down the rougher slopes.

My way is really nothing more than a suggestion. You may decide to walk the heights above the shore from Loch Buie to the precipices of Rubha na Faoilinn, Rubha nam Fear and all the other capes to the mouth of Loch Spelve. Enjoy the place and leave it as you find it − remembering that Laggan belongs to its wildlife.

WALK FORTY-FIVE
Croggan Pier, the deserted villages and on to Loch Buie.

Length: 13 miles
Grade Ⓑ Map on p. 221

In the spring this lochside amble conjures up birds like the great northern diver.

Mull isn't a museum. People live there and work the land and whenever I set out into the hills or along the coast I'm aware of this, just as I am in Wales and Devon. Yet the high ground provides opportunities to escape from the crowds and get back to Nature. Then you discover you are part of creation, not the centrepiece.

The October afternoon was sunlit and so calm I could hear the thrushes on the tideline by Croggan Pier hammering away at the whelk shells to prise out the meat. Mike Taylor, Patrick Blair and I were walking from Croggan above the Firth of Lorn to Portfield. Out to sea gannets were diving, falling from light blue into dark blue. There were also guillemots, cormorants and eiders beyond the wavebreak.

At the house called Portfield the track ended and we climbed up through the birches across the flanks of Maol Buidhe to the deserted villages of Balgamrie and Barnashoag which aren't far apart. Larks sang with a passion that belongs to spring but they failed to dispel the melancholy hanging over the shells of the crofts. The Clearances had left their legacy of nettles, roofless buildings and sadness. But the larks sang on.

The air was warm as we came down between Gortendoil and Kenandroma to Croggan again. Every hill and mountain rose free of cloud in a hazy sky.

The piping of curlew drifted across Loch Spelve and we were on the narrow road marching towards Creach where it stood over the water. Grass hackled the middle of the road, Hebridean style.

Mike was telling Patrick about Banshees. It was not an exercise in scholarship but the sort of bizarre monologue which any eavesdropping stranger would have found disconcerting. The pair of them were shuddering and braying with laughter. Beside the limpid waters of the loch, under the blue sky and surrounded by the brown and yellow hills few things could have been more incongruous – a drunken nun on a dune buggy might have just about stolen the edge on Mike.

We were happy. The road was long and the slopes of Laggan were clothed in silver birch, ash and sunlight. It was a gently rising, falling road running alternately beside the loch, then above it. Waves lapped the shore and streams fell through the trees to our left. On the far side of Loch Spelve was the fish farm and its floating 'pens'. The lisp of rock pipits pursued us and when we stopped to obey a law of nature we saw Balure Cemetery across the loch under Cnoc na Faoilinn.

Young birches grew among mature trees and a couple of burns dashed down the hillside as reminders of the rains of the previous week. The fadeaway of light had begun and a stag roaring from the Laggan skyline proclaimed the close of day. It was very romantic, but Robert Louis Stevenson rather than Walter Scott.

Now we had a view of Creach which would make the compilers of Beauty Spot Calendars weep for joy. Common gulls floated across the mountain's reflection. But our side of the loch had its own attractions. Waterfalls among silver birches, bracken slopes, long high sweeps of grass and then the crags and the deepening of tone as evening advanced.

The deer on the tops of Laggan were motionless and alert as they tend to be at the approach of dusk. A heron flapped up off the shore and a buzzard circled high over the loch. Then we saw the bow wave of a grey seal cutting across the surface. Round black eyes regarded us for a moment before the selkie sank and vanished.

At the end of the loch the road swung away from the water. There was a field between us and the shore and hinds were grouped under the trees in the corner. They broke cover when we neared them and jumped the fence into the next pasture and continued their flight.

The hills grew darker but the sky was bright. We walked beside a hedge of beeches and came to the road that led to Lochbuie. More beeches lined the wayside when we turned left and strode on towards Loch Uisg. A rough track, again on the left, would have taken us up to the sad-looking little church of Kinlochspelve; but we walked on past the war memorial and through the rhododendrons crowding the shores of the fresh-water Loch Uisg. The name means Loch of Water. Whisky comes from the Gaelic Uisg beatha – the water of life.

But making our way towards Creach Bheinn Lodge we were thinking of the Irish Elixir – water of the Liffy. A light shone from an upper window.

The building was half lost in the trees like an example of

late Transylvanian architecture. It had a miniature steeple and weather vane and a walled garden full of soft fruit trees. Maybe the Count was in residence waiting for nightfall.

Dusk wiped out the detail on the steeps of Laggan. Leaves fell through the stillness and a far-off stag began to roar, then another, and twilight brought out the stars. Firs, oaks and birches at the waysides created their own not unwelcome gloom. Then, a little beyond Lochuisg Cottage we found the memorial to Donald MacLean in a gap in the rhododendrons.

'Bloody rhododendrons,' Mike breathed.

We weren't fond of the Himalayan weed. But the air was sweet and the autumn wood crackling with the furtive sounds of deer making their departure. At the end of the loch was the tiny island that I had swum out to during a May heatwave. At the roadside almost opposite the island was the cairn erected by Lochbuie and his Highlanders to commemorate Queen Victoria's Diamond Jubilee.

We swung through Jubilee Wood past the lodge on the isthmus beyond the water and emerged from the trees on the brow of the hill to look down on the half dozen lights of Lochbuie.

Note: We were dropped off at Croggan Pier and walked to Lochbuie and our cottage. Unless you are prepared to make the return trek by the route you came it is advisable to have transport waiting at Lochbuie.

WALK FORTY-SIX
Ben More from the North
and back down the South side.

Length: 5½ miles
Grade Ⓓ

Up to one of Scotland's finest mountain viewpoints.

Pat Blair and I were going to try Ben More from the north, a route that would mean putting hand to rock. Ridge walkers may prefer to begin at the Mile Post a little to the south of the bridge over the Scarisdale River and come up onto Beinn Fhada (Gaelic for the Long Mountain – and rightly named), to follow the tops around to A'Chioch and Ben More. Pat and I wanted to try the rock walls and grass steeps of the North Face.

Around lunchtime on a cold, grey November day we were dropped off on the B8035 at the Mile Post beside the shores of Loch na Keal opposite the Isle of Eorsa. To our left the river, Abhainn na h-Uamha, descended to the loch over a series of falls.

We followed a burn up the slopes towards the shoulder of An Gearna and swung along the flanks of this height in Gleann na Beinne Fada with Abhainn na h-Uamha to our left. It was cold and showery and the mountains looked uninviting but the glen was wide, deep and impressive.

Mull's mountains were thrown up by violent volcanic eruptions. It is an island of 'table-top moorlands' and hill streams. Like most of the other mountains Ben More is composed of basalt which isn't ideal for rock climbing. But the mountain standing at 3,169 feet has pleasing lines and proportions and the views from its summit are splendid.

Walking around the shoulder we startled a stag and his hinds as they fed beside a stream below us. They ran across the glen into a scene that belonged to a Thorburn landscape. Mist sailed in wisps up the mountain sides. Rain beat against us. Ahead the ridge ran dark to A'Chioch under the interplay

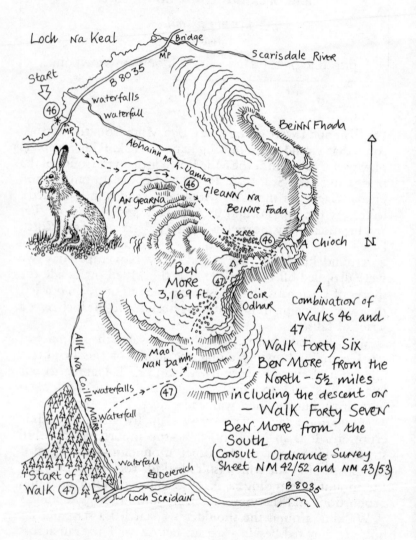

Loch Na Keal

Bridge

MP

Scarisdale River

Start

B 8035

waterfalls

waterfall

Beinn Fhada

MP

Abhainn na h-Uamha

46

Gleann Na
Beinne Fada

An Gearna

46

scree

46

A Chioch

N

Ben
More
3,169 ft.

47

Coir
Odhar

Allt Na Coille Maire

Maol
Nan Damh

A
Combination of
Walks 46 and
47

Walk Forty Six
Ben More from the
North - 5½ miles
including the descent on
— Walk Forty Seven
Ben More from the
South
(Consult Ordnance Survey
Sheet NM 42/52 and NM 43/53)

waterfalls

47

Waterfall

Waterfall

Deierach

Start of
Walk 47

Loch Scridain

B 8035

of sunlight and shadow. The only sound was the rush of the river in the glen.

We rested and ate a couple of mutton pies and a Kit-Kat. From the high place we were able to look back over Loch na Keal to Ardnamurchan and the faint profile of the Skye Cuillin.

The top of the glen ran up against the screes and crags of Ben More. We had the choice of cutting across the screes to the saddle between A'Chioch and the curving north-eastern ridge of Ben More or climbing the North Face direct. The rain turned to snow. The rock was running with water. Then, in the grass under the screes, we found the wreckage of a light aircraft. There was a small crater and evidence of the explosion. Wreckage was scattered for a hundred yards or so. Pat and I exchanged glances and poked about while the snow swirled around us and the cliffs above became black.

The snow stopped and we scrambled up screes of big awkward rock. The actual rock walls of the North Face were like glass. In places water poured over our hands and up our sleeves. We retreated and the snow returned. The screes and rocks below the walls were proving difficult enough so I led Pat up to the saddle between A'Chioch and Ben More. It was a fine, exposed position.

Facing the north-east ridge we had crags and long scree slopes falling to Coir Odhar. On the right were the black, shattered rock walls of the North Face. Ravens cronked and we began the scramble up the ridge path keeping close to the edge and the cliffs which dropped to the screes where the wreckage of the plane crash was strewn.

The ascent despite the taste of exposure was always easy. Snow and hail and cloud drifted around us and on again to open up the views. Soon we were hauling onto the summit sward to enjoy a vision of Mull and the Inner Hebrides that can't be acquired without sweat and legwork. Eastwards was Glen More, Ben Buie, Creach, Laggan and the mountains of the mainland. North beyond Ardnamurchan were the peaks of Skye. Westward lay Coll and Tiree, and to the south, looking over Loch Scridain and the Ross of Mull, we saw the Isle of Iona with its white beaches. The sea off Loch Scridain was a jigsaw puzzle of tiny islands and rocks.

Looking down through the sunlight into the mist-filled greyness of Glen Fada we were treated to a mountain speciality – a Glory. There was my shadow in sphere of light surrounded by a rainbow ring on the cloud below.

Pat and I walked to the cairn and ate a snack and drank some coffee before coming down the south flanks of Ben More to the road at Loch Beg.

WALK FORTY-SEVEN
Ben More from the South.

Length: 5 miles
Grade Ⓑ Map on p. 230

The easy way with The Kinloch Hotel on the return.

On the B8035 which runs to Salen beside the waters where Loch Beg becomes part of Loch Scridain, just before the first forestry commission plantation after leaving the A849 at the bottom of Glen More, there is a parking space to the right of the road. The stream, Allt na Coille Moire comes tumbling and roaring off the slopes on your side of the trees. It is the first part of your route up onto Ben More.

'An t'eilean Muileach', the anthem of Mull composed by the Gaelic bard Dugald MacPhail might have been written as an overture to this mountain walk.

The Isle of Mull is of isles the fairest,
Of ocean's gems 'tis the first and rarest;
Green grassy island of sparkling fountains,
Of waving woods and high tow'ring mountains.

The imagery does not do justice to the reality.

Mike Taylor, Nigel East and myself left the VW Beetle creaking and groaning in the spring sun and made our way up beside the stream. Common blue butterflies were fluttering about with some of the island's various burnet moths. We passed the deer fence and the small waterfall that would have brought Mike to a halt if we hadn't persuaded him to continue. A splashabout on the way back before a pint was logic he understood and accepted.

Shortly after leaving another set of cascades and some rowan trees a little further on we bore to the right into a corrie and made the exit by keeping between two crags. A narrow stream flowed through the corrie and we kept the most prominent crag on our right. But anyone walking these slopes can select their own line. The terrain isn't difficult and there are many approaches onto the big broad ridge.

We ascended a terraced crag and roused a snow hare from its form. It ran uphill as snow hares will if they have a choice. Short front legs and long back legs make ascent easier than the reverse. The creature still had a dusting of its winter coat showing through the summer pelage.

The afternoon was golden. An eagle slanted down and was gone like a meteorite behind the ridge. Maybe it had killed a relative of our hare. On the top terrace of the crag we headed right to a big square rock. The ridge was beyond with a saddle to the right. We walked towards it and the eagle sailed back into view and was joined by its mate. Behind the birds were the heads of Glen More's mountains.

Whenever we paused and looked back the wild country below had pushed out its horizons. The whole panorama was delectable. The sun was hot and there was no wind and not a cloud in the sky. For once distances weren't hazed.

We went up two small gulleys and across a stream to ascend the steeps of Maol Nan Damh with the summit of Ben More above us and the south-eastern buttress falling to immense screes. The sweat dripped off my hair as we mounted the summit ridge and its screes above the crags. Large patches of grass gave easier walking than these slopes of loose stones and rocks. It was a short climb.

Eventually we swung left at two cairns onto the arête for the final stretch to the Trig Point and the top. In the north-east was Ben Nevis, forty-five miles away, and there fifty-six miles to the north was Sgurr Alasdair and the other summits of the Skye Cuillin. West-north-west was Bara Head, sixty-five miles distant. Closer to Mull were the small isles of the Inner Hebrides and Iona magnificent. We stayed on the summit and sunbathed.

In the early evening our thirsts prompted a swift descent over the same ground to the car and a cruise along the edge of the sea lochs to one of the best pubs I know – The Kinloch Hotel on the shores of Loch Beg. In those days it was owned by Frank Meredith, a bearded, retired sea captain with impeccable manners. The new landlord, Angus Brown of Edinburgh, runs it with cheerful regard for his customers, helped by his wife Fionna, daughter Morag and son Gavin. They have probably the smallest pub in Britain.

The inn at the bottom of Glen More has a bar the size of a snooker table. Nothing has been tarted up to suit the day-tripper. There is no muzak or one-armed bandits or juke box. Conversation was encouraged by Frank and the atmosphere his pub created. After the abrasive noise of some of Big Brewery's popular watering holes, Frank's Bar was civilised. You would expect to meet Edward Thomas there. The beer was fine, the malt whisky excellent, the service unhurried and polite. It was refreshing to enter that atmosphere at the end of some of the best mountain walking Mull can offer.

The pub lights were on as we pulled onto the gravel forecourt. Hill solitude imparts calm and you carry it in you at the end of the day. In Frank's Bar the conversation ranged over a variety of topics from the deer to the weather, literature, wildlife, forestry, sheep farming, music and politics, and as the evening gathered momentum – philosophy. Funny how the fifth or sixth pint tends to fuel a pursuit of the profound when the faculties are redundant! But I do not know of another British pub that could boast golden eagles roosting in the trees out the back. One autumn a pair were up in the pines behind the lavatory. They made a pleasant change from pink elephants.

WALK FORTY-EIGHT
Ardura Crossroads, Loch Spelve to Kinlochspelve.

Length: 5 miles
Grade Ⓑ

A walk along the edge of a sea loch.

Dave Abrahams and I had done some groin-testing hillwork and settled for an afternoon wandering along beside the water at sea level. We scrounged a lift to Ardura Crossroads in the sort of spring sunshine that people go abroad to find. Yellow-horned moths were attending the opening of the birch buds at the wayside. Waders were fluting and songbirds competed with each other from the trees.

Where the Lochbuie road meets the Craignure–Fionnphort road there is a monument to Dugald MacPhail of the Mull anthem fame. We walked past it up the single-track Lochbuie road over the bridge spanning Lussa River and on beyond Ardura House. At either hand were woods of oak and birch. Taking the crown of the hill the road dipped beside rough grazing with a wooded glen below on the right and the slopes of Cruach Ardura rising on the left. The hinds, moving over open ground have always kept me occupied with the binoculars. I've never tired of seeing them in the glen or among the trees. Often as I returned at night to Lochbuie they would be running along the road in the headlight beams before clearing the fence and taking to the hills. The vision of them at full stretch was glorious.

The way came down above Abhainn a'choire, crossed the river and emerged from the trees, many of which were in tiny leaf. Craig nam Bodach was on the left overlooking a bay and the salt water of Loch Spelve. Lumpy hill country rolled skywards to our right. We marched past a white and blue house called Seanvaile, inhaling the tang of the seaweed and keeping a lookout for wildlife in or on the loch. It was a good place for seals, mostly grey, and one autumn Pat Blair, Simon Brooks, Ron Walter and I saw an otter on the off-shore rock which is called Sgeir na Faoilinn. Pat spotted it

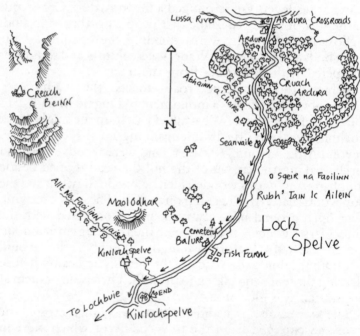

Lussa River

※ Ardura Crossroads

Ardura

Abhainn a'choire

Cruach Ardura

N

Creach Beinn

Seanvaile

o Sgeir na Faoilinn

Rubh' Iain Ic Ailein

Maol Odhar

Loch Spelve

Allt Na Faoilinn Glais

Cemetery Balure

Kinlochspelve

Fish Farm

To Lochbuie

48 END

Kinlochspelve

Walk Forty Eight
Ardura Crossroads,
the shore of Loch Spelve
to Kinlochspelve – 5 miles

first and we soon had our binoculars in position. The animal was lifting its head and scenting, half in and half out of the water among the kelp. Then it slid into the seaweed and submerged to surface again after about a minute. The whiskered pug face was a reminder of other otter watches on Devon rivers and the cry – 'hah' – floating through dimpsey. I also recall how moved we were by the sight of the animal in the sea loch.

Curlew sang out and oystercatchers replied. The pebbly foreshore swept down to the seaweed and the water. Blackface sheep were on the tideline munching dulce (tangle, kelp). In the pasture above the loch hooded crows walked about among other sheep in the hope, perhaps, one would drop dead and become a meal. Then a short distance beyond the white cottage Dave and I saw a great northern diver swimming about twenty yards offshore.

The road went over the bridge and a stream with reedy margins. Every so often curlew lifted from the shore and flew off. Duck and gulls were coming and going and Dave was shaking his head and expressing his delight.

Around the next bend and a small point with a long Gaelic name we saw the hatchery rafts of the fish farm out on the loch. Open hillside swept away on the right and Creach towered above it in the distance. A ewe had chosen to rub her bum on a rock at the roadside. Her eyes were half-lidded as she executed a slow cha-cha-cha. More eider were bobbing about between us and the hatchery pens. The sun sparkle on the water was intense. The hills were burnished and Laggan over the water flickered in the heat ripple. Then we were beside a cemetery that was about the size of a tennis court. Inside its stone walls the turf was short, the headstones few and the fir trees brought the touch of melancholy which, it seems, is necessary to Christian burial places. The curlews coming in to land on the shore loosed their cries and I recalled the maxim: 'The purpose of life is to create more life'. But for humans there can be no having without loss.

We crossed a hump-back bridge and walked past the fish farm. The spring day coaxed the best out of the landscape. Laggan was inseparable from the sky and the loch was a great slab of light scratched with the flight lines of water birds.

Dave and I came below Maol Odhar and we spoke about the wildlife and Robert Louis Stevenson's poetry. A fishing boat was beached at the end of the loch. We could look to the right, up the deep tree-filled ravine where Allt na Faoilinn Glaise was falling from pool to pool off Creach Beinn. The April heatwave had given us a thirst and I went to the stream where we had hidden two flagons of medium dry cider, courtesy of Mr Churchward of South Devon. The water had cooled it to drinkable temperature while we had been walking and we brought the bottles to the grass beside the loch and lowered their levels before sauntering on to Kinlochspelve.

Note: Again it is necessary to be collected at your destination unless you are prepared to walk back along the loch again. This shouldn't cause any hardship, especially in the spring with its wealth of bird life.

WALK FORTY-NINE
The Great Glen – Ardura Crossroads to Kinloch Scridain.

Length: 8 miles
Grade Ⓑ

A superior road walk.

May is the magic month when the island rings to the cries of birds and the greenness has a glow. The deer feed low down on the hills and the wailing of the red-throated and black-throated divers brings a day spent on high ground to the perfect end.

Late one afternoon in the first week of May I asked my friends to drop me off at Ardura Crossroads. I was going to walk the A849, Craignure–Iona Road down Glen More to The Kinloch Hotel. An alternative and probably quieter way is along the Old Road through the valley of the Lussa. It can be picked up near the cattlegrid just up the modern highway

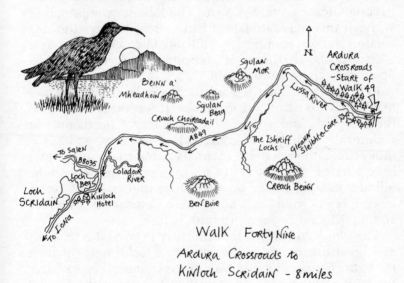

Sgulan Mor

Beinn a' Mheadhoin

Sgulan Beag

Cruach Choireadail

A849

To Salen

B8035

Coladoir River

Loch Beg

Loch Scridain

To Iona

Kinloch Hotel

Ben Buie

The Ishriff Lochs

Creach Beinn

Gleann Sleibhte-coire

Lussa River

Ardura Crossroads - Start of Walk 49

N

Walk Forty Nine
Ardura Crossroads to
Kinloch Scridain - 8 miles

from the turning to Lochbuie. But I was content to walk the new road and enjoy the views it provided.

The conifers reminded me of the forestry commission's massive presence on Mull. Fortunately the part of the island I love best is free of the glum ranks of Christmas trees which now threaten wilderness Britain. When I said one man's profit can be a nation's loss, I meant it.

I danced over the cattle grid above the waterfalls of the Lussa River which will soon be hidden by firs. On my left I could look towards Glais Bheinn, Creach and Beinn Fhada beyond Gleann Sleibhte corrie. The hillsides were streaked with streams and waterfalls. I had marched away from the conifers and was coming downhill into Glen More, the Great Glen that David Balfour of Stevenson's *Kidnapped* trudged up after escaping from Erraid.

In the sunlight and the silence I was walking a Celtic way many pilgrims before me had taken. It was the road to Iona, the Holy Isle and centre of early Celtic Christianity. St Columba would have loved that May day under the mountains although the occasional car and charabanc would have puzzled him. The cry of a bird of prey, the deer on the hillside, hooded crows on the wing, the sound of water leaving high ground in a hurry were elements of his world and a profound relationship with nature.

The Old Road which the saint may have trod on the left and Sguabain, the first of the four Ishriff lochs, were catching the light. The way looped with the river under Torosay deer forest and Sgulan Mor. In the valley below was the derelict shepherd's cottage of Ishriff and Loch Sguabain with its man-made island which was once a Celtic lake-dwelling called a crannog. Behind the loch were the flanks of Beinn Fhada and the sun-washed heights of Creach Beinn with Ben Buie standing alone in blue silhouette. A couple of hooded crows flew away from the rabbit a car had squashed.

I crossed the Old Road and the stream beside a little wooded glen and came uphill past Loch Sguabain. The glen was vast and the mountains at either hand enormous. Streams were running white off the slopes as I walked above the other Ishriff lochs and the Drove Road to Lochbuie.

The Old Road was on the left, then the right as it wound

down the glen. The river glittering below was no longer the Lussa. Waves of grass and rock peaked in places to mountain tops. Here and there was evidence of wayside afforestation which must change the character of the landscape. But even in the teeth of my prejudices it is unfair to question an island economy from a purely selfish tourist point of view. The beauty of the place doesn't give many of the natives a living but forestry guarantees jobs on an island where they are scarce.

A large waterfall on the right was providing piped water for the small dwelling on the left. Beyond it the glen was growing even wider. I passed a deer fence and another waterfall into a vista dominated by the hills of the Ross and Cruach Choireadail. Then I crossed a new bridge by an ancient hump-back bridge with a deep wooded glen to the right. Over the valley huge falls fed by twin torrents were pouring down the slopes. Hillsides rose to the far summit of Ben More and the dwelling on the right was dwarfed by the immensity of its situation.

Black-face sheep watched me stride down into the lap of the glen towards Loch Beg and Scridain. The River Coladoir meandered into the marshy levels at the head of the loch. I went over another bridge with the old one beside it. The wetland levels carried a lot of floodwater and I had forgotten the rain which had fallen on and off for weeks until a few days ago. But now the evening sun was bringing a warm flush to the mountain tops and I had pasture on my left and the delta of the Coladoir on my right. And there beside the road overlooking the marsh and Loch Beg was The Kinloch Inn. My friends were already propping up the bar and the lager was cool and smooth. We sat by the paraffin stove and ate haddies and chips. There were only two other customers.

We had second helpings and more ale while Frank shared the jokes and joined in the chat about hill walking and Mull's wildlife. Darkfall on the island after a sunny spring day was usually very beautiful. At twilight I brought my pint outside and stood on the shore breathing the smell of the loch. The mountains enclosing the glen had created a gigantic bowl that rang with the cries of hundreds of curlew and oystercatchers. The curlew's double notes are the voice of springtime

Mull, and nothing is sweeter than those syllables rising from the marshland at dusk. It is the music of estuary twilights throughout Britain but whenever I think of the Inner Hebrides I hear the piping of the long-nebbed birds, melodious and sad. It is one of Nature's most memorable sounds. Hearing it elsewhere I wait for the mountains of Mull to assemble behind my eyes while the wind shakes light over the loch and deer join the wild goats on the tideline. For me the curlew's cry belongs to beginnings and endings, dawns and dusks. It plays on the emotions and leaves me feeling the world is still marvellous despite human transgression.

I was there in the place where those cries drifted across water that held the last of the sky's glow. My friends joined me but little was said. No doubt it's easy to get moist-eyed about Hebridean springs. Each lost season pushes us closer to the final one, but I find comfort in the curlew cries. I know they will ring out when I'm gone, as part of the celebration of life.

Note: There is only one way back – the way you came and your legs may not be up to it. The Iona bus passes The Kinloch Hotel or you should arrange for your own transport to be there to collect you.

WALK FIFTY
Loch Buie to Carsaig.

Length: 6 miles
Grade Ⓑ

A coastal classic even by Mull standards.

Late April found me at Lochbuie again, glad to be alone with a book growing in my head. The weather was showery and Mull rainbow-hued. My intention was to walk along the coast from Lochbuie to Carsaig, across the Ross of Mull to Pennyghael, lunch at The Kinloch, come up the Great Glen to Ishriff and return to Lochbuie down the Drove Road. You

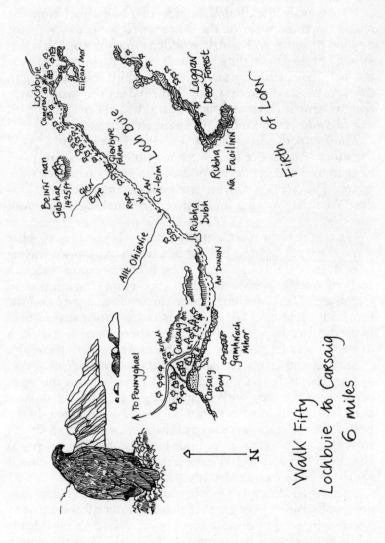

Firth of Lorn

Lochbuie
Cameron
Eilean Mor

Laggan
Deer Forest

Rubha
na Faoilinn

Beinn nan
Gabhar
1,425ft

Glen
Byre

Glenbyre
Farm

Rope
An
Cui-leim

Loch Buie

Allt Ohirgie

Rubha
Dubh

An Dunan

To Pennyghael

waterfall

Carsaig Arches

Gamhnach
Mhor

Carsaig
Bay

Walk Fifty
Lochbuie to Carsaig
6 miles

N

can do it by joining this walk to part of walk Number 49 and the whole of walk 42. It's a long way but most pleasant, especially in the spring.

If you walk the Ben Buie side of Loch Buie from the triangular monument on the shore you'll come to a gate just beyond the burn with a little wooden bungalow on the right. When I pushed open the gate the shower was drifting on over the loch and chaffinches and other small birds were singing in the trees beside the stream. For all the beauty the weather was conjuring up it was irritating because I had to keep putting on my cagoule and taking it off again five minutes later.

The footpath was signposted and it carried me alongside the shore. Across the loch were the gulley-scarred steeps of Laggan and the gentle snoring of the eiders rose from the water. The Scots word for these sea-loving ducks is Coo-doo. And that was the sound they were making: 'Coo-doo, coo-doo'.

Up on the right was Goat Mountain – Beinn Nan Gobhar – and the track went in and out of a wood of summer-leafing trees. It led me through a gate, past low crags and a waterfall and on over a pebbly beach to the empty farmhouse of Glenbyre. Then I walked beside the fence to a gate and the footbridge spanning Glenbyre Burn to join the path in a field over the beach. I was in another copse until a gap in a drystone wall let me back onto the shore beneath the crags.

Such is the character of this walk – stretches of wood against the cliffs and the occasional waterfall and the open margins of the loch with their tidal pools. Another shower petered out and another rainbow bloomed and faded. In the bottom of the crags were several shallow caves and an arm of rock at An Cui'-Leim jutted out into the sea. The drop was about ten feet and would have invited a bit of scrambling if someone hadn't obliged with a fixed rope.

I swarmed down onto a boulder-strewn beach and was greeted by the sight of another slender waterfall and a pair of hooded crows doing some surgery on a dead sheep. Meanwhile things were hapening on the loch. Mallard cruised among the eiders and a goosander was fishing close to the reefs. On the other side of Buie the great precipices of Laggan ran to the point, Rubha na Faoilinn like the frontiers of

Conan Doyle's *Lost World*. South-eastward the Paps of Jura were blue on the horizon. Clouds sailed by, rain fell into the Firth of Lorn and a rainbow arched over the loch. There can be few places in Britain where you will find a grey seal surfacing among ripples left behind by a great northern diver.

The sea beyond An Cui'-Leim was choppier. I came over the rock litter onto grass with some shapely crags above it. I was at the mouth of the loch and Rubha na Faoilinn towered in dark profile. In Gaelic Faoileann is a gravel beach; but Faoilinn is a fold. So is Rubha na Faoilinn the Point of the Sheepfold?

I forded the stream, Allt O'hirnie, by the waterfall, remembering how Mike had re-christened the stream Paddy's Brook after the O'Hirnie bit! He also insisted on calling Rubha Dubh (The Black Point) Rub-a-Dub although the Gaelic pronunciation is soft and lyrical. Beyond Loch Buie the morning was blustery but the showers were less frequent. After Rubha Dubh I passed another waterfall, a wall and a large crag and came upon the tall blunt stac, An Dunan. Through a gap in the rocks was a glimpse of the high cliffs beyond Carsaig. I walked on over the rocky shore, alongside cliffs and more shallow caves some of which had walls across their entrances. These were sheep folds. Hooded crows lurked in them.

The footpath entered a wood with a fine stand of Scots pines on the right and silver birch facing them. I crossed the stream next to the fallen pine that was still alive in one of its great boughs. This branch was about twenty-five feet high, like a young tree.

In places the going was soft but strategically placed stones and planks made it possible to walk the muddiest stretches. Here a shower caught up with me and I was cursing as I struggled to get my cagoule out of the pack and onto my body. Soon I was on the rough way that leads into Carsaig and a more respectable single-track road which ran past the waterfalls, Eas Na Dabhaich. Over Carsaig Bay were the great sea cliffs.

The salt air, the wind and sun had left me with a fine outdoor flush on my face, the appetite of a wolf and a thirst Falstaff would have applauded.

Note: If you haven't any transport waiting at Carsaig and you don't fancy the long trek to Lochbuie via Pennyghael, The Kinloch and the Drove Road, you'll have to retrace your steps. And why not? Think of all the wildlife you'll see.

WALK FIFTY-ONE
The Ascent of Ben Buie, 2,354 feet, from Loch Buie.

Length: 2 miles
Grade ©

A steep ascent with scrambling at the top if you wish.

Night fell quickly in the winter. I built up a fire and had it roaring up the chimney when I closed the cottage door behind me. There was about an hour of daylight left but the sky was clear and I could expect a full moon. The snow lay a few inches deep at the loch-side. I looked up at Ben Buie. The Yellow Mountain was snow-glazed white. A flock of fieldfares smacked into the trees of Cameron. Smoke from the cottages was climbing and flattening in the wind. Lights were on and the curlew were crying. Stevenson's beloved 'whaups'.

Not far from the telephone box I came to the bridge over the meeting of two rivers – Abhainn a'Chaiginn Mhoir and Abhainn an Tomarain – although it was difficult to tell where the one ended and the other began. Beyond the gate close by, the bog was frozen but the river ran free and dark. A pair of hoodies flapped out of the reeds as I followed the water and the Drove Road up past the falls through wet snow. Just before the dead tree I forded the river on large stones where the old deer fence ended, and I took to the lower slopes of Buie.

The snow was deeper on the hillside. I climbed the first of the steeps with a stream on my right to a lump that sprouted a little group of silver birches. Ben Buie was in front of me, the summit wreathed in snowsmoke as it caught the last of the

Ben Buie 2,354 ft

N

screes

Gleann a' chaignn Mhoir

Abhainn a' chaignn Mhoir

Deer Fence

Gate

phone box

Bridge

Old School

to Ardura
via Loch Uisg
and Loch Spelve

Abhainn an Tomarain

Lochbuie

Loch
Buie

Walk Fifty One
The Ascent of Ben Buie
2,354 ft, from Lochbuie
- 2 miles up and down
by the same route.

sun. The cold made my eyes water. Snow devils were raised by the wind and sent hissing away.

I went across the white flanks with most of the light in the sky showing behind Beinn nan Gobhar. To the right were three shoulders of rock culminating in Buie's east ridge. Their symmetry was pleasing.

Creach was behind me. On the tilting snowfield deer had left their slot marks and droppings. In the shallow gulley the animals had been lying in the snow and their body heat had thawed it. I could imagine the hinds dozing on the south-facing slopes and I recalled the sound made by the chomping of their cudding teeth one May evening when I was young and spent every daylight hour in the hills. Snug in their double undercoats they would not be dismayed by the arctic conditions.

I crossed the gulley and the stream and scrambled onto the snowy screes, heading right for a gap in the crags. The trails of mountain hares were printed on the surface. The creatures would be vulnerable now to eagle assaults. My breath came quickly with the exertion of lifting my feet out of the snow which in places was knee deep. I hoped I would find it compacted the higher I went.

Before me were several deer trails and the snow phantoms whispered as they glided off before the wind. And it was a wind that seared naked flesh. The snowsmoke billowed off Creach Beinn. Laggan was white against the haze of approaching dusk. The hills held the sunset for a little while, then settled into shadow.

I tightened my bootlaces and made sure my gaiters were secure. More deer were on the move across the steeps. The lazy lope-away of hinds was the most graceful departure any of Mull's animals could make. And they were close enough for me to see the puffs of breath and hear the grunt of the leading hind. At least a dozen turned up the mountainside and vanished into a corrie which the foreshortening of the ben had concealed.

I had selected a natural path beside a stream onto the ridge to the right of Ben Buie's summit. From there I looked down on the little community at the heel of the loch. The wind slackened to a silence that got into my bones and the mountain was gathering the evening's calm, remote in every sense of the word.

Swinging along, I went up the crag on my left and found the ice, but it wasn't necessary to strap on the crampons although I unbuckled the ice axe from the rucksack. I ascended a natural 'staircase' of snow on grass and heather to a terrace and saw the gap in the rocks.

The summit of Buie was before me, the larger of two huge 'steps' with the smaller on the left. And swinging left under the face I met a mountain hare. It was dusk and the sky was starry. The light in the sky and the snowlight created a supernatural atmosphere. Soon the moon would rise and complete the magic.

The hare emerged from the rock clitter and began to groom itself. I was above it, motionless. It lacked the brown hare's elegant lines and was dumpy, like a big rabbit with black tips to its ears. And it wasn't snow white. I had seen the Ben Buie hares by day. Their yellowish-brown backs had a dusting of grey and their hind legs were silvery. Against the winter whiteness they were good targets for eagles but at least there weren't any foxes on the island to make life even more difficult for them.

I sneezed and the hare departed, lifting crumbs of snow with its back feet. The cold was cracking my lips. Soon I had reached the screes and the problems of the versglas. So I sat down and put on the crampons. (Versglas, according to Collins *English Dictionary* is 'a thin film of ice on rock' but the ice sheathing these rocks was three or four inches thick.) The slopes led me to a view of the Ross of Mull and Loch Fuaran. It was possible, now, to bear sharply to the right under the summit crags. The iced, snow-encrusted scree brought me to the final sloping terrace and the scramble to the top.

The moon rose and frozen snow blazed and the ice gleamed. The deer and the hares would be moving down to feed. The snow crystals were sparking their fire. I kicked through the white crust and reached the cairn. Then I pulled on my mittens and balaclava and did an on-the-spot sprint. The moment held everything. All around me were white mountain tops and beyond them the sea and the islands.

Pinpoints of light marked the dwellings of Lochbuie. A falling star flared and vanished. The wind cut into me and set the snow devils moving. There was nothing to be afraid of. The cold penetrated my long johns and thighs. The feeling had left my features, finger tips and toes. But 'power jogging on the spot' (my son's expression) worked up a bit of a glow and I made the descent back down the way I had come up without incident, shedding the crampons as soon as possible en route.

Around the rim of the sea loch a curlew or two continued to utter their cries. The firelight was waiting for me in the cottage. I turned up the calor gas, made coffee and flopped into the armchair while the stew bubbled. The lid of the saucepan gently rattled as I eased off my boots and reached for the Chivas Regal.

Note: In normal conditions Ben Buie is a steep but easy mountain to ascend. Even the top crags can be avoided although some walkers will delight in the chance to do a bit of scrambling. The route I have chosen avoids crossing any of the private land in Lochbuie.

The route up the north-eastern ridge is rockier and longer.

8

Iona

Iona is a tiny island, three miles long and one and a half miles wide. White shell sands, green machair, some of the world's oldest rocks and the sea unite with the sky and an atmosphere of holy calm to leave the walker spellbound at any time of year. Among the Scottish kings buried here is Macbeth whom Shakespeare libelled. It is the island of white doves, a place that calls you back throughout your life once you have walked its shores and seen the moonrise from Dun I and have knelt in St Columba's Abbey.

WALK FIFTY-TWO
To St Columba's Abbey and Dun I.

Length: 2 miles
Grade Ⓐ

A little pilgrimage.

We drove down the Ross of Mull, along the shores of Loch Scridain and Loch Na Lathaich, through Killunaig and Bunessan to Fionnphort. The hills were on our left and approaching Fionnphort we saw a family of wild whooper swans, beside Loch Poit na h-I. Off the south-east tip of the Ross was Erraid, David Balfour's island in *Kidnapped*.

At the pier we parked the car and boarded the little ferry

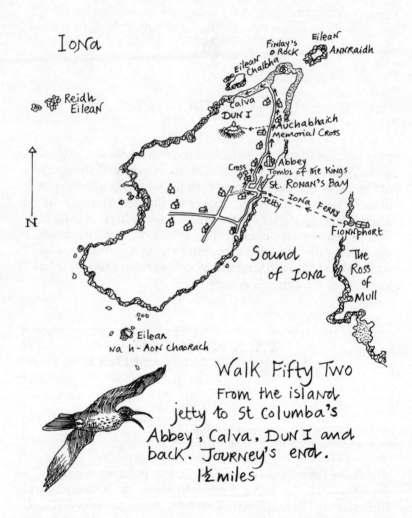

Iona

Reidh Eilean

Eilean Chalbha

Finlay's Rock

Eilean Annraidh

Calva
Dun I

Auchabhaich Memorial Cross

Cross
Abbey
Tombs of the Kings
St. Ronan's Bay

Jetty

Iona Ferry

Fionnphort

Sound of Iona

The Ross of Mull

N

Eilean na h-Aon chaorach

Walk Fifty Two
From the island jetty to St Columba's Abbey, Calva, Dun I and back. Journey's end.
1½ miles

boat, the Morvern, for the mile-long trip across the Sound of Iona to the sacred isle. The clarity of early October was cloud-shadowed but Ben More was catching the rain before it could reach this part of Mull. I was with Patrick Blair, Ron Walter and Simon Brooks and we were travelling the last of the Celtic ways. It was a good place for a wilderness romantic to end his journey. Stepping ashore on the jetty near St Ronan's Bay I wondered if my walks had been a sort of casual pilgrimage with Iona emerging as the ultimate goal. The process was convoluted enough to be Celtic. But it didn't seem that far from Berry Head's limestone to Iona's dazzling white sands – not as the spirit flies.

Columba landed here in AD 563. The saint was a representative of the Celtic Christianity that had entered into spiritual partnership with the planet. There was reverence for Nature even though it appeared to be hostile at times. Columba's faith was the religion of the living world and it didn't divorce itself from the rest of creation.

The saint was of the people and the animals. He was a cheerful, intelligent child of his age. Strong-willed and occasionally aggressive, he was a man who would bless farmstock and dabble in political intrigue.

It was the Irish evangelist Columcille – 'the dove of the church (cell)' – who set foot on Iona at Port na Curraigh determined to convert the Picts. Iona comes from 'I' meaning island and Dun 'I' is The Hill of the Island. Columcille's or Columba's world was a confusion of battles, alliances, betrayals and 'miracles'. But he must have loved the place. They say he slept on rock and drank nettle soup – but surely not all of the time! The beauty of Iona would have filtered through the pursuit of self-denial and there would have been open rejoicing amidst the flagellation of the spirit.

We walked straight up the road through the village with the ruins of the old Nunnery on the right. Columba wouldn't have approved of that community and he certainly wouldn't have endeared himself to today's feminists. The saint is credited with the following quote in Gaelic, translated here:

Where there's a cow there's a woman
And where there's a woman there's mischief.

So cows and lassies were banned from Iona. Women were taken into exile on Eilean Nam Ban – Women's Island. The teenage American girls strolling around the ruins were probably unaware that Columba was a misogynist but maybe the irony would have tickled him.

At the conspicuous white building we bore right and came by the little primary school. Next to it was a rookery in a couple of trees. The road bent to the left passing stone walls and vegetable gardens.

There was a Kirk at the next corner and up on the left some lovely greyish-white outcrops poked from the grass. It was here the full beauty of the island struck me. The grey rock, green turf and dazzling white sands under the autumn wind, the sun and the seabirds were central to something profoundly restful.

Beyond a white house were stretches of sward between rocks and a graveyard. Then the fifteen feet of grey-pink stone that is Maclean's Cross was standing at the roadside. For a man who normally isn't too keen on historical detective work when he's out in the wilds I had gone overboard. Photographs were taken and we moved on – sauntering as becomes pilgrims within sight of Mecca. To the right was the ancient burial ground, Tombs of the Kings, Reilig Odhrain, where over sixty monarchs were tucked away. Only three crosses remained of the 360-odd that once graced the site. One of them was Maclean's. Reformation vandals chucked the rest in the sea.

The white doves flashed through the sunlight of late afternoon and settled on a rock outside St Columba's Abbey. The walls of grey stone brought Samuel Johnson's words to mind. 'That man is little to be envied . . . whose piety would not grow warmer among the ruins of Iona.'

The stone was full of its own light and the abbey building wasn't a ruin. Wrecked by the Vikings it was first restored in the 13th century by the Lord of the Isles when a Benedictine Abbey was founded. Restoration occurred again, this time by the Church of Scotland, in the early 1900s, and the religious brotherhood, The Iona Community, have been there for fifty years, restoring and excavating and 'keeping the candle flame burning'.

We went inside and walked the length of the nave to the choir and the Iona Stone of the altar table. A silver Celtic Cross stood upon it. Sunlight streamed through the windows and we dawdled in the south transept to look at the effigies of the 8th Duke and Duchess of Argyll. Then we did a circuit of the cloister and contemplated the Celtic mind and its pursuit of truth through Nature. The sun was on the grass. Both were part of the abbey.

On Iona it is easy to accept the notion of Christ's love embracing the whole of creation but when we were on the road again and Simon tripped over his own feet to do a funny little dance there were some uncharitable remarks. Passing another white house we could look across the Sound of Iona to the mountains of Mull. Dun I was tall on the left as we passed the Memorial Cross. Haycocks stood in one field, sheep in the other. Backed by the sea and small islands it was typical crofting country.

There were two houses in front of Dun I and more haycocks across the road. But the wire fences caused us some dismay which probably didn't come anywhere near the dismay uncaring tourists must cause the crofting community.

I'm glad access to much of Britain's farmland is restricted. Most ramblers may be responsible people, worthy of the highest praise, but the private corners of the countryside remain sanctuaries for wildlife.

Strolling a little way on we went through a gate and across a field slightly left, towards the island called The Dutchman's Cap. And we found ourselves on the machair which ran into white sand. The murmur of surf lifted from the shore where sheep were browsing the dulce. The sand was the brilliant shell dust which gave Iona its permanent radiance. My companions loved it. This was Ron and Simon's first visit and it must have been very moving to make the transition from dream to reality.

Oystercatchers and turnstones piped from the tideline and a raft of eiders bobbed about on the swells. We walked the shore picking up Iona Pebbles from the shingle. These were Serpentine marble, a mixture of dark green, greenish-grey and pink stone, veined with white and polished by the sea.

Offshore were Eilean Chalbha and Finlay's Rock. At Calva, a little further along the coast, the temptation to climb the west slopes of Dun I was resisted. The fences on the hillside had been put there for a purpose, so we came back to the beach and the road. On our right was the farm, Auchabhaich, and the track beside it went through an iron gate and up over the field to a gap in the lower crags of Dun I. Grassy slopes then took us to the summit cairn and Trig Point.

Clouds drifted overhead and almost as if the incident had been contrived we heard the bugling of wild geese. In the sky above us greylags were arrowing northward. All around the hill were the green fields, the machair and the white beaches. Across the Sound of Iona the rocks on the tip of the Ross were deepening from pink to red.

The view was amazing. Away out in the Atlantic beyond Staffa and Fingal's Cave were the islands of Tiree and Coll; and we could see houses on them holding the sun. The Ross was behind the Abbey and Ben More was huge in the north. To the south were the Paps of Jura. Jackdaws sailed by calling to each other. Then we were treated to a brief aerial display by two of Iona's merlins.

Walking the road back to the Abbey and the ferry we stopped under a telephone wire and listened to a starling imitate a buzzard between snatches of song. The bird could have roosted comfortably in Dafydd ap Gwilym's poetry or in one of Columba's sermons. The shift of hooded crows, the bleating of sheep, the doves and seabirds were all interwoven with the season and the place; and so were we.

Robert Louis Stevenson knew. Some lines of his verse came to me as I stood in the stern of the ferry bound for Oban the following day watching Mull getting smaller on the horizon:

Blows the wind today and the sun
and the rain are flying.
Blows the rain wind on the moors
today and now
Where about the graves of the martyrs
the whaups are crying,
My heart remembers how.